David Ames Wells

Practical economics; a collection of essays respecting certain of the recent economic experiences of the United States

David Ames Wells

Practical economics; a collection of essays respecting certain of the recent economic experiences of the United States

ISBN/EAN: 9783337306328

Printed in Europe, USA, Canada, Australia, Japan

Cover: Foto ©Suzi / pixelio.de

More available books at **www.hansebooks.com**

PRACTICAL ECONOMICS

A COLLECTION OF ESSAYS RESPECTING CERTAIN OF THE RECENT
ECONOMIC EXPERIENCES OF THE UNITED STATES

BY

DAVID A. WELLS, LL.D., D.C.L.

MEMBRE CORRESPONDANT DE L'INSTITUT DE FRANCE, CORRESPONDENTE DELLA REALE ACCADEMIA
DE LINCEI, ITALIE, ETC.

" Experience keeps a dear school ; but fools will learn in no other, and scarce in that ; for it is true we may give advice, but we cannot give conduct.—BENJAMIN FRANKLIN.

NEW YORK & LONDON
G. P. PUTNAM'S SONS
The Knickerbocker Press
1894

TO

The Hon. HUGH McCULLOCH

AS A TESTIMONIAL TO HIS HIGH STATESMANSHIP AND UNQUESTIONED INTEGRITY

IN SUCCESSFULLY DEALING, AS SECRETARY OF THE TREASURY OF THE

UNITED STATES, WITH SOME OF THE MOST DIFFICULT FINANCIAL

PROBLEMS THAT HAVE EVER BEEN PRESENTED TO A FINANCE

MINISTER, AND AS A MEMENTO OF A FRIENDSHIP

THAT YEARS OF OFFICIAL AND PRIVATE

INTERCOURSE HAVE CREATED

AND STRENGTHENED

THIS VOLUME

Is respectfully Dedicated by the Author

iii

PREFACE.

THE essays embraced in this volume—with three exceptions—were originally contributed to and published in the *Atlantic Magazine*, the *Princeton Review*, the *Nation*, and the *N. Y. World*, at different dates from 1872 to 1884. The exceptions are "The Dollar of the Fathers *vs.* The Dollar of the Sons," which was published privately ; the essay on " The Production and Distribution of Wealth," which has heretofore been published only in the Proceedings of the American Social Science Association ; and the fourth chapter of " Our Experience in Taxing Distilled Spirits," which was written specially for this volume, and has never before been printed.

The chief warrant for their republication in a collected form is to be found in the circumstance that, with the exception of the final article of the series, they each illustrate a phase in the recent economic experiences of the United States, which has not as yet been discussed or related as a part of any detailed and consecutive history; an experience in which questions of the highest importance in respect to the use and issue of currency, the imposition of taxes, the collection of revenue, and the regulation of trade and commerce—all involving transactions of enormous magnitude and infinite detail—have been discussed, regulated by legal enactments, and carried to practical results, without, for the most part, any reference whatever to accepted economic principles, and often mainly under the influence of selfish and sometimes of corrupt motives and agencies. A century hence, except for such chronicles of recent tariff legislation as are here given, the writer is of the opinion that the world would find it very difficult to believe that such an illiberal commercial policy and body of tax and navigation laws as now exist could ever have been maintained and defended for any length of time, by a people so free, well educated, and jealous of their individual rights as those of the United States; while in respect to the experience of the United States in the taxing of distilled spirits, it is safe to affirm that nothing similar, viewed from an economic and moral standpoint, ever before occurred in any country of modern civilization, or is likely to occur again.

The author accordingly indulges in the belief that these essays, although fragmentary, will not, as now published in a collected form and with some revisions and additions, be regarded as a wholly unimportant contribution to the existing stock of economic knowledge.

DAVID A. WELLS.

NORWICH, CONN., October, 1885.

CONTENTS.

A MODERN FINANCIAL UTOPIA: HOW IT GREW UP, AND WHAT BECAME OF IT.

Atlantic Monthly, April, 1874.

THERE is one great, plain, practical fact in respect to irredeemable paper money, which in itself is a sufficient answer to all the arguments that may be advanced in its favor. And that is, that there cannot be one single instance referred to in the history of any state, nation, or people, in which its adoption and use has not been wholly disastrous. The more conspicuous examples and illustrations which prove this assertion—namely, the John Law scheme of 1716–1720, the currency of the American colonies before the Revolution, the Continental money, the French *assignats ;* and later and in this century, the paper-money experience of Austria, Russia, Italy, Spain, Turkey, and the South American states—are all more or less familiar ; but there is another example, little known, and rarely if ever referred to, which, occurring within a comparatively recent period, and under conditions analogous to those which in the opinion of many render the United States an exception to all the rest of the world, is no less interesting and instructive. We refer to the fiscal experience of the Republic of Texas, which, during the brief period of its existence as an independent nation, committed on a small scale nearly all the financial blunders, and tried nearly all the financial experiments, which the greater nations of Europe have before and since committed and tried on a large scale, and, as might naturally have been expected, with an almost exact parallelism of results. The details of this curious history were first collected by the late William M. Gouge, of Philadelphia,—an American writer on finance whose reputation was never commensurate with his worth and abilities,—who visited Texas after its annexation, for the purpose of specially studying up this subject ; and whose work, published near a quarter of a century ago, and now a rare volume, constitutes the source from which has been derived the following information.

Previous to the year 1835, Texas was one of the states of the Republic of Mexico ; and its currency consisted of gold and silver, and, to a very limited extent, of the notes of the banks of the United States. As the civilized population was small, no large amount of currency of any kind was required, but as compared with other newly settled countries, money was reported " to have been plenty." A great part of the Texan currency consisted of what were termed " hammered dollars," or old Spanish dollars from which the royal effigy had been effaced by the Mexicans as a testimony of disrespect for their former rulers. Time contracts were however made in new Mexican dollars, which were termed " eagle money," and circulated at one hundred cents to the dollar; while the " hammered dollar," though containing fully as much pure silver, circulated at only ninety cents ; the probable reason for the currency depreciation of the latter being that the destruction of their certificate of value effected by defacing the stamp, also prevented their use in settling foreign exchanges, and consequently their exportation.

After the commencement of the Texan revolution, and the inauguration of a provisional government, in November, 1835, hammered money gradually disappeared from circulation, and bank-notes from the States came in more freely and constituted the chief currency. In 1837, however, the banks of the United States suspended specie payments, and while all of the circulating medium of Texas became greatly depreciated, a very considerable portion derived from the banks of the State of Mississippi became altogether worthless. "Thereby," says the historian above referred to, " many of the people of Texas suffered severely, but their aggregate losses did not equal their aggregate gains, as many of these notes had been obtained in loans, and many of these loans were not repaid."

From the very first the Texans do not appear to have ever allowed themselves to be embarrassed by the idea of Old World bankers, political economists, and doctrinaires, that the circulating medium of a country should be based upon the precious metals. They were wiser than all that ; and they had in their possession something more valuable than gold and silver,—the element and source of all wealth,—namely, an almost unlimited quantity of cheap, fertile land. This was the true thing, in their opinion, to bank on, and bank on it they did. The first bank chartered, nearly six months before the commencement of hostilities, was the "Commercial and Agricultural Bank" of the department of Brazos. Its capital was not to exceed one million of dollars, divided into shares of one hundred dollars each. It was authorized to establish branches anywhere and everywhere; receive eight per cent. per annum on loans not exceeding six months, and ten per cent. on loans exceeding that time; and only the capital of the bank was to be responsible for the notes it issued. But the subscribers were required "*to adequately secure the value of their shares with real estate in the republic.*" In short, it was a most liberal charter, and the only thing any way illiberal about it was the single clause, "that as soon as one hundred thousand dollars, at least, have entered the vaults of the bank, it may commence operations." "Dollars," however, at that time, in Texas, says our historian, "*meant just whatever the people meant to make it mean.*" William M. Strong, of Pennsylvania, Associate Justice of the Supreme Court of the United States, had not then taken his seat on the bench; but the Texans in 1835 had anticipated the sentiments he expressed when he gave the legal-tender decision in 1871, that "*value was an ideal thing*"[1]; that "*it is hardly correct to speak of a standard of value*"[1]; that "*the gold and silver thing we call a dollar is, in no sense, a standard of a dollar*"[1]; in fact, that any thing is a dollar which the law-making powers may imagine it to be, and that it is not at all necessary that their "imagining" for one year should be the same as their "imagining" for some other and subsequent year. And as the Bank of Agriculture and Commerce appears to have commenced operations, and as there is no evidence that the one hundred thousand dollars was ever paid in, we are warranted in supposing that the "ideal" took in every respect the place of the real. That the Congress of Texas had also faith to a large extent in the *ideal* standard of value is made evident by the fact that, by an act passed December, 1836, the secretary of the treasury was authorized and empowered "to negotiate a loan from any bank or banks that may be established

[1] *Decisions Supreme Court of the United States*, 1871.

in this republic, of sufficient amount for the payment of all just claims " held by certain creditors against the government ; and lest the Bank of Agriculture and Commerce, with its capital of one million of "ideal" dollars, and the value of its shares made good by the pledge of real estate, should not be able to afford sufficient banking facilities to a population not exceeding fifty thousand, the " Texas Railroad and Navigation Banking Company " was in 1836 incorporated in addition.   The capital of this company was fixed at five millions, to be increased if desired to ten millions, with the right of connecting the waters of the Rio Grande and the Sabine by means of internal navigation, and the privilege of making branch canals and branch roads in every direction ; and this too at a time when the Republic of Texas had not the means of supporting a navy sufficient to protect its coasts from the attacks of one small sloop of war beloging to the Mexicans. The five millions of stock were immediately subscribed by eight individuals and firms; but the operations of the banking company were exceedingly limited, and are thus reported :   None of the subscribers paid in any thing.   One sold his interest, however, to a firm in New York, and took his pay in store-goods.   A second sold his for ten thousand dollars ; while a third swapped his for three leagues of land, which he subsequently sold at ten dollars and a half an acre, " The rest of the subscribers retain their original stock to this day."   Other projects of a like character were brought forward ; namely :   "A Joint-Stock Company for the Erection of a Hotel and Bath House at Velasco, with Banking Privileges "; "The Texas Internal Improvement and Banking Company"; "The Red River and Aransaso Bay Navigation, Railroad, and Banking Company"; and finally, one for establishing a bank on the faith of the government.   All these projects were favorably received ; but before the necessary laws could be passed, to put them in operation, news was received of the general failure of the banks of the United States (1837), and the republic was deprived of its prospective capital, enterprise, and consequent development.   To supply the necessities of a circulating medium occasioned by the discredit of bank-notes issued in the United States, individuals and municipalities commenced in 1837 to issue "shin-plasters," or notes for the fractional parts of a dollar, and continued to do so until 1840, when an end was put to them by the bankruptcy of the issuers.

It is now desirable to turn back and consider more directly the means by which Texas provided funds to carry on the war. At the outset the new republic had, apart from the pledge or sale of its lands, but few financial resources. A financial report made to the provisional government or council in November, 1835, brought out the fact, that although an army was in the field, engaged in active operations, yet " our finances, arising from the receipt of dues for lands, as will appear on file in Mr. Gail Borden's report, which were in his hands, are fifty-eight dollars and thirty cents. This money has been exhausted, and also an advance by the president of the council of thirty-six dollars. There were also several hundred dollars in the hands of the alcalde of Austin. Upon this money several advances have been made ; as such you may consider that at the present moment the council is out of funds."

But it will never do to despise the day of small things.   The men who had undertaken to make of Texas a free and independent republic were, in respect to audacity, enterprise, and self-reliance, typical emigrants from the great American nation, and having put their hands to the plow had no intention of stopping half-way in the furrow.   But to succeed in their undertaking "ways and means " were indispensable ; "and finding," says Mr. Gouge, "that other nations in their periods of exigency had resorted to taxing, borrowing, begging, selling, robbing, and cheating, they determined to try all six," and he might have added, they in all six succeeded.   The first feasible and ready way of collecting a revenue through taxation, that suggested itself, was by duties on imports, and the Texan legislators accordingly took to the tariff after the most approved American fashion ; enacting a given rate of duties on the 12th of December, revising the same on the 15th, and making a new tariff on the 27th.   In the ten years that Texas existed as an independent republic, it had no less than seven distinct tariffs.

Export duties on cotton were also recommended.   The chief reliance of the government was, however, upon loans, and commissioners were early appointed to borrow one million of dollars at a rate not exceeding ten per cent., on bonds running for not less than five or more than ten years ; the commissioners being authorized to pledge the public faith, the public lands, the public revennes, and in short every thing that Texas possessed in the way of security, for their repayment.

The idea that "a national debt was a national blessing" was one for which it had been generally supposed an agent of Jay Cooke & Co., employed to write up the 5-20 bonds, in 1863, was entitled to a patent for originality; but the records of the Congress of Texas show that the unexpatriated Yankee was after all but a poor though probably unconscious imitator, and that his conceptions of the felicity of owing somebody nationally never began to rise to the height of those indulged in by a Mr. Chenoweth, who, as chairman of the national committee on finance, submitted to the first Congress on the 16th of December, 1835, a report, of which the following is an extract :—

"At present our indebtedness is small, and our liabilities almost entirely to private individuals, whose claims, your committee are of opinion, may properly be merged and cancelled by the creation of substantial loans. An outstanding national debt may in many respects be looked upon as beneficial, by a community isolated and dependent as Texas, if the creditors, as such, can afford us substantial patronage. And until we can stand immutable among the nations of the earth, your committee would advise *that the pecuniary interests of our creditors will excite for us the sympathy and protection of mankind.*"

In one sense Mr. Chenoweth's "advice" proved correct, though not altogether in the manner he anticipated; for the various debt certificates of Texas being largely disposed of in the United States, an earnest sympathy for the republic was thereby naturally created among the holders; and this sympathy ultimately was most powerful in securing the annexation of Texas to the United States, and subsequently an appropriation from Congress of the sum of $10,000,000, with the understanding that the same should be used in the payment of the debts of the republic.

Under the head of "selling," as an expedient for providing ways and means, the public lands were offered by the Government of Texas at low prices and in any quantity; but as the cash value of the article was small,—the price fixed by the Mexican Government before the war being less than four cents per acre,—and as, furthermore, until after independence was fully established it was a question whether the vendor could pass an adequate and sufficient title, the receipts from this source were inconsiderable.

Under the head of "begging," the foreign agents of the republic were authorized to receive money or donations of any kind that might be given by citizens of any country they might visit; and that the hat thus passed round did not return empty is evident from the circumstance that on the 30th of November, 1835, formal resolutions of thanks were passed by the council to John Hutchins of Natchez, Mississippi, for his liberal donation of one hundred dollars " for the use of Texas in her struggle for liberty."

Under the head of " robbing," the council, on the 17th of January, 1836, enacted, that whereas it was impossible for the troops at Bexar " to drive beeves and procure provisions for their use without horses; *Therefore be it resolved*, that the commandant be authorized to employ as many Mexicans, or other citizens, for the purpose of driving up beeves, and procuring provisions, as may be required for that purpose." Letters of marque and reprisal were also early authorized and issued; but in this department of robbery the Texans could plead the precedents of the best-established and most Christian governments.

Under the heading of "cheating," Mr. Gouge groups the several acts and proceedings of the republic in respect to the manufacture and issue of paper money. The national treasury was first established, so far as the election of a treasurer could establish it, in November, 1835. Previous to this there had been a fiscal committee, and this had made a report, which, as the first official financial document of a *de facto* government, destined in the course of the following year to come into possession and control of a territory larger than France, deserves to be handed down to posterity. The report related to a matter of extortion and swindling on the part of certain contractors, and alleged, that one Thomas Bray, for furnishing " Cole's company of wagoners with one hundred and seven pounds of bread, had charged twenty-five cents per pound, or twenty-six dollars and seventy-five cents, whereas he should have charged but fourteen cents per pound; and that one Madison M. Stevens had charged an extortionate sum for " carrying one express to Nacogdoches." It was accordingly recommended that Bray be allowed but fifteen dollars and seventy-eight cents, and Stevens but ten dollars and fifty cents in full of all accounts, and the report was ordered to lie on the table. A month afterwards, by some skill of manipulation not unworthy of these later days, the committee made another report, in which it was recommended that Messrs Bray and Stevens be paid in full, —and paid in full they probably were. How good a field there would have been for modern adventurers to have operated in is illustrated by the following extract from a message which the first governor, Henry Smith, about this same time sent in to the "*Honorable President and Members of the General Council.*" He says:—

"Instead of acting as becomes the counsellors and guardians of a free people, you resolve yourselves into low, intriguing, caucusing parties; pass resolutions without a quorum, predicated on false premises ; and if you could only deceive me enough, you would join with it a piratical co-operation. You have acted in bad faith, and seem determined by your acts to destroy the very constitution you are pledged and sworn to support. I have been placed on the political watch-tower, and I hope I will be able to prove a faithful sentinel. You have also been posted as sentinels; but you have permitted the enemy to cross the lines, and you are ready to sacrifice your country at the shrine of plunder. Mr. President, I speak collectively, as you all form one whole, though at the same time I do not mean all. I know you have honest men there; but you have Judas in the camp—men who, if possible, would deceive their God.

"Notwithstanding their deep-laid plans and intrigues, I have not been asleep. They will find themselves circumvented in every tack. I am now tired of watching scoundrels abroad and scoundrels at home, and as such I am now prepared to drop the curtain.

"Look around upon your flock ; your discernment will easily detect the scoundrels: the complaint, contraction of the eyes ; the gape of the mouth ; the vacant stare ; the hung head ; the restless, fidgety disposition ; the sneaking, sycophantic look ; a natural meanness of countenance ; an unguarded shrug of the shoulders ; a sympathetic tickling and contraction of the muscles of the neck, anticipating a rope ; a restless uneasiness to adjourn, dreading to face the storm themselves have raised. Let the honest and indignant part of your council drive the wolves out of the fold. Some of them have been thrown out of folds equally sacred, and should be denied the society of civilized men.

"But, thanks be to my God, there is balm in Texas, and a physician near."

And the governor then, in the capacity of a physician, proceeded to administer the balm by ordering the council to be forthwith prorogued, "unless your body will make the necessary acknowledgment of your error, and forthwith" (before twelve o'clock to-morrow) "proceed" (by issuing a circular and furnishing expresses) "to give it circulation and publicity, in a manner calculated to counteract its baleful effects."

But the council would n't be prorogued, and refused to accept the balm. They referred the governor's message to a committee, who forthwith reported: "That they are unable to express any other views than indignation at language so repulsive to every moral feeling of an honorable man, and astonishment that this community should have been so miserably deceived in selecting, for the high office of governor, a man whose language and conduct prove his early habits of association to have been vulgar and depraved." The report concluded with resolutions that they would sustain the dignity of the government, and that Henry Smith be ordered forthwith to cease the functions of his office. The next day they issued an address to the people, in which they repelled the charges brought against them in "that impudential document," and brought counter-charges against his excellency himself. A single paragraph is given by Mr. Gouge to show the character of this address: "All these acts of stubbornness and perverseness were not sufficient to gratify his thirst for sole dominion. His dignity was insulted at the idea of the existence of the co-ordinate branch of government to curb his acts and check his usurpation. He became more and more restless, until, enraged at the presumption of the council, in the exercise of a constitutional right, he ignites; his fury, in a blaze, consumes his prudence (what he had); he orders the council to disperse, shuts the door of communication between the two departments, and proclaims himself the government."

At this rejoinder and counter-attack Governor Smith seems to have been considerably astonished; and sought to reconcile matters with the council by sending the next day a message, in which, after confessing that he had used "much asperity of language," he concludes as follows:—

"Believing the rules of Christian charity require us to bear and forbear, and as far as possible overlook the errors and foibles of each other, in this case I may not have exercised towards your body that degree of forbearance which was probably your due. If so, I have been laboring under error, and as such, hope you will have the magnanimity to extend it to me, and the two branches again harmonize to the promotion of the true interests of the country." But it was of no use; Governor Smith's "Christian charity" was exercised too late. The council deposed him so far as they could, and for the remainder of the session Lieutenant-Governor Robinson "reigned in his stead."

The formal establishment of a national treasury was one thing; the filling it with money was quite another and different thing. And as sufficient funds for defraying the expenses of the government and the army did not come from any of the expedients of taxation, loans, the establishment of companies with banking privileges, the sale of lands, begging, or seizing private property by land and sea, the republic next undertook to pay its way by drawing drafts on itself. To give these drafts credit and circulation an act was passed, December, 1836: "That it shall be the duty of the several collectors (of customs) to receive the orders of the auditor upon the treasury of the republic when offered by importers in payment of duties at the time of importation"; and in June following it was enacted: "That properly audited drafts on the treasury of the republic shall be received in payment of taxes imposed, except on billiard tables, retailers of liquors, and nine-pin alleys, or games of that kind." By these two acts, Texas gave her audited drafts a greater value than they would otherwise have possessed, and caused them to pass into hands that otherwise would not have received them. From first to last, the issue of these audited drafts amounted to about eight millions of dollars ($7,834,207). They do not appear to have ever to any extent answered the purpose of currency; and the circumstance that they were issued for odd numbers of dollars and cents, and when passed from hand to hand required a calculation, doubtless contributed to prevent such a result. They gradually depreciated in value, and in December, 1837, one year after the passage of the act authorizing their reception for customs dues, another act was passed declaring that the state would no longer receive such drafts in payment of debts due to itself.

The greatest and best stroke of financial policy on the part of the new republic was, however, reserved to the last; and in November, 1837, when borrowing, begging, selling land scrip, and issuing audited drafts had been exhausted as expedients for raising money, the government commenced the issue of treasury notes. These notes were in the form of bank-notes, and by law were required to be printed *" in neat form."* They were also for round or even sums, and mainly for small amounts, and specified on their face *" that they will be received in payment for lands and other public dues, or be redeemed with any moneys in the treasury not otherwise appropriated."*

And here commences by far the most valuable of all the lessons deducible from the study of the fiscal experience of the Republic of Texas—a lesson, moreover, exceptionally interesting, from the circumstance that we find in it a showing and demonstration that the working and effect of a system of irredeemable paper money is one and the same, whether the field of its influence be a rich, densely populated old country like Austria or France, or a disturbed, thinly populated community, with little accumulated capital, and occupying, as it were, the very border line between barbarism and civilization.

The first noticeable and most interesting fact connected with the history of these Texan treasury notes is, that although the credit of Texas at the time of their issue was so bad that a foreign loan could not be negotiated, and the audited drafts on the treasury had so far depreciated as to have but a nominal value, and that of less than *fifteen* cents on the dollar, yet the notes themselves, though practically unredeemable, were when first issued at par, or nearly par, with specie, and furthermore were kept so for months, or until their issue exceeded in amount half a million of dollars. The explanation of this curious phenomenon is, that the people of Texas, at the time of the authorization of these treasury notes, had practically no circulating medium for effecting exchanges, or none that was really worthy of the name; and

although a community can get along in its business without a
currency, as it can without horses and carts, ships and steam-
engines—all alike instrumentalities for effecting the interchange
of commodities—there is no community that will dispense with
any of these agencies if it can help it.   With the outbreak of the
revolution the hammered money and the eagle money soon disappeared.   With the failure of the banks of the United States in
1837, the notes of the banking institutions of the Southwestern
States, which had come in like a flood and had supplied to Texas
the void occasioned by the disappearance of its specie circulation,
became worthless ; while the issue of shin-plasters or fractional
notes of persons and firms, although continued, was by law for-
bidden.   The want of some medium that should have *one* value,
and would regulate prices and facilitate exchanges, was therefore
much felt ; and when the government gave the people the best
medium they could, threw around it all the guaranties that it was
in their power to supply, and issued no more of the " medium "
than was necessary to meet a specific want, the people in turn ac-
corded to the medium a value proportional to the work it performed,
or the necessity it supplied.   The first issue of notes, in addition
to a pledge of government faith to receive them in payment of all
public dues and to redeem them as soon as there was any thing to
redeem them with, carried also a promise of *ten* per cent. interest ;
a rate easily calculated, and which offered an inducement for
hoarding the notes, to such Texans as could afford it and had
also faith in their ultimate payment.   The whole revenue from
customs was also devoted to sustaining the credit of these treasury notes, and about this time the laws for raising a revenue from
imports began to be effective ; the gross revenue accruing from
the customs for the quarter ending September 30, 1837, having
been about sixty thousand dollars.

The Texans were, moreover, exceedingly wise in their day
and generation in another matter.   The original treasury notes,
although intended to serve as currency, were nevertheless, from
the fact that they carried ten per cent. interest, in reality a
species of national " bond " ; and being issued in round sums of
small amounts, as low even as one dollar, they were taken up as
investments, or speculated in by persons of very small means,
who never regarded themselves in any sense as capitalists.   Very

considerable sums thus found their way into the United States and were permanently held there, and even the negroes of New Orleans were enabled to enjoy the luxury of speculating in foreign securities. It is also curious to recall that at the time of the formation of the syndicate in 1870–71, for the purpose of funding the national debt of the United States at a lower rate of interest than six per cent., this very same plan that worked so successfully in Texas in 1837 was brought forward and urged before the committees of Congress with great ingenuity and ability by the then head of a European banking firm, as a condition precedent and essential to placing permanently a large amount of Federal securities among the masses in Europe, at a very low rate of interest. According to Mr. Gouge, Texas treasury notes continued to be at par, or nearly at par, with specie, until their amount exceeded half a million of dollars. If we take the population of Texas at that time as about *forty* thousand, and suppose that one fifth of the entire issue of half a million was hoarded, or floated off into the United States, then the result affords a very striking and curious confirmation of the theory, held by many of the best informed bankers and economists, that an average of about *ten dollars per capita* is the utmost limit of paper money that a community can permanently float, and at the same time keep on a level or par with specie.[1] It is also a fact in regard to the Continental money, that, so long as its issue was not in excess of thirty millions, or at the rate of about ten dollars *per capita*, or up to January, 1778, its maximum depreciation was not in excess of five per cent., as compared with specie.

But all history shows that when a nation has once embarked in a scheme of irredeemable paper money, it is extremely difficult, if not wholly impossible, to resist the current and drift of its influence; and the experience of Texas constitutes no exception to this general rule. The five hundred thousand paper treasury dollars had done good service; they had doubtless been printed in a " neat form " as the law provided; had proved attractive to the masses, and had relieved the most urgent financial necessities

---

[1] The theory is that if the notes are redeemable in specie on demand, and more than ten dollars *per capita* is issued, the excess will be presented for redemption and be thus voluntarily retired. If the notes are not redeemable on presentation, the moment the line of excess is passed, that same moment indicates the commencement of permanent depreciation.

of the republic. Why should not the people of Texas have more of so good a thing? They accordingly, through their legislative agents and representatives, determined to have more; and in the spring of 1838, a bill, bearing the familiar title of "*An act to define and limit the issue of promissory notes,*" was reported in the House of Representatives, which authorized an additional issue of one hundred and fifty thousand dollars. The Senate, however, increased the existing amount to one million, and as thus amended, the bill passed both houses by large majorities. Sturdy and honest Sam Houston was then President, and when the bill came up for his signature, he promptly vetoed it, and gave his reasons therefor in a message so full of common sense and sound principles that there is nothing which people everywhere, who are attracted by the idea of paper money, could to-day read with greater profit and instruction. He says: "When the (treasury note) currency was projected, both the government and the country were without resources. National existence and freedom had been achieved, but the struggle had left us destitute and naked. There were no banks! There was no money! Our lands could not be sold, and the public credit was of doubtful character! To avoid the absolute dissolution of the government, it became necessary to resort to some expedient that might furnish temporary relief. This could only be effected by creating a currency that should command some degree of credit abroad.

"It was hoped and believed that, if *a small issue of government paper* was made, with specific means of redemption pointed out, which appeared to be ample and well guaranteed, and the government should evince a prudent and discreet judgment in its management, it would command such articles in the market of the United States as were indispensable to the country.

"The result has justified the expectation."

But he continues, and his words are as full of truth now as then: "*The government will never be able, by all the issues it can make, to satisfy the demands of private speculation and interest.* The vast issues of all the banks in the United States (reference being here made to the condition of things in 1836–37), in their most extended condition, failed to attain this object. There has not probably been in circulation at any time more than half a million of dollars. The present bill requires the secretary of the treasury to increase the issue to a million. No time or discretion is allowed to that officer. The circulation of the country is to be doubled in as little time as is required to issue the paper."

The objections of the executive for the moment prevailed; but another bill was passed a week after, which allowed the president to increase the amount of treasury notes to one million, if in his judgment the interests of the country required it; and at the same time it specifically appropriated four hundred and fifty thousand of such notes, or an amount nearly equal to the whole existing issue, to the payment of army, navy, and civil indebtedness. The barriers against unlimited inflation were thus indirectly removed, and from this time there does not appear to have been any effort to restrain further action in this direction. The first issues of these notes, as already stated, carried interest. The new issues were without interest, and on account of a red impression on their back, were everywhere known as "red-backs"; thus curiously anticipating the name—"green-backs"—applied to the paper currency of a later generation.

As might have been expected, with the authorization of the new issues the notes began to depreciate; and the depreciation increased with each additional emission. In all, paper money in the form of treasury notes to the nominal amount of $4,717,939 was issued. In January, 1839, these notes were worth no more than *forty cents on the dollar;* in the spring of 1839 they were worth thirty-seven and a half cents; in 1841, from twelve to fifteen cents; and in 1842 they fell to ten cents, to five cents, to four, to three, to two, and finally became utterly worthless. In the characteristic language of the times, it required, before the close of President Lamar's administration, "fifteen dollars in treasury notes to buy three glasses of brandy and water, *without sugar.*" To the treasury notes succeeded what were termed "exchequer bills"; but they were comparatively few in number, and never passed to any extent into circulation. "By this time," says Mr. Gouge, "there was little circulating medium of any kind in Texas; but this was no great calamity, as the people had but little left to circulate. The evils this system did were immense, and such as for which, even were it so disposed, the government could afford no compensation to the sufferers. They no doubt, however, like others in similar circumstances, attributed to the want of circulating *medium* the evils they suffered from want of circulating *capital.*" In all, from first to last, the amount of "promissory notes," "audited drafts," "exchequer bills," bonds, etc., issued by the Texan treasury, and serving to a greater or less extent as "circulating medium," amounted to $13,318,145 ; or, reckoning the population at fifty thousand, more than two hundred and sixty-six dollars per capita. If paper issues could, therefore, have made a people rich, the Texans ought to have been the richest people in the universe.

One other thing in connection with this subject ought specially to be mentioned in all honor to the Texans. In the midst of their poverty, and crushed almost to the earth with their burden of financial necessities, they never made their government paper a legal tender in the payment of private debts ; but every man was left at liberty to refuse or receive treasury notes at his option. The result was, that when "red-backs" were almost the exclusive circulating medium, specie was the standard of ultimate reference. If a man bought an article on credit, he gave a note promising to pay dollars in silver, or so many treasury notes as should, when the note fell due, be worth an equivalent of the amount owed in silver.

But another and no less curious part of this history yet remains to be told. The experiment of paper issues, not redeemable in specie on demand, to supply the office and function of money, or circulating medium, had been fully and fairly tried in Texas, and the people, one and all, were so entirely satisfied with their experience that they wanted no more for all time like it. They accordingly did not content themselves with mere ordinary legislation ; but when the convention came together, immediately after the consummation of the act of annexation to the United States, to form a State constitution, the delegates, by one of their earliest acts, inserted in the constitution the following sections, which were afterward ratified by the people [1] :—

" *In no case shall the Legislature have power to issue* ' *treasury warrants,*' ' *treasury-notes,*' *or paper of any description intended to circulate as money.*"

" No corporate body shall hereafter be created, renewed, or extended, with banking or discounting privileges."

" The Legislature shall prohibit by law individuals from issuing bills, checks, or promissory notes, or other paper, to circulate as money."

" It is never," says Mr. Gouge, in noticing the peculiarities of this constitution of Texas, " without deep experience of the evils of paper issues that the people impose such restrictions on their rulers."

And the first Legislature that convened after the adoption of the constitution, or in the succeeding year, made the following further enactment :—

" No person or persons within this State shall issue any bill, promissory note, check, or other paper, to circulate as money."

" Every person who may violate this act shall be subject to indictment therefor, by a grand jury, as for a misdemeanor, at any time within twelve months after so offending ; and shall be subject to a fine of not less than ten dollars, nor more than fifty dollars, for each and every bill, promissory note, check, or other paper, issued by them in violation of the first section of this act."

These measures practically put an end to the paper-money system of Texas. Various subterfuges were afterward resorted to, and by means of them paper money, to a very limited extent, found its way into circulation in Texas after its annexation to the United States. But, as a rule, the generations of Texans who had had this experience of " fiat paper money " never again looked with favor upon any other currency than specie. The result of such a policy on the development and business of the State was thus reported by Mr. Gouge in 1852,—seven years after its adoption : " The result of this hard-money policy is, that business in Texas rests on a more stable foundation than it does in many other

only safe expedient for governments—a hard-money currency as a circulating medium." In accordance with this recommendation, the Congress of Texas, in almost one of its last acts, forbade the further issue by the government of " any description of paper representing money intended for circulation, or to be received in payment of any class of revenue " ; and required the secretary to cause to be destroyed all the exchequer bills received at the treasury department.

parts of the Union. That it is absolutely free from vicissitudes is what we do not assert. But, unbolstered by bank-credits, and governed by that best of all regulators, gold and silver, her merchants limit their purchases of goods abroad by the actual demands of the planters at home, measuring that demand by the surplus crops the planters have to dispose of. Exchanges are regular. The maximum rates never exceed the cost of transporting specie, and often fall below it. A gentleman at Austin told us that he had in the course of years negotiated bills on New York, to the amount of two hundred thousand dollars, and had seldom given either premium or discount. At Galveston, exchanges on New York have not for years been at any time more than one and a half premium."

Prices, Mr. Gouge observes, were not low, but quite as high as they are (other things considered) in the most paper-loving portions of the Union ; thus showing that " hard money and high prices are not incompatible."

" The rate of interest is high, because the profits of trade are great. Money is scarce, as money ought to be, for without scarcity it would lose its value. But gold and silver is in Texas quite as plentiful, in proportion to other circulating wealth, as paper money is in New York or Massachusetts."

Mr. Gouge also, in his record, brings out two other series of facts in connection with the history of the paper money of Texas, which from their parallelism with results obtained on a larger scale, but under similar circumstances, in the United States and other countries, are especially worthy of notice. The first relates to the incentive given by paper money to national extravagance and increase of expenditures ; and in this respect the experience of Texas was as follows. The revolution broke out in 1835. From that time until the close of 1838, the period covering the main military operations and the practical achievement of independence, the Republic of Texas incurred a debt of less than two millions of dollars. This small amount was not due to the circumstance that the government had any objections to running in debt ; "but because few would trust, except such as could not well avoid so doing." In 1838, Mirabeau B. Lamar was elected president, and held office for three years, or until December, 1841. The period of his administration was one of comparative peace, but it was also the era of paper money and profusion. Lamar in his three years' term increased the national debt from less than two millions to upwards of seven millions. The average annual expenses of his government were also $1,618,405.

In 1841 General Houston took office as president for a second term. The paper-money bubble had exploded, but Mexican hostilities, which in General Lamar's administration only threatened, now actually broke out. Yet in General Houston's last administration not only was the national debt not increased, except by increments of interest and by the bringing in of back accounts, but the average annual expenses of the republic were reduced from $1,618,405 to $170,361. Mr. Gouge claims that this experience of the republic under President Houston, from 1842 to 1844 inclusive, shows "that if it had been possible for the Texans to be hard-money and prompt-payment men, they might have achieved their independence and defrayed all the expenses of the republic, at a cost of two hundred thousand a year. But the Texans never became economical until constrained by necessity." So long as they could borrow, or induce any one to take their paper money, they were extravagant; but when they could borrow no longer, and their paper money refused to circulate, then they became saving.

The second series of facts relates to the influence which an excess of paper currency in Texas exerted in encouraging imports and discouraging exports. Thus during the administration of Lamar,—1839–1840,—when treasury notes were the circulating medium, and money was, as it is termed, "abundant," the imports were nearly six times as great as the exports; or an average of $1,442,733 of imports per annum as compared with an average of $247,459 of exports. On the contrary, in two years of Houston's second term, 1843–44, when such notes were no longer current, the exports nearly equalled the imports; the average annual import being $578,854 as compared with an average annual export of $506,444.

The memory of the events and experiences thus recorded was furthermore kept alive for a long period after the annexation of Texas (in 1845) to the United States; and continued to exercise so great an influence, that during the whole period of the Rebellion (1861–65) the paper money issued by the Southern Confederacy found little favor among the people of that State, and circulated only under the pressure of military law and of necessity. And even after the war was ended, and the supremacy of the Federal Government was firmly established and everywhere acknowledged, it was found very difficult for a long time to make the average Texan of the interior recognize the green-back, or accept any thing but specie in exchange for his cotton and his cattle.

THE TRUE STORY OF THE LEADEN STATUARY; OR, A CURIOUS CHAPTER IN ECONOMIC HISTORY.

" A story as amusing as a novel is scarcely what we are accustomed to expect from the sedate pen of our excellent economist, Mr. DAVID A. WELLS. But that is precisely what we are indebted to him for this morning, as the brightest of our fairest readers will admit, who hate figures, skip statistics, and would disclaim the ballot if it involved learning economics. Mr. WELLS has dug up and relates for us the True Story of the Leaden Statuary. Its moral draws itself, as in the case of all good and well-told stories."—*New York World*, May 11, 1874.

THERE is an amusing old story told of the magistrates of a certain country town in France, who, before the days of street lamps and gas, and as a better security against the unlawful act of "vagrom men," passed an ordinance that "no citizen should walk out after dark without a lantern," and that disobedience of the law should entail a heavy penalty. The watch, vigilant in the performance of duty, accordingly arrested, the first night after the law took effect, a well-known and estimable individual, but of waggish propensities, and hauled him up before the local Dogberry on charge of having broken the statute. The defendant, however, on being asked why punishment should not be inflicted upon him, made answer, that he had committed no offence, and in support of his plea produced a lantern. It being rejoined that the lantern had no candle, he next declared that the law did not require that the lantern should contain any candle ; and the statute being examined and the defence found valid, the arrested party was dismissed and the law so amended as to read, "that no citizen should hereafter walk out after dark, without a lantern and a candle." The next night the same person being again found walking in darkness was again arrested and arraigned, but as before maintained that he had committed no offence ; and, in proof thereof, produced a lantern and showed that it contained a candle. "But the candle,"

said Dogberry, " is not lighted." "And the law," rejoined the
wag, "docs not require that it should be"; and this interpre-
tation being found correct, the accused was once more discharged
and the statute further amended so as to read, " that no citizen
should hereafter walk out after dark without a lantern and a
candle in it, and that the candle should be lighted."

But the very next night the same incorrigible and troublesome
person was again brought up before the Court, and this time both
watch and magistrate thought they had a sure thing of it ; for, to
all appearances, he had not on this occasion made even a pretence
of complying with the law. The triumph of the officials was,
however, of very brief duration, for, to their utter disgust and
amazement, the accused drew from his capacious coat pocket
a dark lantern, and showed that it not only contained a candle,
but that the candle was lighted and burning. Warned by this
threefold experience, the statute was for a third time amended,
and this time so fully and clearly that no further practical
jokes were attempted, and the majesty of the law remained
unassailed.

As thus told the above story is manifestly a broad burlesque,
even in its application to stupid French " country officials," and
without further foundation than the imagination of its author.
But it is nevertheless a most curious and amusing circumstance
that it has been reserved to the United States to furnish out of
the history of its fiscal legislation a record of actual experience
which, in many respects, is the exact and truthful counterpart of
the French burlesque; and, as the incidents involved have often
(but always incorrectly) been alluded to on the floor of Congress,
and in the columns of the Press, and may be found pertinent to
prospective legislation and debate in respect to custom-house reforms and irregularities in all countries, it is proposed to now embody them for the first time, and, as a contribution to economic
literature, in the form of a complete narration.

Between the years 1816 and 1828, encouraged by the imposition of a low duty on imported metallic lead, the manufacture of
white lead as a basis for paints came into existence in the United
States and developed with great rapidity, the principal seats of
the business being the cities of New York, Philadelphia, and
Baltimore. But about the years 1826–28 the discovery of the

lead mines at Galena, Ill., became generally known, and as the
first reports were to the effect that the deposits were of such un-
paralleled richness, purity, magnitude, and easy accessibility as to
make it only a question of time when the whole world, from sheer
inability to compete, would become wholly dependent for its supplies of lead on this one locality, it was at once considered desirable by many people to establish, so far as fiscal legislation could
do it, a most extraordinary economic principle, and one which,
from that day to this, has proved popular in all tariff enactments
in the United States ; and this was to make the discovery or
recognition of the existence of any great natural advantages—
either in the way of mines, soils, climatic advantages, forests,
means of intercommunication or national characteristics—the
immediate occasion for cursing the country by the creation and
imposition of some new tax, thereby making dear what was before cheap, and endeavoring to work up to a state of abundance
through conditions of scarcity, artificially created and unnecessarily perpetuated. In this particular instance the principle was
exemplified by raising the duty on lead imported in pigs and bars
from one cent a pound to three cents; and to this extent increasing to the consumer the price of the raw material, whether of
foreign or domestic origin, and of all manufactured products in
which lead entered as the principal constituent.[1]   As the duty

[1] Among other illustrations to the same effect, drawn from actual and subsequent
experiences, the following are especially worthy of mention. From the foundation of the
government to the outbreak of the civil war in 1861, the imports of crude or unmanufactured copper into the United States were free, or subject to a mere nominal duty.
In 1861, however, in order to help meet the enormous expenditures occasioned by the
war, a duty of 2 cents per pound on such imports was imposed ; but subsequently, and
after the requirements for war expenditures had ceased, at the demand of the owners of
the richest copper mines in the world (which had been discovered on public lands on
Lake Superior, and sold by the government for a mere nominal price), the duty was
increased to 5 cents per pound ; a rate so prohibitory, that in 1878 only one pound of
foreign copper, yielding a revenue to the treasury of 5 cents, was imported.   The
further results of such legislation were, that the owners of the Lake Superior mines,
on an investment of a few hundred thousand dollars, received from fifteen to twenty
millions of dollars in dividends ; copper was made higher in price in the United States
than in any other civilized country ; and the product of the mines being in excess of
any domestic demand, the resulting surplus was regularly sold in Europe at a much
less price than the mine owners controlling the domestic market would allow it to be
sold to the American consumers.   And so the discovery of these rich mines of Lake
Superior, on the public lands of the nation, in place of having proved a benefit, have
actually resulted in misfortune and detriment of the whole people. Similar experiences,

was not at the same time correspondingly advanced on the import of white lead, and as the lead-mining interests of Galena were not prepared to supply at any price the immediate demand thus artificially created for their products in the domestic market, the American manufacturers of white lead all at once found their business threatened with utter destruction ; and, with intellects preternaturally sharpened by a prospective loss of a large invested capital, they looked shrewdly about to see in what manner they could save and protect themselves.

And putting on their spectacles, and scrutinizing carefully the entire tariff, as modified by the special act of 1828 referred to, they soon discovered that the government, while effectually closing and barring up the big door by which foreign lead could be imported, had inadvertently left wide open a smaller door beside it, inasmuch as while Congress had prescribed a duty of three cents per pound on lead imported in pigs and bars, they left a prior duty of fifteen per cent. *ad valorem* on the import of *old lead* fit only to be manufactured, unrepealed and in force. Those were the days of packet ships and slow communication with the Old World ; but we may readily believe that no time was unnecessarily wasted by those interested in this discovery; and at the earliest practicable moment afterwards agents of nearly every important American house engaged in the importation of metals—Barclay & Livingston, Boorman, Johnson, & Co., Hoffman, Bend, & Co., Phelps & Peck, William Wright & Co., and many lesser firms—were ransacking the markets of Europe for the purchase and shipment to the United States of old lead. Of course, the legitimate market supplies, never great, of this peculiar article soon gave out, but the agents and correspondents of the American houses being Yankees, proved fully equal to the emergency, and a scheme was forthwith devised to replenish the

though on a smaller scale, have in like manner followed the discovery in the United States of rich mines of bichromate of iron (from which chromate of potash, and yellow and green paints are made) and of nickel ; and would also undoubtedly have been the case with tin, had this metal been discovered in former years. For when, about the year 1870, enormous deposits of tin were reported to have been found in the Ozark Mountains of Missouri, attempts were at once made, on the mere basis of report, to remove tin as an importation from the free list, and make it subject to a duty ; and the effort was only abandoned when it was ascertained that what was supposed to be *tin*, was something else, and of no value.

stock by exchanging new lead for old, and contracts in more than one instance, for example, were actually entered into and carried out for stripping from extensive factories in different parts of England their old lead roofing—lead being then used more extensively than now in the place of slate—and replacing it without expense to the owners with new roofing on condition of receiving the old material.

In the course of time the old lead thus collected began to make its appearance on this side of the Atlantic, and arriving in large quantities—almost by the ship-load—at the ports of New York and Boston, naturally attracted the attention of the custom-house authorities, who at first demurred to its entry at the low duty of 15 per cent. *ad valorem.* The matter, however, being referred to the Treasury Department at Washington, an answer soon came back that the position of the merchants was unimpeachable, but the Department would have the law amended as soon as possible.

But the merchants by this time, in studying up the fiscal legislation of Congress in respect to lead in pigs and old lead, had made another discovery—and that was that the tariff act in force was mandatory to this further effect, namely, that if any person or persons should import musket balls or leaden bullets into the United States they should pay to the customs authorities a duty on the same of 15 per cent. *ad valorem,* and, in default thereof, the goods should be forfeited and the importers be punished. Like good citizens, therefore, the merchants made haste to obey the law, and their agents in Europe being duly instructed, lost no time in buying up all the musket balls and leaden bullets they could find for sale, and when the foreign markets were exhausted they had musket balls of the regulation weight and calibre largely manufactured, and all were duly shipped as fast as possible to the United States. Again the custom-house authorities objected, but again came back the response from Washington that the law was explicit in respect to the 15-per-cent. duty, and that nothing could be done in the way of restraining the importation of leaden bullets in place of pig lead until Congress had provided further legislation on the subject.

But the tariff acts in force from 1828 to 1832 were, however, almost as much a mystery and a muddle of perplexity as are the acts under which the customs are at present administered, and it was only after continuous study and investigation that their full depth of meaning and of wisdom could become evident. But the success attending the import of old lead and musket balls had been so remarkable, and the preservation and resuscitation of the " white lead " business so encouraging, that the merchants were stimulated to further fiscal investigations; and again putting on their spectacles, they discovered two other remarkable provisions of the then existing tariff which heretofore had not been considered of much importance. These provisions related, the one to " leaden weights " of all descriptions, and the other to " sounding leads," and were to the effect that if any person imported any of these articles into the United States he should pay on the same a duty of fifteen per cent. *ad valorem.*

It seems almost unnecessary to relate in detail the consequence of these discoveries, but it sufficeth to say that those were the good old days when false standards were far more of an abomination than they now are, and it was astonishing how great a demand all at once appeared to have been created in the United States for full, fresh, and new sets of leaden weights (from half an ounce to fifty-six pounds and upward, but notably of the heavier denominations), which had not had their accuracy impaired by continuous use and abrasion. If the exact truth, moreover, could now be known, it might also appear that many persons at that time (especially in the cities of New York and Boston) had somehow become indoctrinated with the idea that the possession of more " weights " would in some way increase the quantity of things to be weighed—in the same way as the progressive men of the present day have brought themselves to believe that the possession of more paper money will increase the value and quantity of the things that this same money can buy. Those were the days, also, when clocks were high and stood in corners rather than upon mantels, and were moved by weights rather than by springs, and our ancestors of forty years ago—and none knew better than they that " time is money "—all at once seemed possessed with the desire to have more clocks, for the import of heavy leaden clock-weights, with iron hooks neatly fitted to one end, and which *prima facie* could be only used for the manufacture of clocks, all at once increased and rapidly became a business of magnitude.

Navigators also about this time, it might be inferred, became more intelligent ; or, if not more intelligent, then, through a desire to save their insurance premiums, more cautious ; or, if not these, then the desire of American geographical students to study more accurately the sea bottom, might have been abnormally stimulated ; for in what other way could an excessive and unusual import of deep-sea sounding leads be accounted for ?—leads small, leads large, leads of two ounces weight, leads of seventy pounds weight, leads a few inches in length up to leads two feet in length—all with an eyelet at one end for the sounding line attachment and a cavity at the other for the reception of the tallow, by the agency of which specimens were to be brought up from the sea bottom.

But the custom-house authorities were practical men. They indulged in no philosophical reflections as to any abstract possible uses of the imported articles in question. They saw in all of them lead and lead only—and on lead, in the interests of the Galena mines and of the revenue, they wanted a duty of three cents per pound. They accordingly, as opportunity offered, seized and refused to deliver the exceptionally large invoices of "clock weights," "scale weights," and "sounding leads," and the appeal, as usual, from their proceedings went up from the merchants to Washington. But if the custom-house officials were practical men, the Treasury magnates at the capital, on the other hand, were strict constructionists, and as they found the statute written so they interpreted it ; and in all cases the arrested importations of the merchants were, after a little delay, restored and admitted to entry ; and in at least one case, where three cents per pound had been paid under protest on the above-mentioned leaden articles, the difference between that sum and fifteen per cent. was returned to the merchant by the Treasury. In fact, as " sea stores " of all descriptions were then on the free list, "sounding leads " might have been claimed to be exempt from all imposts ; but the merchants were generous, and this question does not appear to have been raised.

It is not to be denied, nevertheless, that by this time lead had got to be a very irritating topic to a Federal official ; and indeed it was only necessary to say " lead " to a United States district attorney, a collector, or revenue inspector, to seriously disturb his mental equanimity. An opportunity to retaliate upon their mercantile tormentors was therefore earnestly sought for, and before long such an opportunity seemed to present itself. A prominent New York house in the metal trade, which, in connection with some half dozen or more leading firms, had been engaged in importing old lead, musket bullets, sounding leads, clock weights, and the like, and passing them, under a strict but legal construction of the statute, at fifteen per cent. *ad valorem*, imported on one occasion, during the period under consideration, but subsequent to the events narrated, an invoice of stereotype metal. Now, stereotype metal was then on the free list of the tariff, and subject to no duty, and in this particular instance the importation had been made in consequence of a direct order received from one of the largest type founders in New York; but as it came in pigs or bars, was in unusual quantity, and consisted merely of lead mixed with comparatively small proportions of antimony and bismuth, the custom-house officials conceived the idea that it was only a new device of the enemy to take advantage of the faulty statute, and that the ultimate intent was to remelt the stereotype metal, separate its several constituents, and then dispose of the lead independently. The whole invoice was accordingly seized, and suit commenced in the United States District Court for its forfeiture, the government having previously ascertained, by means of an analysis of a sample bar, made at their request by the then famous New York chemist, old Dr. Chilton, that the metal contained somewhat more than eighty per cent. of lead. The District Attorney at that time was Price, afterward best known for some financial irregularities. The merchants, of course, resisted, and on the day of trial appeared in court with the type founder on whose account the metal was ordered, and other experts to prove that the import and prospective use of the metal were entirely legitimate. The government opened their case by stating their assumption that the metal was not imported for the manufacture of stereotypes, but for the purpose of defrauding the revenue, and, calling as their first witness Dr. Chilton, examined him somewhat as follows:

District Attorney—What is your profession? Dr. Chilton—A chemist.

Q. Where were you educated? A. In Edinburgh, and have followed for many years my profession in New York.

Q. Have you made an analysis of this imported metal [at the same time referring to one of the bars included in the invoice]? A. I have.

Q. Of what does it consist? A. Of some eighty per cent. of lead; the remainder, antimony, bismuth, and tin.

Q. Is it possible to separate these several constituents, as thus mixed, so as to use and sell them separately? A. Perfectly so.

Q. Please tell the Court what, in your opinion, would be about the expense of the operation. A. Rather more than all the materials are worth.

There was silence for a few moments. The District Attorney did not seem to be possessed of a further inquiring spirit. It was a warm summer's day, and the Judge (Betts), after mopping his face with his handkerchief, stretched his head forward, and, somewhat brusquely, asked if Mr. Price had any rebutting testimony, and, on receiving a negative reply, fell back in his chair with the remark: "Then the case had better be dismissed." And dismissed it was.

But the troubles of the custom-house officials were not yet ended; and here comes in that portion of this curious series of events which is best known to the public, is the most comical, and which, as has already been remarked, is often referred to in Congressional debates, when topics of the tariff, smuggling, or under valuations are under consideration.

The wicked merchants, encouraged by their complete success as law interpreters, had continued their tariff investigations, and had further found among its provisions in force one to the effect that "metal statuary and busts" might be imported free of duty. It was thereupon immediately determined by the merchants that if the American people desired to cultivate their taste, or keep alive the memory of the good and great of former days by adorning their houses and grounds with metal statuary, they ought to have the opportunity of so doing; and, accordingly, large orders were sent to Europe—at that time the exclusive seat of high art —for the manufacture of busts—mainly colossal—of Washington Lafayette, Napoleon, Moses, and the prophets, and not forgetting, also, duplicates or reproductions of the great works of antiquity; and as lead, of all the metals, seemed to possess in the highest degree the qualities of durability, tenacity, cheapness, and facility of being moulded, the statuary in question was directed to be made of lead. It should also be remarked in this connection that lead statuary fifty years ago was not the abnormal exceptional thing it now is. In fact it was then the common material for cheap imagery throughout Europe, when something less expensive than bronze or marble was desired, and filled the place which is now supplied by cast iron and zinc, but which materials fifty years ago were not thought susceptible of ornamental adaptation. And that the lead statuary in question was really ornamental is proved by the circumstance that some of it thus imported is yet in use for ornamental purposes, one piece embellishing, as recently as 1874, the garden of an eminent banker in New York. From such an æsthetic point of view, also, did the prosaic custom-house officers regard the first importations of these leaden images, and so might they long have continued to regard them, had the persons in Europe intrusted with their shipment been more careful in respect of packing. But when Washington came up out of the hold of the vessel after a rough voyage with his nose punched in, and Napoleon with his eyes sufficiently askew to require an operation for strabismus, and Moses looking very much like a subject on whom the law ought to be administered rather than an author and administrator of the law, suspicion was naturally excited, and forthwith the statuary was seized and held for forfeiture by the customs authorities. In answer, the importers, as before, pointed to the clear and explicit provision of the tariff then in force—" Metal statuary and busts free "—and urged the government, if they doubted, to institute a suit. But Mr. Price, the district attorney, had once burned his fingers with cold lead, and persistently refused to bring the matter into court. Thereupon one of New York's then best-known merchants and publicists, caused an invoice of the questionable statuary to be imported into Boston, and arranged with the district attorney of that port to try the issue in respect to its dutiable character. When the trial came on Daniel Webster appeared as counsel for the defence. His speech in answer to government was very brief but to the point, claiming the law provided for the admission of metal statuary, busts, etc., free, with no limit as to the kind or quantity, and that the imports in question were metal statuary, though made of lead.

When the case closed Mr. Webster requested the judge to charge the jury that they were to decide whether the articles were metal statuary, and if they found that they were, they must bring in a verdict for the defendants. The judge substantially did as requested, and the jury, in a few minutes after retiring, returned with a verdict for Mr. Leavitt.

The decision in this case practically put an end to the whole controversy. The lead statuary under seizure was released, the import was allowed to go on unrestricted, and, as soon as circumstances permitted, Congress amended the tariff by equalizing the duties on all forms of lead, and at the same time satisfied the white-lead manufacturing interest by fully protecting their products from foreign competition.

As this curious story has been heretofore told, the importation of the leaden statuary has been popularly attributed to the agency of the former well-known New York firm of Phelps, Dodge, & Co. This is, however, an error. The firm of Phelps, Dodge, & Co. was not, at the time of the occurrence of these events, in existence; and the old firm that preceded them—namely, that of Phelps & Peck, —although large importers of metals, were not concerned in this matter of the leaden images.

It would be a mistake, furthermore, to infer that like muddles and perplexities cease to characterize the tariff when Congress, taught by experience, successively remedied the omissions and commissions of the act of 1828. On the contrary, there has been hardly a tariff enacted since that time which has not the absurdities of the old lead, the musket balls, the clock weights, the deep-sea leads, and the leaden images in some form repeated. Thus, for example, in the tariff of 1846 a duty was imposed on flaxseed of twenty per cent., but in the tariff of 1857 linseed was made free, while flaxseed was charged fifteen per cent. duty. As might have been expected, the import of linseed was always large, but that of flaxseed very small.

When the manufacture of cloth-covered buttons began to be established in New England, one great obstacle in the way of producing an article sufficiently cheap and sufficiently nice to attract and build up a domestic demand, which had hitherto been mainly supplied by imported buttons of wood, metal, or bone, was the difficulty of obtaining at reasonable cost the essential

varieties of cloth ; the fabrics of wool and silk most suitable for
covering "button-moulds," or frames, being almost exclusively of
foreign manufacture, and subject on importation to such extreme
rates of duty as to make their use exceedingly costly. Rags,
however, could be imported free of duty ; and the shrewd Yankee
manufacturer took advantage of the situation by having his
foreign-made "button cloths" technically reduced to rags, by
cutting them up into small pieces, or by systematically perforating
the goods in the piece with holes previous to importation, a process which did not impair the value of the cloth for use as button-
covers, and really only anticipated one step in the process of
manufacturing. It is hardly necessary to say that the profits on
the device, so long as it was not interfered with by the officials,
were extraordinarily large, and constituted the foundation of a
large fortune; which, in part at least, was subsequently devoted
to the education of missionaries for the work of Christianizing
the heathen of other countries.

Again, in 1864, the manufacturers of spool thread, anxious to
shield themselves against all foreign competition, obtained a prohibitory duty on the import of unwound cotton thread or yarn.
When the law went into effect it was found that the result of the
new duty would be the destruction of the manufacture of fine
elastic fabrics, suspenders, gaiters, etc., as well as of certain
worsted fabrics, which were dependent on Europe for certain
qualities of warp yarns not then manufactured on this side of the
Atlantic. The difficulty was, however, got over by an absurd
Treasury ruling, that cotton warp or yarn intended for use in the
manufacture of elastic worsted or woollen fabrics was not unwound thread or yarn, but a manufacture of cotton "not otherwise provided for."

And, coming down still later, Congress, in 1872, enacted a
general reduction of ten per cent. in tariff rates on metals and
manufactures of metals—watches and jewelry excepted. It was
clear, however, that "watch cases" are not "watches," and
neither are springs, escapements, wheels, etc., etc., considered
separately. The course of trade, therefore, in respect to imported
watches, soon adjusted itself as follows : The movements taken
out of the cases, packed in separate cartons, but carefully num-
bered, were, when thus imported, clearly manufactures of metals,

and as such entitled to the rebate of ten per cent. In like manner the cases, without the essentials of a watch in them, were also held to be nothing but manufactures of metal (gold and silver), and so treated in respect of duty. Watches, of course, when they come in as watches, pay full duty ! ! !

Thus the old, old story of the effect of impolitic and absurd restrictions on trade and commerce, the lesson of which Europe through centuries of experience learned and profited by, continues to repeat itself in the fiscal policy of the United States. Let us hope that the result here, too, at no distant day will be what it has been elsewhere—namely, to force men to the conclusion that the best system of taxation is to tax but a few things, and then leave those taxes to diffuse, and adjust, and apportion themselves by the inflexible laws of trade and political economy —and, furthermore, to recognize that no system of government has any just claim to the title of free, which arbitrarily takes from its citizens any portion of their property for any purpose other than to defray the necessary expenditures of the State.

THE SILVER QUESTION.

THE DOLLAR OF THE FATHERS *versus* THE DOLLAR OF THE SONS.

THE substance of this essay appeared originally in the columns of the Cincinnati *Commercial*, July 2, 1877, in the form of a letter addressed to the editor, Murat Halstead, Esq. The motive that mainly prompted its writing, was a desire to set forth the inconsistency and absurdity of the attempt to win popular support for unlimited silver coinage, and its enforced circulation as currency through the invention and use of the term " *The Dollar of the Fathers*," and inferentially claiming thereby, that because in the old days of low prices and limited cash transactions the cumbersome and bulky silver dollar had suited the requirements of the fathers, it should, therefore, be venerated and used by their sons, notwithstanding the changes in the methods and mechanism of business, consequent on a higher civilization, clearly demanded something radically different and better. A continued demand for the essay in a more permanent and readable shape, and the continued interest on the part of the public in Europe as well as in the United States, in the question of the future use of silver as a material for coinage, subsequently induced its republication, with additions, in a pamphlet form; but the edition of this last soon passed out of print.

WHY THE CHINESE DO NOT COIN THE PRECIOUS METALS.

IN China the Government long ago ceased to coin the precious metals or regulate "the value thereof." Gold in China is not money. Silver is money; but neither are coined. Both are merchandise, and pass by weight and fineness. But although the Chinese Government has abandoned the coinage and regulation of the value of the precious metals, it has not absolutely and entirely abandoned all coinage.

It provides one coin, and one only, for the use of its people, namely, an ugly, coarse, and comparatively heavy disk, composed mainly of iron, with a little copper; cast, and not stamped, and bearing some rude characters, letters, or signs upon its surfaces. This coin, which is known among foreigners by the name of *cash*, has a value of about one mill, American money, and is made with

34

a hole in the centre for convenience of stringing in tens and its decimal multiples. It occasionally drifts into the regions of Western civilization, and doubtless often suggests the inquiry, "How can any people use a coin so heavy and of such trifling value to any advantage in making their exchanges?" The answer is a very simple one. The wages of manual labor in China do not in general exceed fifteen or twenty cents per day (our money); and these wages serve for the support and tolerable comfort of the great mass of the people, because, in part by reason of the great stability of values, but mainly because of the fact that labor itself is the real standard of value, to which the prices of all the products of labor adjust themselves; so that in China, upon apparently small wages, a man may live as well as in other countries upon nominally larger wages. But whatever may be the wages of a day in any country, they must be capable of division into many parts, in order to be exchanged for the many necessities of an individual or a family. In most countries this division is effected by the use of coined (metallic) money. But with wages at twenty cents per day, the use of coined gold would obviously be impracticable. The equivalent of a day's labor in gold would be too small to be handled conveniently; the equivalent of an hour's labor in gold would be no bigger than a pin's head. And in a smaller degree would be also the inconvenience of using coined silver for effecting the division of wages ruling at the rate of 15 to 20 cents per day. A quarter day's wages would be represented by a silver coin not so large as our 5-cent piece; and an hour's wages, which in turn might buy a pound of rice, and perchance a chopstick to eat it with, by a piece of silver no larger in circumference than the flat surface of a small split pea. Therefore the Chinese intelligently discard the use of coined gold and silver, and in their place have substituted the bulky and cheap, but at the same time admirable, because well adapted and useful, *cash,* which sustains the same relations to their low nominal wages and prices that gold and silver coin sustains to the nominally high wages and prices of other countries; 200 pieces of *cash* dividing a day's wages of 20 cents into 200 equal parts for convenience in exchange for commodities and for the payment of taxes, estimated by a correspondingly low standard. Now all this comprises a lesson of experience, which those interested in the question to what extent can or shall silver be made the circulating medium, and an instrumentality of exchange in the United States, may do well to consider. That it is possible also to debase and over-issue a currency or circulating media of as low a type and of as small absolute value as the Chinese "cash," and that the resulting consequences of such "debasement" and "over-issue" will be precisely the same in character and influence, as when entailed upon a currency representing larger specific exchanges and greater specific values, is shown by the following curious story of Chinese experience, which has been told to the writer by an American merchant, resident in China at the time of its occurrence, and who was not only personally cognizant of the facts but also an eye-witness of some of the involved transactions.

Shortly after the termination of the first Anglo-Chinese war (1838), the authorities of Pekin delegated the government of the great city of Foo Chow—one of the five commercial ports—to a mandarin of great reputation and learning, who, though invested with despotic power, governed on the whole so well that the people regarded him in the light of a father, and in his visits to the city, from his official residence outside the walls, were accustomed to receive him with the utmost respect and deference—standing in front of their houses, arrayed in their best garments, making low obeisances as he passed, and crowning him and his retinue with garlands of flowers. But, after a time, the love of gain taking possession of the ruler, he sought to gratify it by secretly withdrawing the "cash" in current circulation, having a market value as metal of about a tenth of a cent, and re-issuing the same in larger quantity and of lighter weight, and placing the difference in value in his pocket as private property. The first thing the shop-keepers, the market-men, and the laborers knew about it was, that they all at once found themselves rather abundantly supplied with "cash" currency. The abundance did not, however, at first disturb them, because legitimate Chinese cash, like all other true money, flows where it is most wanted, and so finds its level. But in this case, the quality being inferior, the natural and legitimate "flow" was checked, the "cash" accumulated, and its value rapidly declined, so that at first 12, then 14, 15, and, finally, 16 cash were required to purchase what formerly could have been obtained for 10,—in the same way as the purchasing power of our "greenbacks" declined during the war in proportion to the abundance of their issue.

The people saw this, knew the cause of the depreciation and who was responsible, and proceeded to execute justice after the Chinese fashion ; for, when on a certain day the mandarin visited the city, as by previous notice, the people in unusual numbers turned out to meet him ; but not this time with flowers and obeisance, but with strings of the debased money, which they threw at him and his retinue ; and also so beat them with it, that while some were killed, the ruler barely escaped with his life. Returning, however, to his palace without the city, he immediately despatched a courier to Pekin, informing the Government that an insurrection had broken out, and demanding troops to seize and punish the offenders. But the Government was not much alarmed ; it is used to this method of impeachment by the people, it knew there was something wrong, made no haste to send force, but decided to wait for further information ; and in about three weeks the people's courier, travelling by slower methods, arrived and communicated the other side of the story. Thereupon an investigation was made, and the statement of the people having been found correct, the mandarin was deposed and ordered to Pekin, where he was publicly informed that, having sinned in the highest degree, inasmuch as he had abused his official power and trust to wrong and defraud the people, there was no longer any fit place for him among the living ; but that, in recognition of his former services, he would be permitted to effect his own departure rather than put the state to any trouble —an intimation which, there is every reason to believe, was speedily complied with.

PRICES, WAGES, AND CUSTOMS IN 1792.

In 1792 (when the dollar of the fathers was first established), the average price of the ordinary labor of adult males was not in excess of 40 and 45 cents per day. [The pay of soldiers in the army was $4 per month, and one ration per day of the value of 12 cents. The military storekeeper at Springfield, Mass., received $40 per month ; artificers and armorers at posts on the frontier, $5 per month ; United States District Judges, $1,000 per annum ;

messengers in the Government offices, $150 per annum.] The prices of all commodities, conforming then as now to the prices of labor, were also correspondingly small, while cash transactions were exceedingly limited. The fathers, moreover, were a stay-at-home people, and made but few journeys, or journeys of any considerable distance. Under such circumstances, the gravity of silver was a matter of very little consequence, and a bulky, cumbersome coinage (the dollar of the fathers) was not then an inconvenient instrumentality for making exchanges, and for the same reason that the heavy cheap Chinese *cash* is not an inconvenient instrumentality for making the present retail Chinese exchanges.

The present conditions of affairs, comparing 1885 with 1790, or with even 1840, a period of fifty years later, is, however, entirely different. The prices of labor and of its products have greatly advanced. [The pay of soldiers in the army is $13 per month, and one ration. The military storekeeper at Springfied, Mass., receives $200 per month ; armorers, from $1.75 to $3.50 per day ; United States District Judges, $4,000 per annum ; messengers in Government offices, $750 to $1,000 per annum.] Now everybody travels. Comparatively, and probably absolutely, more people go every year from the Atlantic to the Pacific, and *vice versa*, than fifty years ago went from State to State. Negroes now travel in the Southern country ten times as much probably as did all the people in that section before the Revolution. Now cash transactions are numerous and often very extensive. Everybody carries more or less money in his pocket, and it is far from unusual for individuals to carry habitually as much as $100 on their persons. No one would think of starting upon any considerable journey with any less sum of money at his immediate command. Under such circumstances the weight or "tonnage" of silver becomes an element the importance of which has thus far been overlooked in considering the extent to which this metal can in future be used as currency.

THE WEIGHT OF SILVER.

Eighteen dollars and fourteen cents, represented by the present subsidiary silver coinage of the United States, weigh a pound ; one hundred dollars weigh five and a half pounds, and for every thousand dollars that a man is paid in silver, a wheelbarrow would become necessary if he proposed to remove it. The wheelbarrow, in fact, will become the essential, and possibly the fashionable, portemonnaie for all who propose to engage in any considerable moneyed transactions, if the dollar of the fathers is to be made by law the principal circulating medium. If a business was extensive, and it became desirable to pay at once $300,000 (in the dollar of the fathers), then the wheelbarrow would have to be discarded, and the railroad car called into requisition.[1] And if silver is to be made the basis of banking it is well to consider that there is not probably a bank vault in the country that can hold and sustain a single million of coined silver weighing more than twenty-five tons. If silver is to become our practical single standard, a new style of bank architecture must be adopted.

RELATION OF NATURAL LAWS AND NATIONAL NECESSITIES TO THE SILVER DOLLAR.

While silver, therefore, is not an inconvenient coin in countries of low prices and limited internal exchanges, and however it may once have favorably answered to conditions in the United States, our present condition of affairs—our high nominal wages and prices, and the necessity that exists for the carrying of comparatively large sums of money upon the person—would obviously seem to preclude the possibility of its use for the bulk of even the retail business of the country. And if by law silver should now be made the exclusive standard for money values in the United States, no law could enforce its use for general circulation. Substitutes of paper money would be resorted to and speedily replace it.

Again, if it is proposed to do business with all the world on terms of equality—and the great trouble with us as a nation to-

[1] The following table, prepared for the writer by Mr. E. B. Elliott of the United States Treasury Department, represents the weights in pounds avoirdupois of various sums of United States Silver coinage :

Number of dollars.	Weight in pounds, avoirdupois.
100	5.51
1,000	55.12
10,000	551.16
30,000	1,653.47
50,000	2,755.78
100,000	5,511.55
300,000	16,534.66

day is, that by reason of various circumstances we are not so able, and, therefore, cannot dispose of the excess of our commodities—we must make use of those instrumentalities of trade of every kind (ships, engines, railways, and more especially the money) which the commercial world has adopted. Now the money of the commercial world, of all international trade, is mainly gold ; and the United States has little commerce with any country which uses a silver standard. To some this may appear as a matter of very little importance ; but this opinion will not long be entertained if it is remembered that so sharp is the competition of various countries for trade, and so completely have the barriers of space and time been broken down by the steamship, the railroad, and the telegraph, that the question as to who shall take the lead in supplying the world with certain great commodities is going to turn in the future, not on cents, but on fractions of cents, per yard, pound, or bushel; and that the opportunity for employment and for the earning of a comfortable livelihood may be denied to thousands by the apparently trifling fluctuations in the purchasing power or the inconvenience of the money which the country may use in making its exchanges.

And if the American laborer—if the masses of our people now seeking employment, and painfully realizing that in the midst of abundance the nation cannot market its abundance, and because it cannot market it, production stops and poverty increases—could also realize how much of all this trouble is connected with the attempt to make the United States adopt and use forms of money, or media of exchange, which our own experience and the experience of other nations teaches we should not use, the advocacy of any thing but most stable, non-fluctuating, and commercially valuable currency would be any thing but popular.

As a condition of national defence, furthermore,—to enable the nation to carry on a future war, foreign or domestic, offensive or defensive—a full supply of the most valuable coin that is purchasable and salable without discount in other countries (and so available for settling international balances) is more necessary than a full supply of arms, ships, or forts. And the safest depositories of such coin are not the vaults of banks or of the Federal Treasury, but the pockets of the people ; and the conveniences of the people would prompt them to employ more coin, and so keep up a greater supply of the essential munition of war, if gold was the standard, than if the standard was exclusively a commodity so cumbersome as silver.

But the remonetization of silver, or the proposed restoration of the "dollar of the fathers," if silver continues depreciated, would be equivalent to abolishing the use of coin to any large extent as a circulating medium; or, in other words, natural laws have ordained that the use of silver, in any highly prosperous commercial community, shall be limited to its use as a subsidiary token coinage; while sound policy and the dictates of national interest require that it shall not be made legal tender except as a token of currency for small amounts.

REMONETIZATION OF SILVER A QUESTION OF NATIONAL CONVENIENCE.

Remonetization of silver is, therefore, a question of convenience, of tonnage, of gravity, and cost of transportation. The kind of coin a country should have and use must depend upon the value of its transactions, the prices of its labor, and the rapidity and magnitude of its exchanges. Iron was not ill adapted to Sparta as a metal for coinage. It would not, however, suit Chicago; and everybody in Chicago and elsewhere who will take the trouble to understand why it would not suit, will at the same time see that it is not the dollar of the Spartan daddy or of the fathers that we want, but the dollar of the Yankee sons that the country requires; and that it ultimately must and will have, if it proposes to prosper.

THE FALLACY OF A CHEAP CURRENCY.

But the advocates of the remonetization and extended use of silver as currency plant themselves on what they regard as a fundamental axiomatic principle—namely, that it is necessary and desirable to have a cheap currency. But, as a matter of fact, no commodity currency (gold, silver, copper, iron, or cabbage) of one kind can be relatively cheaper than one of another kind. The value of each (if not a token currency, and minting is free) will depend upon the amount of labor embodied in or that will be required to purchase it: and no legislation can give to it any other value. If a gold dollar cost on an average one day's labor, and a silver dollar nine tenths of a day's labor, a dollar and ten cents of nominal silver will sell for the same price as a dollar in gold. Whatever nominal value, therefore, legislation may give to gold or silver, it will have no influence on the price of any commodity in the open (or world's) market. Neither gold nor silver can be made *fiat* money as to future transactions; and the amount of labor expended in their production will establish their final and permanent value. If this value should fail to be recognized for a time, labor will go into other channels, and the production of these metals will cease until their labor value is again recognized.

NO NATIONAL ECONOMY IN RESTORING THE DOLLAR OF THE FATHERS.

As these truths are, however, persistently ignored by the majority of those who have undertaken to agitate for a renewed use of the dollar of the fathers, and as the force of the argument against the use of silver by reason of its cumbersomeness may be attempted to be met by assuming that it is proposed to use silver as a basis for the issue of a (paper) circulating medium, and not as a medium directly, it is desirable to still further elucidate this subject by illustration.

Thus, if it requires $500,000,000 to supply an exclusively gold currency for this country, and silver is depreciated ten per cent. in comparison with gold, it will require $550,000,000 in silver to perform the same work ; and it will require the same amount of commodities or embodied labor to buy the exclusively gold currency that it will to buy the exclusively silver currency. Whatever may be the dollar or the unit of coin adopted by any country, it will have no effect on future transactions, for prices will adapt themselves to the amount of labor embodied in the new coin, whether it be of great or small value, nominal or real. No one will be deceived by a mere nominal dollar. If it represents less embodied labor than the real dollar, it will depreciate just in proportion to the difference in the amount of labor embodied in the real and in nominal coin, and prices of every kind will advance just in proportion to the depreciation of the coin unit that is used.[1] If the

---

[1] The volume of the French assignate (the irredeemable paper of the French revolutionary period) is said to have at one time reached the extent of 45,000,000,000 francs, or $9,000,000,000 ; and the prices of services and commodities so adjusted themselves to this condition of fiscal affairs, that 6,000 livres (about $18\frac{1}{2}$ cents each) was the usual fare for a ride in an ordinary hackney coach.

gold dollar should be made to contain double the amount of pure gold contained in the present dollar, prices, measured in dollars, would immediately depreciate one half, and it would require only a mental operation to reduce the prices of commodities to the new standard. On the other hand, if a depreciated silver dollar currency should be adopted, it would only require a like mental effort on the part of the seller of property to advance his prices in proportion to the depreciation of the new coin, and no one would be deceived in either case. The aggregate nominal silver circulation would, however, be increased in proportion to the comparative depreciation of silver, and would cost in exchange for other products just the same amount as an aggregate gold circulation would cost. In other words, an exclusively aggregate gold currency can be bought as cheaply and with as little burden to the country as an exclusively aggregate silver currency, for they are both worth what they embody of labor—no more or any less on the average.

When the Connecticut Yankees counterfeited the wampum which Peter Stuyvesant made currency in New Amsterdam, it continued to depreciate in value until it sold at a price which barely remunerated the counterfeiters for its manufacture and counterfeiting only ceased when the price, or exchangeable value, was reduced below the cost of its manufacture. If we permitted counterfeit notes to pass as legal tender, they would finally come down to represent the mere cost of the material of which they are composed, and of their manufacture, and would then become a commodity currency.

From these considerations, therefore, it would seem clear that there is nothing to be gained as to future transactions by having the coin currency of the country composed of one or the other of the two metals—gold or silver,—except so far as one may have an advantage over the other in respect to convenience, adaptation to the business of the country—domestic and foreign,—portability, and the like; and on all these points the balance of advantage for all transactions above $20 (a sum weighing more than a pound in silver) is largely on the side of gold; as will be evident when it is remembered that it requires sixteen times more time to count silver in any considerable quantity than it does to count a like value in gold; sixteen times more strength to handle it;

sixteen times more packages, casks, or capacity to hold it, and sixteen times more expense to transport it. In other words, in this saving age, to use silver for large transactions, in the place of gold, is a misapplication and waste of fifteen sixteenths of a given unit of effort, time, expense, and capacity, when one sixteenth would accomplish the same result.

SILVER INCONVENIENT BOTH FOR GENERAL CIRCULATION AND FOR BANK RESERVES.

Whatever coin is held as a reserve, or basis for banking, must at times be counted and at times transported from bank to bank, from city to city, from State to State, and from nation to nation. Bank-notes must be redeemed somewhere and at some time, and if the redeeming coin is inconvenient for general circulation and inconvenient to handle, count, and transport, or to use as a bank reserve, its value as a redeeming coin will be diminished to the extent of all these inconveniences. The value of a redeeming currency consists largely in its adaptability to general circulation ; but if the currency is bulky and ponderous, its value is diminished, because it is a constant menace to the creditor, who, at the arbitrary will or caprice of the debtor, can be compelled to bring his wheelbarrow, cart, or freight-car, and receive the cumbersome coin. It may also be here pertinently asked, If silver is never to be counted, handled, weighed, or transported, why remove it from its native bed in the mines ?

THE RELATIVE VALUE OF GOLD AND SILVER DETERMINED BY NATURAL AND NOT ARTIFICIAL LAWS.

One element of confusion that has been introduced in the recent discussions of the question of the use or disuse of silver as a material for currency has been the proposition soberly put forth, that the permanent and ultimate value of whatever is used as money depends on legislation ; or, what is the same thing, that the value of a commodity can be established by law, and is not necessarily based upon the amount of labor employed in its production. But if all countries should demonetize both gold and silver, the market value of both metals must ultimately, by natural laws, be the same as now, when they are almost universally recognized as money. Universal demonetization would at first produce a surplus of the precious metals in form of coin. Production would cease—that is, the mines would be closed—and the coin in existence would finally be absorbed in the arts and for ornaments. Loss and abrasion would, however, continue, and at length new demands for the arts would arise, which could only be supplied by a remuneration for labor sufficient to induce a re-opening of the mines, or what would be equal to the remuneration obtained by following other employments. When railroads re-placed stage-coaches, there was in some sections of the country for a period a surplus of coaches and horses. But natural laws in process of time restored the equilibrium, and now horses and coaches cannot be bought at any less prices, or even as cheap, as at the period when the displacement occurred.

Authorities differ as to the cause of the present depreciation of silver. But the drift of opinion with political economists, and those who have made the subject a study, is that the present de-preciation is not permanent, but has been produced mainly by the action of certain of the governments of Europe demonetizing it, and forcing its sale as a commodity upon the world's market. From 1857 to 1873 (which latter year was the time when the Ger-man Government announced the demonetization of silver), the variations in the market price of bar-silver in the London market were between $60\frac{5}{16}$ and $61\frac{11}{16}$ pence per standard ounce, or, in other words, during the whole of this period the silver dollar (of $412\frac{1}{2}$ grains) of the United States was worth more than its gold dollar ; and for a period of six years (1858–1864) it exceeded it in value by over four per cent. Since 1873 the decline in the value of silver has been rapid ; the fall being from $59\frac{1}{4}$ pence in 1873 to an average of 50.79 for 1883, and to $49\frac{1}{2}$ in April, 1885, which is equivalent to a reduction in the value of the silver dollar in com-parison with gold, from 100.45 in 1873 to 85.57 in April, 1885. At present the annual production of silver is somewhat in excess of the annual product of gold ; the value of the world's production of the two metals (stated in dollars) for the year 1883, according to the estimate of Mr. Burchard, the Director of the Mint of the United States, having been $94,027,901 of gold, and $114,217,733 of silver. From 1877 to 1883 inclusive, the aggregate world's production, according to the same authority, was, however, $743,-166,783 of gold, and $678,884,932 of silver.

All the more productive silver mines are now producing a large percentage of gold in connection with silver ; and the improved machinery for working ores of silver are equally applicable to the working of ores containing gold, while one process, largely profitable for the working of gold—washing under hydraulic pressure—is not at all applicable to the working of silver. Of course it is not possible to foretell with certainty whether silver may not be hereafter produced more abundantly and with less labor than at present, or formerly, and less in proportion than is now required for the production of gold. But be this as it may, the amount of labor expended in producing either metal in the future must, as in the past, regulate the relative value of each. If silver should cease to be a legal tender throughout the world, it would still continue to be used as money, until a substitute in the form of gold could be obtained. Silver-coin is a non-perishable article, and the amount of pure silver contained in such coin is well known. It would, therefore, continue to be used at the convenience of every community—at its market value in exchanges—until an ample supply of the metal made, legal tender in the form of coin, was obtained. Stage-coaches continue to be used after the introduction of railroads until the supply and service of railroad cars are ample. The theory, therefore, that the demonetization of silver will produce a sudden vacuum of metallic currency, or a demand for gold, more than sufficient to cause its production to the extent required, is chimerical and without foundation.

THE GOLD STANDARD OF THE COMMERCIAL WORLD A NECESSITY FOR THIS COUNTRY.

As already pointed out, the principal cause of the *present* depreciation of silver has been the discarding and sale of its silver currency by Germany ; and as the great commercial nations of the world did not require this discarded silver, and would not purchase it for any purpose, depreciation has been the inevitable temporary result. The foreign commerce of the East Indies, to which countries this surplus of silver must ultimately be exported, is limited ; and these sections of the world, however much they may want silver, cannot suddenly receive and pay for large quantities of it. They must pay for what they receive with their exports, and these exports, with their limited foreign commerce, cannot be suddenly increased. But at the same time it is not improbable that the East, after a while, will absorb all the present apparent surplus silver of the West, a result which the recent extension of the Russian dominion over Central Asia will undoubtedly accelerate ; for it is admitted that one result of such dominion has been to give security to life and property to large sections of country and to great numbers of people where such conditions did not formerly exist, and these, in turn, must result in great extension of production and exchange, and the consequent increased demand for and use of (silver) money.

At present the East seems to require annually at least $50,-000,000 of silver[1] ; for the years 1875–6, the exports from the West to the East exceeded $75,000,000.

If now the United States should ally its destiny to a silver currency, and we should find at any time that we had an excess of silver, we should be in the present predicament of Germany— with no immediate purchaser or reservoir in the commercial world with which we have intimate relations to receive it.[2] We should be not less embarrassed if for any reason we needed suddenly an increased amount of silver; for then we should be obliged to draw it back through the same narrow and distant channels, requiring both time and expense.

WHY GIVE TO OTHER NATIONS AN OPTION TO TAKE OUR GOLD AT LESS THAN ITS VALUE IN THE WORLD'S MARKET ?

Again, for the United States to now abandon the single and present exclusively gold standard, and adopt the bi-metallic standard (both metals being made legal tender in the form of coin), would amount to practically giving to all the world the privilege of taking all our gold at a nominal price in silver, or all our silver at a nominal price in gold. For arbitrarily fix what relations of value we will between gold and silver, there will

---

[1] Mr. J. Hector, Deputy Secretary of the Bank of Bengal, has recently estimated that British India absorbed $820,000,000 of silver in the twenty years prior to June, 1875, in excess of her exports of that metal.

[2] *This prediction, made when this essay was written in 1877, has since been abundantly verified.*

always be a liability to such changes in these relative values as to create an opportunity for a profit by interchanging the one for the other in the form of coin, the value of which has been arbitrarily established (temporarily) by law. Now, what object can the people of the United States have in giving to the rest of the world such an option, when none of the commercial countries with which we are on intimate commercial relations propose to extend to us any such privilege? The creating of conditions whereby such an option can be given to foreign countries will unquestionably entail upon us as a nation great inconveniences in the future, as it has in the past. At times it may siphon out of the country so much of our entire circulation as may be silver and replace it by gold; and at another time by the change of temporary market values, or changes in the legislation of other countries, the gold may be siphoned out and the silver return. Any sudden influx of foreign coin—gold or silver —would not, however, be readily and at once practically available, as the people would not at once willingly receive and admit the coins of foreign nations into general circulation. But as the capacity of our mints will be inadequate to meet these extraordinary demands that may arise, the necessities of the people may compel them to receive foreign coins for a time, whose value they are incapable of suddenly appreciating; thereby producing endless confusion and uncertainty, as was the case previous to 1853, when the country was flooded with old Spanish and Mexican depreciated coin, and when silver of American coinage of full legal weight flowed out of the country as fast as the mints could issue it. If France should admit free coinage and unrestrained circulation of silver, and silver continue depreciated, she would have to immediately mint anew not less than $700,000,000 of silver, which, by the competition of bullion brokers, would be sent to her in exchange and for the supplanting of the $700,000,000 of gold which she now possesses. This vast sum is more than sufficient for all the available silver in the world to cushion upon, if France should again adopt unlimited coinage of silver, and maintain her standard of $15\frac{1}{2}$ to 1. Nor could we under such circumstances retain in this country a single dollar of silver, if it was remonetized here according to the standard of 16 to 1. In fact, with a bi-metallic standard we cannot control and say what kind of coin we will have in circulation; for other countries can at their will draw from us either all our silver or all our gold, and substitute the one metal for the other. Long before we nominally demonetized silver, it was practically demonetized and banished from our territory. The recent depreciation of silver is, however, due to the recent action of the German Government; *and if any debtor therefore, has now a grievance by reason of the demonitization of silver, it is a grievance against the German Empire and not against the Government of the United States.* Prudence, therefore, would seem to dictate that whether debtors have or have not a grievance, we should not again, by adopting the bi-metallic standard, permit the practical demonetization or monetization of either silver or gold in this country to be absolutely under the control of other governments. We cannot be masters of the situation with a bi-metallic standard. We can only control the kind of coin we will use by utterly refusing to give the option which the bi-metallic standard implies, and the real question of the whole controversy is: "Shall we have the coin of our choice or the coin which other nations may select to dole out to us as their caprice or interest may from time to time dictate?"

On the other hand, the great commercial countries with which we are in intimate relations, and which recognize the single gold standard, have great reservoirs of gold, and ability through their foreign commerce to either receive our surplus gold and pay for it, or send us their surplus gold and receive our products in exchange. These great reservoirs of gold, furthermore, immediately respond to any deficiencies or demands for gold in the various commercial countries using gold as a standard, and so, by the law of supply and demand, keep the volume of gold in equilibrio with the volume of commodities to be measured, and greatly aid in maintaining, in respect to most articles, a uniformity of prices. It would seem to be apparent, therefore, from these considerations alone, that for this country to now reject the coin of the great commercial nations as a standard of value, and adopt another standard, or two standards, would inevitably entail upon it great and incalculable loss and inconvenience, and powerfully contribute to arrest our future industrial and commercial development.

THE DOLLAR OF THE FATHERS AND THE PAYMENT OF DEBTS.

The question of next and final importance to be considered is: Is it desirable to provide by legislation that debts [1] incurred prior to 1873, when silver was demonetized, may be paid in either gold or silver, as the law authorized before that period? If silver is to be permanently and largely depreciated relatively to gold, in consequence of a diminution in the amount of labor required to produce silver, this is a practical and important question of constitutional law and morals. But if the present price of silver is owing to temporary influences, and if within a few years it is likely to resume its old price in the markets of the world; or if the adoption on the part of the United States of the bi-metallic standard will, as soon as our mints have coined all the silver presented for coinage, restore silver to par, or nearly par, with gold, the question is comparatively unimportant. For the debtor cannot show that he has been injured unless he can prove that silver, as merchandise, would be depreciated, relatively to gold, after restoration of the bi-metallic standard, as it existed at the time his debt was contracted. Let us, therefore, examine the question from the standpoint of constitutional law and morals.

Debts payable in coin are in effect payable in commodities. A coined dollar before 1873 in this country was not an imaginary unit, but a physical actuality, composed of 412½ grains of silver, or 28.8 grains of gold. In all commercial transactions common honesty also requires that the dollar shall always be treated as a commodity—that is, that its name shall always indicate a given fineness and weight of metal. A bushel is not an imaginary measure of capacity; a yard is not an imaginary measure of length; a pound is not an imaginary measure of weight; and a dollar ought not to be regarded as in any sense an imaginary measure of value.

Again, debts payable in coin dollars are stipulated rights to specific property, and in both law and morals should be held equally sacred with property itself. Any interference with the rights of contracts is only a form of theft or robbery. It is true that there has never been any national law requiring that coin contracts shall be payable in gold and silver coins of the weight and fineness established by law at the time the contracts are

---

[1] *Railroad and other mortgage bonds, Government and State securities, and the like.*

made, but it is generally recognized, nevertheless, as a moral and constitutional obligation to pay in the same number of grains of pure metal as the law required when a given contract was made. And it is time that Congress should act and proclaim that this hereafter must be the known, conceded, and recognized rule. There is no reason, furthermore, why this rule should not be applicable to all debts contracted when silver was a practical legal tender, even if silver is permanently depreciated, and if its full remonetization will not restore it to par with gold.

THE ADOPTION OF THE BI-METALLIC OR ALTERNATE STANDARD IS A VIOLATION OF THE NATURAL LAW OF SUPPLY AND DEMAND, WHEN ONE COIN IS MORE CONVENIENT THAN THE OTHER.

It is claimed by some that the demonetization of silver, and the adoption of a single gold standard, will so far appreciate the price and value of gold, as to greatly increase the burden of existing debts, and diminish the supply of useful instrumentalities for effecting national exchanges. But this, although a specious, is an utterly false theory, unsustained by either facts or logic. Any demand, where human industry is left free, will be met by a corresponding supply. The fact that there may be at a given time an increased demand for gold, and a diminished demand for silver, does not necessarily indicate or prove, that the cost in labor of producing gold has increased, or the cost of producing silver has decreased. It simply indicates the direction that natural laws are giving to production, and also that the same laws are interposing obstacles in the way of producing things inconvenient or useless. It is undoubtedly true that the cost of producing both gold and silver is much less than formerly. Every railroad and other modern improvement, which gives cheaper clothing and food to miners, as well as all labor-saving machinery employed in mining, enables labor to produce a larger amount of gold and silver in a given time. Hence the great depreciation of both gold and silver during the last third of a century. And the probabilities are that this depreciation in the value of this precious metal will further continue; and creditors must submit to such results. Within the next quarter of a century, instead of one railroad crossing our continent (as in 1877), there will probably be half a dozen, with several branches, further

developing our natural reservoirs of gold and silver.   In fact the
recent abundant, or, what is the same thing, cheap production of
both gold and silver, is the sole cause which has necessitated the
partial demonetization of silver—the most cumbersome metal—
by countries maintaining a high scale of prices of wages and
commodities.   In other words, it is the abundance, not scarcity,
of the precious metals that has given rise to the controversy as
to what metals it is expedient to use at this time for circulating
media.   No one can suppose that this controversy about demonetization of silver has been occasioned by any abstract desire
for discussion; it has been forced on the world by the necessities
of the situation.   There is a natural law by which both labor
and capital tend to the most profitable employments, and
if there is a temporary increased demand for gold and a temporary diminished demand for silver, labor and capital in the
production of gold will be supplemented, until an equilibrium is
established, and without any reference to the permanent cost
of the production of either metal.   Supply and demand are to
production what waves are to the ocean ; and notwithstanding
the depressions created always and everywhere by these waves, all
scientists agree that the general and average level of the ocean is
constant and unvarying.   It is by the natural laws of supply and
demand that the introduction of the most desirable commodities
is always stimulated, and the production of surplus and unsuita-
ble articles is checked and discouraged, without reference to their
cost of production.   Thus far all the evidence tends to show that
the cost of producing silver relatively to gold has not been
apparently diminished.   Now, applying these principles to the
problem under consideration, it follows that the adoption of the
bi-metallic, or alternate standard may, for a period, create an artificial demand for a coin not suited to the wants of some com-
munities, the result of which may be the indefinite production of
an article not well suited to certain human wants.   Nature has
created an abundance of both gold and silver.   If man refuses to
produce the metal best adapted to his wants, and persists in
producing another, ill-adapted to his wants, by an artificial, bi-
metallic standard, he makes warfare upon the beneficence of
the Almighty.   Therefore the conclusion :—that the adoption
of a bi-metallic standard is a violation of the natural laws of

supply and demand, and an attempt to provide for the survival of unfittest.

Again, the gold-producing power of the earth is abundant and unlimited, and the supply of this metal will be no more limited in the future, than the supply of milk or whiskey; and if left to natural laws will always be equal to the demand. The employment of coin is not an absolute necessity, for commerce can be carried on by barter. But food and clothing are absolutely necessary for the sustenance of human beings. And yet we find that these absolutely necessary articles are best supplied when their production is left to the natural laws of supply and demand. Value is the relation or ratio between two articles or services; and there is no more propriety in establishing a relation between silver and gold, than between iron and lead, or rye and wheat ; or between silver or gold and brass, copper, and all other commodities. When economic laws and the efficacy and value of individual judgment were less understood than now, governments were logical, and established prices, or the relations of all labor or commodities to gold and silver. But now, in the main, prices and production are left to individual judgment and competition, and an arbitrary regulation of the relations of silver to gold is now the sole relic of governmental interference in regulating the prices of articles; or, in other words, in establishing the relation of things as expressed in money. The reason why gold and silver are the best standards of value is, that they are the products of human labor, and that their production will always be regulated by demand. They are, therefore, not a *fiat* currency. The quantity produced is not regulated by the arbitrary actions of any government, but is determined by individual judgment and the natural influence of competition. The production of gold in the United States is at present [1885] about thirty millions per annum. There is no reason why this domestic product of gold should not be augmented to more than one hundred millions per annum, if there is a demand for it—and all there is wanting to produce it, is demand. We have capital and abundance of labor craving employment, and gold-bearing rocks and fields without limit. Here is an unlimited opportunity for debtor or creditor who wants to "root" or labor at the remuneration afforded by the prosecution of other similar labor; and it is not proposed to compel him to root or labor at something that is less profitable. Furthermore, if it is gold rather than silver that is wanted in this country, every pound of our silver product, as well as our other commodities, can be used to buy gold in the markets of the world: and thus the gold resources of the world are at our command.

THE LAW OF SUPPLY AND DEMAND.

A brief word further on the law of supply and demand in respect to currency, and in answer to the frequent assertion that unless the Government freely coins silver and assists its circulation, the country will suffer for lack of sufficient currency. If there was a real or anticipated scarcity of wheelbarrows in the country that man would be considered a fool who should seriously propose that Congress should undertake to regulate the supply by statute. And yet there is one and the same law governing alike the supply of gold and of wheelbarrows. They are both tools or commodities, and the country will have and use all of either that it can use profitably. The dentists and jewellers of the United States have never, even at the time when gold commanded the highest premium, experienced any difficulty in getting all the gold they wanted. We have never heard that any of them ever contemplated petitioning Congress on the subject, or that they lay awake nights for fear that their business would be interfered with by reason of a deficiency. And if they had wanted ten or a hundred times more gold than they actually used, and their customers had been willing to pay for it, they could easily have had it. In short, there can never be a permanent scarcity or surplus of gold and silver in a country which adopts the world's currency, any more than there can be a scarcity of milk or wheat; for the law of supply and demand regulates the quantity and adjusts the prices of one of these commodities just as much as it does the other. If, in the next twenty-four hours, one hundred millions of legal tenders were to be added to the circulation of the United States, domestic prices, other things remaining equal, would on the average be affected to the extent of not less than one seventh, and currency would remain in respect to scarcity or abundance relatively as before. But if one hundred millions of gold, without labor, were to be mysteriously showered down upon us in the form of coin, it would not affect prices appreciably, for the disturbance from the increased quantity would be diffused over the total coin circulation of the world, estimated at upward of ten thousand millions. The world's currency may therefore be compared to a reservoir like the broad ocean, capable alike of quietly absorbing any surplus or supplying any deficiency in the circulation of any locality without disturbing the general level of prices. Any increase, on the other hand, in the volume of currency which owes whatever it has of legal-tender character to statute enactment rather than to a universally recognized value, must be subject to local rather than general laws, and, like an accumulation of water escaping from a broken reservoir, will prove powerful for disturbance just in proportion as its volume becomes disproportionate to the channel in which it is compelled to flow. Hence the extraordinary gambling fluctuations which of necessity attend the use of any currency whose circulation is local and does not partake of the universality of the world's currency; and experience must inevitably sooner or later show that there can be no permanent prosperity in any country that undertakes to do business with any other currency than the world's currency.

THE MASS OF THE PEOPLE NOT DEBTORS BUT CREDITORS.

It is also pertinent to call attention, in connection with this general subject, to the opinion which so generally prevails, that the mass of the people of this country are debtors, and that their interest naturally arrays them in opposition to any policy that does not favor what is popularly termed " cheap money "—the real significance of which to the majority of those who use it is " poor money." Now, so far from this hypothesis being warranted, the exact contrary is the truth. The great mass of the people in this and every other country do not possess sufficient of credit, through the ownership of property or amount of income, to enable them to become debtors—however much they may desire to be—except for such insignificant amounts as the application of a few days' labor or the practice of a brief economy would suffice to liquidate. The great mass of all who work for wages—from the fact that the wages are paid periodically—are also, from necessity, nearly all the time creditors and not debtors; while in the case of that much smaller portion of our population whose annual receipts exceed their annual expenditures, the surplus in their hands, at any

one time, for investment is so small that the only profitable way
open to them for using it is by assuming the position of creditor
—*i. e.*, by loaning either directly on a promissory note, bond, and
mortgage, or by the purchase of some evidence of indebtedness
issued by the Federal or State governments or by corporations,
or by loaning indirectly as stockholders or depositors through
banks or institutions for the management of savings. Hence the
origin of the eleven hundred millions of dollars standing to the
credit of depositors in our savings banks. Hence, also, the even
more striking fact that in New York City, where the multitude of
banks is popularly supposed to be due to the accumulation of
large wealth in few hands, the average amount of bank stock
owned by individual shareholders does not exceed a par value of
$3,000. The only class of debtors whose instincts, therefore,
naturally prompt them to cry for abundant and cheap money, irrespective of quality, are what may properly be termed " bloated
debtors," or those who, by reason of large property, have claimed
and obtained large credits, and have used those credits, or, what
is the same thing, have run in debt partially on account of legitimate enterprises, but in the majority of cases for the furtherance
of illegitimate speculations whose existence and maintenance
have worked to the discouragement of honest productive industry.

CONCLUSION.

There can be no objection to the use of silver as a subsidiary
or token currency, issued only in exchange for gold at nominal
values, or at all times redeemable in gold at nominal value, not
legal tender in excess of $10 for any one specific payment, to any
extent the people will desire. But when it is proposed to go
further, and compel the sons to accept the dollar of the fathers
to an unlimited amount, then an answer to this proposition, simple and conclusive, is that the dollar of the fathers is not, on
grounds of convenience, adapted to our use. The " sons " want
something better—the most improved tools of trade,—as they
want better methods of conveyance, of warming, of lighting, ventilation, printing, and communication of news, than did the fathers.
They want, as a condition for success in business, the coin receivable without discount by the great commercial nations with which
the bulk of our foreign commerce is conducted. And herein is

another point that ought not to fail of receiving full consideration, namely, that whereas, in most cases, the first cost of an improved tool is greater at the outset than that of a poor and unimproved one, in this case the conditions are reversed ; for the first cost of the good tool—a gold currency—will be no greater at the outset to the country than the first cost of the poor one—a silver currency ; while in all subsequent respects the advantages are immeasurably in favor of the gold. Any attempt to restore the old silver dollar to its place as lawful money, without qualification or limitation,—to adopt a coin currency not suited to our wants or the age,—is as foolish and absurd as an attempt to displace through legislation railroads by stage-coaches, and steamships by sailing-vessels. Sovereign power can violate natural laws, the same as individuals can : but the penalty of violation is inevitable in both cases.

ARE GOLD AND SILVER INDISPENSABLE AS MEASURES OF VALUE.

AN EPISODE OF THE DAYS OF CURRENCY INFLATION AND PAPER MONEY.

IN a discusssion which occupied no small part of the columns of the newspaper press of the United States in 1875–77 on the maintenance, further inflation, or redemption of the then "legal-tender" (irredeemable paper) currency of the country, the Rev. Thomas K. Beecher, a prominent clergyman, settled in Elmira, New York, in a communication to the *N. Y. Nation* (October, 1875), submitted the propositions, as to whether *there is any valid distinction between gold and legal tender* (paper) *as a measure of value;* and whether the use of gold and silver as a measure of value is an indispensable prerequisite for a sound and correct system of exchange ; and supported the negative view of the same by the following course of argument and illustration.

"Agreeing that gold is a measure of value that has attained an almost world-wide acceptance, does it follow that gold should be the only legal tender, and that all currencies or other debt-certificates of whatever kind should be "redeemable in gold only?   I detect in the general flow of commerce phenomena which I will call closed circles of exchange—*i. e.*, circles of exchange, within which the same currency may revolve for ever, independently of gold.   Such circles are indeed little short of countless.   Some of them are very small, as, for instance, the dealings of a grocer with his milkman ; the grocer taking five dollars' worth of milk-tickets and crediting the milkman accordingly, and the milkman redeeming the tickets in milk—gold meanwhile serving the use of a measure both of the groceries and the milk.

"Am I safe in asserting that whenever a closed circle like this can be demonstrated, there is need of neither gold nor silver as a legal tender? True, if either party dies and the business be wound up by strangers, there must come in an outside currency. But so long as the milkman and the grocer continue in their respective relations, have we not a trade of say one hundred dollars a year, in which milk-tickets serve all the uses of currency? From this smallest circle step at once to the largest circle—a sovereign government like the Government of the United States, with an undisputed right to tax the people—say two hundred million dollars a year. The people at large are to pay to the national treasury, in the course of a year, two hundred millions of dollars. The Government is to disburse precisely the same sum to the people. Have we not here a closed circle—foreign creditors excepted?

" Where lies the fallacy, then, in asserting that any stable government may wisely meet its obligations by issuing its notes promising to pay, just as our greenbacks do promise to pay? And inasmuch as by the tax law every citizen must pay to the Government, and these notes of the Government by their very face are receivable for taxes, why not make them, for all purposes of internal commerce, legal tender, their volume to equal at least the amount of the annual budget?

" The Treasury notes thus issued are, on a large scale, what the milk-tickets were on a small scale.

" If the Government has a legal right to take from citizens at large two hundred million dollars, I am not able to see that there is any unwisdom or injustice in requiring citizens to recognize Treasury notes—which are legal tender to the Government—as legal tender also in the settlement of private accounts, etc., etc."

To these interrogatories and deductions, Mr. Wells returned through the columns of the *Nation* the following reply, which, at the time, attracted considerable attention, and was the occasion also of no little merriment on the part of the public.

It was prefaced by the editors of the *Nation* with the following title :

" DR. WELLS' OPINION IN CONSULTATION ON MR. BEECHER'S CASE."

" Mr. Beecher says he detects in the general flow of commerce what he is pleased to term ' closed circles of exchange,' and asks why some currency other than gold may not be used and continue to revolve for ever independent of gold in such circles. To this I reply that I, for one, see no objection to the use of such other currency, under the conditions specified. For example, take the illustrations which Mr. Beecher brings forward ; and, *first*, that of the grocer and the milkman, who exchange between themselves groceries for milk-tickets. What objection can there be to their so doing, or why should any one interfere to prevent this little arrangement, any more than any other mutually agreeable trade or bargain the grocer and milkman may choose to make ? So, in the *second* case supposed by Mr. Beecher—namely, that of the Government issuing notes promising to pay and made receivable for a year's taxes—I can see no objection to that either, further than that, as a general rule, it is better for Government and individuals alike to pay cash down, rather than issue their I. O. U.'s or get trusted. And if the Government wishes to obtain commodities or services, and promises to pay for them in its own notes or cabbage-leaves, and people are found *willing* to take such notes or cabbage-leaves in exchange, I see no reason for entering any protest against it, or calling on any one to prevent the Government from issuing, on the one hand, or the people from receiving, on the other. The highest right of property is the right freely to exchange it for other property ; and the highest attribute of personal freedom is for each person to determine for himself under what conditions he will render service. Thus far, then, there is no disagreement in our respective positions. But when Mr. Beecher goes a step further, and says he is unable to see ' any unwisdom or injustice in requiring citizens to recognize Treasury notes [whether the same be greenbacks or cabbage-leaves], which are legal tender to the Government, as legal tender also in the settlement of private accounts,' then Mr. Beecher and I walk apart ; and it is just here, in my opinion, that Mr. Beecher's mental obscurity about money and legal tender begins, for he seems unable to recognize any broad distinction between ' may,' or the *permissive* sense, and ' must,' or the *compulsive* sense, in its application to money. To make this clear let us take an illustration.

   "Suppose I go on a certain Saturday to Elmira, to hear Mr. Beecher preach. Time hanging heavy while waiting for Sunday to come, I stroll on Saturday evening to Smith's pleasant gambling-saloon to have a little amusement, and being at the same time on 'frugal thought intent,' I conclude to risk but five dollars for my evening's diversion, and so bet but fifty cents at a time on the green cloth. To enable me to do this, I get a five-dollar green-back exchanged at the cashier's desk for ten red ivory counters, or '*chips*,' as they are technically called ; and after playing to my heart's content I leave, and Sunday morning finds me at Mr. Beecher's church. (I acknowledge that my conduct is rather in-consistent ; but it is not my conduct that we are looking after just at present.) The sermon pleases me so much that at its close, when a collection is taken up to help pay Mr. Beecher's well-earned salary, I determine to contribute ; and finding one of those red chips I received in exchange the night before in my pocket, I put it in the hat. When the money comes to be delivered over to Mr. Beecher, he very naturally expresses some surprise at find-ing this strange-looking visitor nestled in among the bank-notes, the fractionals, the cabbage-leaves, and the milk-tickets, and asks what it all means.

" To this I may be supposed to respond that the chip is cur-rency, 'revolving perfectly in the closed circle' of the faro-bank, and fulfilling within that circle all the offices of money, indepen-dently of gold. Mr. Beecher has only to go, after church, down to Smith's saloon, and present the red chip I have given him to Jones, the cashier, and Jones will either allow him to bet with it or, if the bank was not cleaned out the night before or seized by the police, will probably redeem it in a fifty-cent scrip. ' But, my dear sir,' responds Mr. Beecher, ' I am a minister, and I don't want to be seen going into Smith's saloon.' I answer : ' I suppose it would be somewhat disagreeable to you, but you can give this chip to the milkman, the grocer, or the Government tax-collector to-morrow morning. They understand all about these " close circles " of exchange ; they will take it.' ' But I am not so certain of that,' says Mr. Beecher. ' How will they, any more than I, know what its value is, or whether it will be redeemed in any thing else ? ' 'Don't trouble yourself about that matter,' I rejoin ; ' I have fixed all that. I happened to be a member of Congress last year, and after devoting two weeks' earnest study to the subject of finance, I was not able to see, any more than you now are, "that there is any unwisdom or injustice in requiring

citizens to recognize Treasury notes" and gambling chips—the
one of which is legal tender to the Government, and the other
legal tender in the faro-bank—"as a legal tender also in the settlement of private accounts." More than this, the ivory chips are
prettier than the greenbacks, and more convenient for carrying;
and what better device can there be for indicating their difference
in value than by a change in their color? They have also in per-
fection another attribute of really good money, inasmuch as they
are non-exportable; and if we take into consideration the number
of fights, feuds, and murders that take place in gambling-saloons,
I think that we are fairly entitled to claim for the chips that they
are "battle-born" and "blood-stained." So I accordingly persuaded the National Legislature to pass a law making Treasury
notes, gamblers' chips, milk-tickets, and every other instrumentality of exchange which is capable of revolving perfectly in a
closed circle, legal tender in payment for all private debts. 'You
see it now, don't you, Mr. Beecher?' 'I rather think I do,'
responds Mr. B.; 'but at the same time I wish that when you
next come to hear me preach, and feel that I have rendered you
a service and strengthened you up to further good work in
Washington, you would give me something that don't belong
to a closed circle of exchange—something that I shall not feel
obliged, before accepting, to examine a statute-book, read my
Bible, consult the resolutions of the last political convention, or
wait the news of an election in Ohio, to decide whether I had
better take it, and, if I do take it, how much I can get for it.'

   " Seriously, however, the trouble with Mr. Beecher and a good
many other persons is, that they fail to recognize, that 'legal
tender,' whose father is Government and whose mother a Statute
Law, is a suspicious character, and has been engaged in all manner of disreputable transactions ever since he was born; whilst
gold and silver, of acknowledged weight and purity—*i. e.*, coined
money—are nature's noblemen, whose patent of honesty is so
written on their front that they require no passport, in the shape
of a legal-tender statute, to find acceptance everywhere, as the
universal equivalent for all exchangeable commodities and services, and as the universal solvent for all debts; and, furthermore,
that no matter how great may be their recommendation on the
score of cheapness, it is very poor economy for a man or a com-

munity to work with poor tools or dishonest, tricky servants if good tools and honest servants are available.

" Money existed before statutes, and owes its origin to man's instincts or natural promptings. Gold and silver came into use as money also before statutes, and were made choice of for use as money for exactly the same reason that men have made choice of cotton, flax, wool, and silk as materials for clothing, and stone, brick, and timber as materials for houses; because they best of all things supply certain wants and necessities.

" If the Government will confine itself simply to the business of saying how much pure gold and silver shall be entitled to use the name of 'dollar'; that the standard of a dollar once judiciously fixed shall never be changed ; that everybody who talks dollars shall always and under all circumstances be understood to mean but this one kind of dollar ; that any promises to pay, without specifying what the payment is to be in, shall also be interpreted to mean the acknowledged standard—if the Government will do these things, and these things only, then all legal-tender laws may be wiped at once off the statute-books, and everybody will be better for it. And when that day comes, if the milkman, grocer, keeper of faro-bank, or children on a rainy day up in an old garret, want to trade, swap, barter, or exchange, and use milk-tickets, ivory chips, or pieces of old newspapers respectively, to serve as memoranda, checks, counters, or symbols, I will promise Mr. Beecher that no one will object ; unless the milkman, grocer, faro-bank keeper, or garret children want to make them legal tender, and compel him, and me, and all other persons, because of the artificial character thus given them, to take them in payment of commodities and services, when we don't want to."

" I am yours, most respectfully,

"DAVID A. WELLS."

TARIFF REVISION: ITS NECESSITY AND POSSIBLE METHODS.

I.

THE old writers, before the discovery of America, were accustomed to indulge in all manner of fanciful speculations respecting the conditions and actions of the people on the "other side" of the world, or their antipodes, supposing, indeed, that there were any. It was generally agreed that they must walk with their heels upward and their heads hanging down, and do everything in a reverse order from that which was then regarded as proper and natural in the Old World experience. A little practical experience, however, in enlarged navigation soon showed the absurdity of such imaginings; and yet if the old speculators had restricted the sphere of their imaginings to the mental rather than the physical actions of the "other side" men, they might not have been considered by posterity so far out of the way in their conclusions. For America, or rather that part of it known as the United States, has always been to Europe a country of surprises or contraries, in most matters political, financial, economic, and theological. And of these surprises none could be more remarkable than that one of the two great parties into which the country is politically divided should regard the continued maintenance in time of peace of an extraordinary, onerous, and unnecessary system of taxation as a policy likely to insure to it a popular favor and support; while the other great party, either through ignorance or cowardice, shirks the issue, hesitates to boldly array itself in favor of exempting the masses from excessive public burdens, and through some of its chief leaders even favors the policy and tries to do business on the capital of its opponents. In short, taxation in excess of any legitimate

requirements of the State—the thing which in all other countries
has heretofore been regarded by politicians and statesmen as
the certain precursor of popular wrath and party defeat—has
really in the United States come to be looked upon as a good
thing in itself, and as politically and economically expedient.
"*If there were no public debt, no interest to pay, no pension-list,
no army or navy to support, I should still oppose ' tariff for revenue only' and favor protective duties*" (*taxes*). (*Speech of Hon.
Wm. P. Frye, Senate of the U. S., Feb.* 10, 1882.) Again in a debate in the U. S. House of Representatives, March 4th, 1882, on
a proposition to reduce or abolish the oppressive and obsolete
fees, exactions, and formalities of the existing consular system
of the United States, Frank Hiscock, a representative of the
State of New York—a State that is pre-eminently commercial—
after admitting the existence of the grievances alleged, nevertheless declared himself in favor of their continuance, and simply
for the reason that they were an obstruction to commerce; and
if removed it might be difficult to replace them with other equivalent obstructions. Out of such a curious state of things have
come certain results so plain "that he may run who reads,"
and which may be enumerated in part as follows:

First. The annual gathering through the tax-gatherer of a
surplus revenue of from one hundred to one hundred and fifty
millions of dollars in excess of any legitimate requirements of
the government; the same constituting a constant incentive
for needless and corrupt expenditures, the multiplication of
offices, and the enlargement of the sphere of influence of the
federal government. The rapid reduction of the public debt
occasioned by the war has been a never-ending theme of national self-congratulation; but taking taxation as the measure
of the burden of obligation which the war entailed upon the
country (and it is the only proper measure), the war debt has
in reality been diminished by a sum which in comparison with
the national receipts of revenue is very inconsiderable.[1]

[1] Thus the current burden of the war debt (omitting the repayments of the principal of the debt, which is not in the nature of a demand obligation) is the annual
taxation required to provide means for the payment of interest on the debt, and
the requirements for pensions. The largest obligation incumbent on the United States in any one year on account of national debt-interest was in 1867, and
amounted to $143,781,000. The disbursements for pensions during that same

Second. A condition of things in which the country depends
almost exclusively on its harvests for its prosperity, and has
no export trade worth mentioning except in the raw produce
of its soil, representing in the form in which it is exported the
minimum of embodied labor. In place of an annually increasing ability on the part of the nation to withstand foreign competition in respect to the production of the so-called products of
manufacturing industries, all the evidence points in the opposite
direction ; our exports of manufactured articles forming a considerably smaller percentage of the total exports in 1879–80 than
they did in 1859–60.[1] Never, moreover, in the history of the

year were $20,936,000. In 1871, six years after the termination of the war, and
when it is reasonable to infer that nearly every person who had a legitimate claim
for injuries *directly* and *immediately* contingent on his service in, or to, the federal armies had presented the same and made a settlement with the government,
the pension disbursements amounted to $34,443,000; and after reaching this
maximum, the annual expenditure on this account, in accordance with all former
experience of the United States and other countries, and also with the life-expec-
tation tables of life-insurance companies, began to rapidly decrease, and in 1878
had become reduced to $27,137,000. The payments on account of interest during
this same year were $125,576,000. The direct aggregate burdens of the war debt,
as measured by taxation and expenditures, were therefore $164,717,000 in 1867 and
$152,713,000 in 1871; on the other hand, the obligations on the part of the govern-
ment for interest on the public debt ($57,360,000 on the 1st of July, 1882) and for
pensions ($100,000,000 actually appropriated) will probably amount for the current
fiscal year to about $150,000,000; thus making the aggregate burden of the present
war debt but little less than it was soon after the close of the war. For the future,
some who have made a very careful study of the matter do not hesitate to predict
that the enactment of the so-called "arrears of pensions" law (in accordance with
which every man who served in the army or navy of the United States during the
war and was discharged in fair health is practically considered to have a valid
claim for a pension against the United States on account of personal disabilities
contingent on advancing age) will entail, from first to last, a further aggregate
expenditure on the country of not less than two thousand millions of dollars.

[1] The ratios which the exports of the unmanufactured and manufactured products from the United States have sustained to each other during the three decen-
nial periods included between the years 1859–60 and 1879–80 are as follows:

	1879–80. Per cent of total.	1869–70. Per cent of total.	1859–60. Per cent of total.
Unmanufactured products	87.5	86.6	82.3
Manufactured do.	12.5	13.4	17.7

Unmanufactured products have risen, therefore, from being 82.3 per cent of
the total exports in 1859–60 to 87.5 per cent in 1879–80; while, during the same
period, manufactures have fallen from 17.7 per cent to 12.5 per cent.

country has the import—responsive to domestic demand and ready sale—of the products of foreign industries into the United States been greater than at present (1882)[1]; while, on the other hand, the stocks of American manufactured products continually tend to accumulate and bring on the stagnation and disaster consequent on what is termed " over-production."

Third. The " merchant marine," or carrying trade, of the United States upon the ocean—a branch of national industry once second only in importance to agriculture—has practically ceased to exist. Differ as men may as to the proper remedial legislation for such a state of things, there ought to be no difference of opinion as to its cause. Commerce is the interchange of commodities and services between men and men and countries and countries ; and its one essential condition of existence and growth is that such exchanges shall be reciprocal. To sell we must buy, and in order to buy we must sell. Now for many years the policy of the United States has been to impose taxes with the avowed purpose of restricting so much of the commerce of the country as is carried on by the agency of ships upon the ocean ; and that it has been eminently successful in its results will not be disputed. If it were not a most serious matter, it ought to be regarded as a huge joke, to propose, as has recently been done, to assemble the several American States by their representatives in a Congress, and try to get them to reverse the principles of human nature by agreeing, on account of neighborhood and good feeling, to permanently trade at the United States shop, when a shop across the way offers to sell cheaper and take the products of the purchaser in barter payment. It can't be done.

Fourth. That the market for the products of the manufacturing industries of the United States is practically limited to the requirements for home consumption, and that the power of domestic production in all branches of industry, consequent

---

[1] The imports of merchandise have never been so large as in the fiscal year ending June 30, 1882. The largest imports of any one year prior to 1880 occurred in 1873 and amounted to $642,136,000. For 1880 the aggregate was $667,954,000, but for the fiscal year 1882 the imported values were returned at $724,623,000; of this increase, $10,533,000, or 12 per cent of the present aggregate import of $93,000,000, occurred in the class of metals, and $23,731,000 in articles of clothing.

upon the application of machinery, conjoined with high intelligence, to our great natural resources, continually tends to exceed the power of domestic consumption, are facts too evident to be disputed. The natural, nay more, the inevitable, outcome of such a condition of affairs is an effort on the part of the producer to prevent the accumulation of a surplus, by restricting production and keeping a part of his machinery idle; and this in turn means limitation of the opportunity for employment to the laborer. The manufacturer also sees clearly, that if he could produce and sell cheaper he could enlarge his markets, and at least maintain if he did not enlarge the sphere of his business activity; but having become thoroughly indoctrinated with the idea that the maintenance of a system of national taxation, which abnormally augments the cost of all his services and supplies, is absolutely essential to his industrial prosperity, and even existence, he naturally opposes any reduction of taxes, denounces as unpatriotic and visionary those who favor such reductions, and as naturally seeks to avail himself of the only other avenue open to him for cheapening the cost of his products, namely, that of cheapening his supply of labor. This the laborer resists, and the outcome of this resistance is seen in strikes, local disturbances, and the extensive interruption of the business and exchange of the country such as has characterized the history of the present year. But what chance has the laborer for successful resistance, with a limitation of market for the sale of the products of his industry and an annual import of 700,000 foreign laborers, ready to compete for and embrace every opportunity for domestic employment? Under such circumstances there is no possibility of any strike or resistance on the part of labor being successful; and the result of recent experience might have been predicted in the absolute certainty at the commencement of the present year, as can be at present predicted of the future.

One of the most notable of the strikes of the year, that of the freight-handlers upon the piers and at the railroad termini of New York, is full of teachings of the utmost interest and importance. The question was put at the commencement of the difficulties, by the writer, to the foreman of a body of freight-handlers—not participating in the strike—on one of the steam-

boat piers of New York: "Is the strike likely in your opinion
to be successful?" "There is not a ghost of a chance for success," was the prompt reply. "Why not?" *Ans.* : "Simply
for the reason that two men stand ready to do the work that
offered for only one." "Have the laborers, then, no remedy
for their grievances?" *Ans.*: "Yes; let us have a law pro-
hibiting the coming in of all those laborers from Europe."
"Do you think the enactment of such a law possible?" *Ans.* :
"Yes; if the laborers all over the country were united in demanding it, the politicians would soon bring it about." Now,
whatever may be thought of the remedy proposed, there can be
no doubt that the man thus interrogated had a clear view of
the situation, and its utter hopelessness so far as it concerned
the strikers.

But let us further consider this matter. The strikers were,
it is understood, in receipt of seventeen cents per hour, and
demanded twenty, on the ground that the former sum was inadequate for the support of themselves and their families.
Popular sympathy was unquestionably on the side of the
laborers and adverse to the railroads. The general public, in
their indignation at the result of railroad management on the
part of certain individuals, are prone to overlook the great
service that the railroad system of the United States has rendered; to forget that no other one agency in all time has been
more productive of benefit to the laborer—using the term in its
ordinary sense,—by enlarging the sphere of his employment,
cheapening product, and creating abundance ; and that by it
the cost of transportation has now been so far reduced, that one
day's wages of the most ordinary laborer in New York will
suffice to pay the cost of the movement from Chicago to New
York of all the meat and grain that he can consume in a year—
thereby placing such laborer in New York, so far as the prime
cost of his food is concerned, on a par with the laborer that
lives where food is the cheapest on this continent; and that in
comparison with these benefits, all the injury that has resulted
from "stock-watering" and diversion or squandering of railroad
capital or receipts, great and reprehensible as this may have
been, is relatively but as "the small dust upon the balance."
But in the frame of mind that the public then were (and now

are) the expression was most common, that the demands of the
strikers were most reasonable, and that the railroads ought willingly to accede to them.   Now if these expressions were anything more than mere sentiment, the " *ought* " must have had
a foundation on the principles of either "charity" or "equity;"
if the former, then the issue pertains to the province of the
moralist or philanthropist rather than to the economist ; and if
the latter, the economic question most pertinent is, according to
what principles of justice or equity *ought* a railroad or any other
corporation to be asked or expected to pay more for what it
desires to buy and use—be it material or labor—than the current rates established for the same in the open market ?   And
if public opinion could force such a reversal of the laws of trade,
does any one suppose that such an arrangement could be permanent, and not utterly disastrous to the general business interests
of the country ?   But had not the strikers any real grievances?
Most certainly they had.   They had found out that their ability
to earn a comfortable livelihood for themselves or their families
was becoming impaired; they had learned generally by hard
experience what scientific investigation has demonstrated specifically, namely, that what of grain, meats, dairy products, sugar,
other food, clothing, metals, and lumber an expenditure of $1.08
would have given them in November, 1878, would have required an outlay of $1.28 in November, 1880—before the drought
influences of the succeeding year—and $1.44 in June, 1882, for
the obtaining of the same quantities ; or that, wages remaining
the same, the fall in wages owing to a decrease in their purchasing power, comparing the first half of 1881 with the first half of
1882, was equivalent to ten per cent.   And becoming painfully
sensible of such results, without recognizing their causes, both
strikers and the public made haste to put the blame on the railroads, when the railroads, through their management, were no
more responsible than any other portions of the body-politic.
Had the situation prompted the inquiry of how it was that the
strikers, while receiving the full market rates for their labor, and
probably the highest nominal wages that are regularly paid for
similar services anywhere on the face of the globe, should yet
feel themselves unable to live comfortably on their wages ; and
how it is that this land of abundance, which is ever ready to

supply the food deficiencies of all other nations, has been made one of the dearest countries of the world to live in,—had these inquiries been instituted and intelligently prosecuted, a rational, and indeed the essential primary step in the way of bettering the situation would have been taken. And as indicating in part what such an inquiry would have brought out respecting the influence of the present system of excessive Federal taxation, attention is asked to the following facts:

Federal taxes, both direct and indirect, with very few exceptions, are levied on commodities, fall on consumption, and must be paid by the consumer in the increased price of the things he consumes. Hence it follows that the burden of such taxes must be disproportionately heavier on the man who from necessity expends all, or nearly all, of his wages, salary, or other income in mere living, than on he who only expends one half, one third, or a smaller proportion of his income for like purposes, and lays up the surplus for increasing his resources. Under ordinary circumstances any disproportionate taxation falling upon the entire class of laborers would be speedily equalized by an advance in wages; but with a tendency to the limitation of employment through limitation of markets, and the present extraordinary influx of foreign competitive labor, such equalization is very difficult, if not absolutely impossible. Every dollar raised by the government by taxation for any other purpose than to provide revenue for its most economical administration constitutes, therefore, a heavier burden on the recipients of small incomes and wages than upon any other class of the community.

Recent investigations have shown that, accepting the highest reasonable estimate that can be made of the value of the annual product of the nation, and supposing the same to be divided equally among our present population, the average income of each person—out of which subsistence, savings, education, means of enjoyment, reparation of waste, and taxes are to be provided—would not be in excess of *fifty*, and probably not over *forty* cents per day. But as a practical matter, we know that the annual product is not divided equally, and never can be, and that some receive the annual average as stated multiplied by hundreds and thousands; which of course necessitates that very many others shall receive proportionally less. When now it is further considered that the present aggregate of federal, State, and municipal taxation in the United States probably amounts to seven per cent on the value of the entire annual product of the country, and that the unnecessary taxation of one hundred millions which the federal government now collects from the people is equal to fifteen or twenty per cent of what the whole people annually save from the product of their labors (taking no account of the additional burden which the imposition of such taxation entails through increase of prices, taxation which the people pay but which the government does not receive), it is possible to form some idea of how a fiscal policy of large taxation, which so many politicians and so-called statesmen advocate as in the interest of the masses, fearfully intrenches on the narrow measure of comfort which the masses under the most favorable circumstances can obtain. Such "taxes," says Mr. Atkinson, alluding to the fact before noticed, that the federal taxes fall on commodities, "take from the many what they may actually need for a bare subsistence; they must fall with greatest hardship on those whose earnings for their families are less than the average dollar a day to each adult man and woman; and while our present excess of national taxation may be equal to only *fifteen* per cent of the possible savings of the whole people, it may take *a hundred per cent*, even the little all, of what the poor may save." Doubtless some may point to the great immigration that flows in upon us from other countries, and claim that this fact is a sufficient answer to the above statement; inasmuch as it proves that the masses in this country have advantages which are not to be found elsewhere. Now so far as these advantages are natural this claim is not be denied; but its admission does not affect or answer the real question at issue, which is, To what extent have our great natural advantages—which ought to insure comfort and abundance to every industrious person—been neutralized or impaired to the masses by the economic policy which we have as a nation adopted? The multitudes who during the past summer, from Nebraska to New York, "struck" for alleged insufficient returns for their labor—as, for example, the coal-miners of Pennsylvania, whom Hon. Abram S. Hewitt in the United States House of Representatives in March, 1882, declared to be, from his own personal knowledge, "absolutely suffering for the necessities of life"—were all, undoubtedly, the European immigrants of a few years ago. And if so, do not their proceedings prove that they are no more content with the existing state of things in this country than they were in the countries of the Old World from whence they emigrated?

The plea has recently been put forward in defence of the continuance of our present system of tariff taxation, that it is the best system for accomplishing a desirable thing, namely, the taxation of capital for the benefit of labor. It would, however, probably puzzle the proponent to tell, how such taxes can be made to "stick" upon capital in any greater proportion than upon labor; or even in anything like as great a ratio. For all experience shows that when capital is thus taxed it simply advances the tax, and requites itself for the advance by taking two or three times as much for itself. The most effectual way of primarily doing the thing, which a candidate for Congress from New Jersey has recently proclaimed to be most desirable, is to adopt the "Sicilian" or "Greek" economic method, of forcibly abducting capital as represented by the individual, carrying it off to a cave, and compelling it, under fear of prospective loss of ears or hands, to disgorge, and then sharing the proceeds of the assessment among the laborers. But the ultimate trouble here would be, that as soon as capital found out that it was liable to be thus arbitrarily treated, and could not easily requite itself for forced contributions, it would run away to some place where it could be better treated; and if there were no such places, as was the case in the middle ages, then it would hide itself in holes in the ground, or other secret places, as it does now in Turkey and Egypt—countries where the New Jersey principle is especially exemplified, thus narrowing the sphere if it did not wholly deprive the laborer of profitable employment. Certainly, to borrow an expression of the late H. C. Carey, the activity of "societary circulation," the cause of all material development, would be greatly impaired under such circumstances.

The paramount necessity of the hour—whether the masses under the education before alluded to, which they have received, respecting the blessings of taxation, as yet fully appreciate it or no—is the reduction of Federal taxation, and any political party which fails to recognize it will, sooner or later, have reason to repent of its lack of sagacity. That an abatement of one hundred millions in the taxes now annually collected by the Federal Government, or one seventh of the entire present burden of taxation upon the whole country, can be made without in any way deranging the national finances or reducing to a corresponding extent the national revenues, will not probably be questioned. It should not be overlooked, however, in considering this whole prospective work of revenue reform, that the question of immediate importance is not so much how large a sum shall be abated, but rather by what method shall the abatements be effected; for under the existing fiscal policy of the nation, which has been also long continued, many vested interests have grown up and been fostered which are entitled to the largest and most generous consideration, and which cannot be arbitrarily and suddenly interfered with, without occasioning such changes in the direction of industry as may work great temporary injury to not a few persons. With the most honest intent, it will be only too easy for tax reformers to arrest by injudicious action the tide of public opinion now setting strongly in their favor, while those in favor of maintaining substantially the present system would do well to bear in mind, that by resisting moderate reforms at present, and by continuing the rapid reduction of the public debt, they cannot fail to ensure the sudden enactment of far more radical measures in the not distant future.

So much, then, in the way of exposition of the necessity of prompt and large reductions in the number and amount of Federal taxes. It is proposed to next ask consideration to the methods by which an abatement of taxes may be most safely and judiciously effected under the tariff—the department of revenue in which abatements are most urgently needed.

The tariff of the United States as it now exists, and considered entirely apart from any economic policy which it may be intended to subserve, is a disgrace to our civilization. The honor of the nation, the interests of ordinary morality, the necessities of business, and the claims of civil-service reform, all alike demand that it be reconstructed with a view to simpli-

fication and intelligibility. If it be replied that this is the lan,
guage of a partisan and a theorist, we would ask, if it is not a
libel on good government, and an outrage, that constant suits
at law and appeals to the Treasury on the part of merchants
should be made necessary—some 18,000 of which are now
reported as on file—in order to settle the meaning and construction of the mere words in which the statutes imposing the
rates of duty have been expressed? That, in deciding upon the
rates of duties to be imposed upon certain fabrics, the difference of a shade of blue or brown, or the weighing in a damp
atmosphere, makes the same quality of merchandise just enough
heavier to turn the scale and largely augment the assessment of
the duty; that a constant espionage of the mails and an examination of the contents of sealed letters is necessary to protect
the revenue; and the mere misplacement of a comma, as in the
case of a former tariff enactment in respect to dried fruits,
makes a difference of hundreds of thousands of dollars in the
receipts of the Treasury.

France has a tariff of the kind needed in the United States, if
its taxes are to be imposed on many articles, embodying the protective policy : extensive, but so scientifically constructed as to be
almost free from ambiguity or the possibility of misinterpretation.
The Walker tariff of 1846, the best tariff in respect to administration and adaptation to the end designed which the United States
has ever had, was a model of simplicity and conciseness. It
was not an attempt to amend anything that had previously
existed, but was an original construction, framed after much patient inquiry, with the aid of the best experts, and recognized the
ad-valorem system exclusively; all imports subject to duty being
arranged in eight alphabetically designated classes, to each one
of which an ad-valorem rate was assigned, ranging from 5 to 100
per cent. To attempt to now reconstruct the tariff as a whole,
and make it simple and harmonious, we must, it would seem, take
either the French or the " Walker" system as a model. To attempt to do it on the principle that has alone been recognized
since 1860, namely, that of establishing a separate and varying
rate for every article or limited class of articles, and endeavoring at the same time to balance the reciprocal relations of a multitude of industries and make compensation to each for a pro-

gressive and unequal taxation of its respective elements, is impossible, simply because it would demand superhuman knowledge to do it. A volume almost might be written full of incidents which would be most amusing if they had not been often most disastrous, of influences unexpected (even by those well acquainted with the subject) and most remote in their effects, which have been the result of attempting to impose tariff taxes in this country in this manner. Hence those who know most of the tariff are, as a rule, the most conservative and the least inclined to advise radical and arbitrary legislation. But what chance is there for a commission not more than two members of which bring any fund of previous knowledge to their work, and whose attention has been mainly occupied with statements submitted, as Adam Smith once expressed it, " with all the passionate confidence of interested falsehood," of reporting any complete yet simple and intelligent system? As well expect an equal number of well-meaning, moderate men, as the result of six months' desultory experience, to be able to revise an intricate code of civil or criminal law, to make a geologic survey, or lucidly expound the best method of managing a complicated competitive railroad system. Or supposing, by some gift of inspiration, they were able to submit such a report ; what chance would there be for its adoption by Congress? A single amendment, offered by some member whose main interest in the tariff was to know what some influential and selfish constituent desired, might prove as destructive of all harmonious adjustment and working as would the interposition of some rude fragment of wood or metal among the delicate wheels and levers of some nicely constructed machinery.[1]

---

[1] As an illustration of the difficulties unavoidably connected with the control or direction of economic or fiscal legislation by men whose ideas of trade and commerce have been largely gained by an experience of selling nails by the pound, molasses by the quart, and tape by the yard, the following story may be related: By the act of June 30th, 1864, the duty on imported bituminous coal was fixed at $1.25 per ton. By the act of 1873 this duty was reduced to 75 cents per ton. A merchant of Boston interested in the coal-mines of Nova Scotia, happening to be in Washington shortly after the change in the law, called on a prominent member of Congress who had been instrumental in effecting the reduction, with a view of expressing thanks to the latter for his action and vote. In the course of the conversation which ensued it was incidentally mentioned that

It seems, therefore evident that no general reconstruction of the tariff is possible at present, or even in any not distant future; and that no general propositions for relief from the abatement of excessive taxation in this department of our revenue are likely to be ever entertained, except for an increase of the free list, and a recognition of the principle embodied in the celebrated "Compromise Tariff Act" brought forward by Henry Clay in 1832, under political and industrial circumstances not unlike what exist at present, and subsequently adopted by Congress: which provided in the main for a reduction of 10 per cent in all duties in excess of 20 per cent at three successive intervals of two years.

A United States Senator from Massachusetts—Mr. Hoar—has been pleased to say of this latter method "that there never came out of a lunatic asylum propositions so monstrous, so indefensible, so destructive," and that its adoption " will be to create a business revolution not equalled " by anything in our experience. But such assertions may be passed by as the utter-

the Washington Capitol building itself was lighted with gas derived from the very Nova Scotia coal which had been mainly affected and cheapened by the reduction of the duty in question. Some surprise being manifested by the Congressman that such should be the case, the merchant explained its happening in this wise : Small vessels sailed in the first instance, mainly from New England to ports of the British North American Provinces, laden with miscellaneous freights—furniture, hardware, glass, coarse textiles and carpets, drugs, medicines, paper, machinery, etc.—the product of our domestic industries. These shipments directly or indirectly paid for Nova Scotia coal, especially adapted to the economical manufacture of gas, which coal was then transported in American bottoms to the Potomac and sold to the Washington Gas Company. A cargo being unloaded, the vessel was immediately reloaded with coal from the Cumberland mines of Maryland, especially desirable for blacksmithing or steam purposes, which coal in turn was transported and sold in the Boston market; and the circle of exchanges being thus completed—each movement of which brought profit to American labor and capital, and enlarged the sphere of employment for our merchant marine—a new and similar series of commercial transactions were at once entered upon with the same recurring results. To all this the only reply which the Congressman vouchsafed to make was, " Well, I had no idea that Nova Scotia coal could be used in Washington. Had I been aware of it I certainly should have voted against the reduction of duty. I think I made a mistake in voting as I did." And this story is true, almost *literatim et verbatim*, and the Congressman in question still holds his seat in the national halls of legislation and is never weary about talking of the necessity of encouraging our domestic industries.

ances of an intellectual crank who has persuaded himself that the continual taking of excessive portions of the product of the labor of the masses under the name of taxation, and using a large part of the taking for extravagant expenditures, is equivalent to the creation of wealth. The argument that successive percentage reductions of the tariff would compel the manufacturer to conduct his business for a series of years on a falling market is more rational. But if it has any value at all, it is conclusive against all reductions of taxation. The real objection to the Clay " compromise" plan is that it gives little or no immediate relief from the present burden of tariff taxes, and practically will not reduce the revenues. Its recommendations are that it will work no real injury to any one, will be in the nature of a tentative experiment, and a positive step in the right direction, and, apart from general action, in accordance with the two plans above mentioned. The only further method for reducing and amending the tariff that would seem to be possible is that of taking up and considering its multiplied provisions in detail, and legislating separately in respect to the numberless articles or classes of articles taxed; having reference in so doing to two points: first, the reduction of national taxation; and second, of making such reductions, severally and in the aggregate, instrumentalities for cheapening the cost of all domestic production and of living, enlarging the market for our manufactured products, widening the opportunities for the employment of labor, and bringing back to its former status our now all but extinct merchant (ocean) marine. And in respect to this latter point, Prof. Siemens, in his recent address before the British Association, tells us that the time is near at hand when there is to be a revolution in the construction and propulsion of ocean ships analogous to what occurred when iron was substituted for wood, and steam for sails; a statement which may be construed as saying to the United States, "You are to be relieved, by the progress of invention and discovery, from your present disabilities in respect to equipment for prosecuting the ocean carrying trade, and may have an equal chance in starting against all competitors under the new conditions, if you will only not continue to neutralize the inventive skill and business enterprise of the nation by the creation and maintenance of artificial obstructions in the path of progress." And with a view of aiding in this work, it is proposed to next submit some points that may be worthy of consideration on the part of Congress and the public.

TARIFF REVISION: ITS NECESSITY AND POSSIBLE METHODS.[1]

II.

IN a certain and at the same time correct sense, all loyal and patriotic citizens are ultra-protectionists. That is to say, every American with one spark of patriotism and national loyalty in his composition prefers the interest of his country to that of any and every other country, and is ever ready with heart and hand to support every measure that tends to promote the development and prosperity of his country and insure the maximum of abundance and comfort to his fellow-citizens. But altho thus united as a whole people in the desire for a common object, the greatest divergence of individual opinion at the same time exists in respect to the methods by which such object can best be attained. On the one hand, a large number who especially arrogate to themselves the title of protectionists (to American industry) assume by their action, if they do not openly proclaim by their speech, that national industrial development can be most speedily effected and permanently maintained by creating and imposing artificial obstructions—mainly in the nature of excessive or discriminating taxes—upon the work of producing and exchanging; while, on the other hand, a not inconsiderable number of citizens, in view of the great and varied resources of our country, the intelligence of its people, their wonderful skill in the invention and use of machinery, and their readiness to adapt themselves to circumstances, believe with equal sincerity that the largest and truest protection to American industry is to be obtained through the removal to the greatest possible extent of taxes and obstructions of every kind on the work of producing and exchanging; and that such pro-

[1] *Princeton Review.*

tection, if attainable, is certain to be most stable, because it will be most simple and natural. It is rather difficult to assign any good reason why those who accept the former of these opinions should be always so ready and so uncharitable as to impute improper motives and eminent lack of patriotism to those who believe in the latter. But be this as it may, it must be admitted that the present necessity for making large reductions in national taxation, for reasons independent of any theoretical considerations, affords a most excellent opportunity for safely determining by practical experiments which of the two methods of protection referred to is likely to prove most effective; and with a view of helping to such determination and assuming, in accordance with the deductions of a former article, that the immediate work by Congress of abolishing tariff taxation will be mainly confined to legislation in respect to certain specific taxes, it is proposed to next ask attention to a review of the condition of some of our great branches of industry, and of the requirements essential to give them a further healthy growth or extension; the *first* example selected being that of the *Manufacture of Cotton.*

This industry ranks third or fourth in importance among the manufacturing industries of the country. It has been long established, enjoys special advantages in the supply and cost of its raw material, and produced goods in 1880 to the value of $192,773,000. In 1879 a representative of *The British Textile Manufacturer* (a trade journal of established authority), thoroughly qualified for his task, visited the United States for the purpose of ascertaining through extensive personal investigations what the British cotton manufacturers had to fear from American competition in the world's markets. He reported to his employers in December, 1879,[1] " that in the matter of wages America is as cheap as England." (The census returns show

---

[1] It is somewhat curious that this report, which was not private and is one of the most interesting of recent economic publications, seems to have wholly escaped the attention of the multitude of writers and speakers, in Congress and out, who have discussed the question of the relative wages of the United States and Europe. It was, moreover, not even alluded to in the recent report on wages issued by the Treasury and State Departments, in response to a call by Congress for information on this subject.

that the average wages paid to the hands employed in the cotton manufactures of the United States for 1880 were $245.47 per annum. The best available statistics for the United Kingdom for 1882 make the annual average for British cotton-spinners and weavers a trifle over $250. See also U. S. Consular Reports for 1882, to the same effect.) The average relative cost per pound of manufacturing print cloths was returned, with full data for verification, at 11.99 cents for Rhode Island, 12.16 for England, 13.72 for Lowell, and 15.59 for Pennsylvania. It is also most interesting to note, in connection with this matter, that while this English reporter shows the cost of cotton manufacture (print cloths) to be less in New England than in Pennsylvania, the U. S. census for 1880 shows that the general average wages paid in the cotton-mills of New England is about seven per cent higher than the general average paid for similar service in the whole country. In the matter of weaving, in which department the wages paid "amount to as much if not more than all other processes combined," the rates in England were found to average from 22 to 25 per cent more than in the United States; but as the American weaver (working by the piece) attends to more looms and turns out more work per week than his English competitor, the average earnings of the former are much higher than the latter: thus illustrating the economic principle that is now beginning to be recognized, that where machinery is employed to any great extent in the work of production, high rates of wages and low cost of production are correlative results. The advantages enjoyed by American over English spinners were further reported to be "that people in America work longer" (on an average, 66 hours per week, or within a fraction of an entire working day each week more than is allowed by law in Great Britain); attend to their work better; drink less; are less influenced by trade-unions; and have the necessaries of life cheaper. In the matter of raw material the English expert showed that American cotton manufacturers have a decided advantage over the English to the extent of 0.7 cents or ¾d. per pound. American experts fix this advantage on our coarser cotton fabrics at "not less than one half cent and oftener three fourths of a cent a pound;" which in turn is said to represent an ability on the part of the manufacturer to pay at least 20 per cent higher wages, and yet produce a given kind of cloth at an equal cost with English competitors. It is also asserted by experts that the question as to what cotton manufacturers shall supply the bulk of the world's consumption is likely to turn on as small a margin as an eighth of a cent a yard. Under these circumstances the United States has long ceased to *import* the goods necessary to meet the wants of the million, but does import very largely of such finer cotton fabrics as depend mainly on style and fashion for their use; the value of the total importations for the fiscal year 1881–2 being $34,351,000, an increase over the previous year of about ten per cent. Of these imports, $7,501,000 represented hosiery, shirts, and drawers; $2,257,000 jeans and drillings; and $22,164,000 goods not specially enumerated, mainly fine fabrics and fancy articles. On the other hand, in the matter of supplying foreign countries we do not transact as large a business as we did twenty-two years ago. The United States has never exported as much as 150,000,000 yards in any one year; while Great Britain exports year in and year out nearly *five thousand* millions of yards, or its equivalent. In 1880 we exported *raw* cotton to all countries to the value of $239,000,000, and thought we did a big business; but during the same year Great Britain, besides supplying her own domestic consumption and with a general depression of her industries, exported *manufactures* of cotton to the value of $377,000,000. In the business of making cotton goods for export, altho, in addition to other advantages, we are by natural location a cheaper distributing centre than England for a large part of the world's consumption, we may be said to have as yet but barely scratched the ground. Now what more important matter could claim the attention of Congress and the country than the ascertainment of the reason of this remarkable industrial condition of affairs? What better starting-point of inquiry for a national commission authorized to investigate the relations of the tariff to the varied business interests of the country? In most other countries this matter would be considered of sufficient magnitude to warrant the creation of a commission for its special investigation and nothing else. New England ought to take the greatest interest in having such an investigation; for just as bright, sharp Yankees, just as skilled in the construction and use of machinery, are now scattered all over the West, the South, and the Pacific States, as still live within her borders; and these men, prompted by self-interest, have constantly the objective before them of emancipating their own sections from dependence on New England for supplies of manufactured products. And if current reports are to be accepted, the day is close at hand when the South will seriously break in upon New England's present prerogative of supplying the bulk of the domestic consumption of coarse cotton fabrics, and compel the latter, if she would continue her industrial growth or even maintain her present status in this department of production, to seek for other and larger markets than she now enjoys. Could the United States participate in the existing cotton-fabric export of Great Britain to the extent of only one third, we could at once greatly increase the number of our spindles, give employment to at least one hundred thousand additional operatives, plant factories beside many a now unutilized water-power or coal-mine, and render much substantial help in the way of resuscitating our commercial (ocean) marine. Experts tell us, moreover, that there are from five to eight hundreds of millions of people outside of Europe and the United States who are clothed mainly in cotton manufactured by slow and toilsome hand processes. One skilled female operative in a first-class American factory can produce more and better cloth in one day than the most skilled of these hand-loom workers can in fifteen or twenty days. Could we reach one half of these consumers we should need forty million spindles in addition to our present eleven millions, and 600,000 operatives more than our present 185,000. Under such circumstances what folly it is to talk about relative wages; as if any hand product of even the poorest paid labor of China or India could compete with our machinery : and of what importance it is that we should study and arrange our system and our instrumentalities for foreign commerce, so that the pauper labor of other countries could be induced to give us something satisfactory in exchange for the products of our machinery; and how much longer are we as a nation, in obedience to "wrong end foremost" notions of protection, to let this enriching opportunity of exchanging with " foreign paupers" slip out of our hands?

The result of such an inquiry would probably be in accordance with the conclusions at which most American investigators have for some time arrived ; namely, that the tariff has ceased to be a factor of the slightest importance in determining the source of supply of the great bulk of the cotton fabrics required for the domestic consumption of this country, and that American manufacturers would fully control this supply were every tariff enactment at once swept from our statute-books; but that, on the other hand, the existing tariff and our navigation laws constitute an almost insuperable obstruction to the command by the same manufacturers of any other than the domestic market. The opinions of the English expert on this point, as expressed in the report to which reference has been made, were as follows: " The general impression made upon me," he says, " by what I saw of cotton manufacturing in the United States is that at present England has little to fear from its rivalry, but that it lies in the hands of the people of America to make a considerable change in the state of things, whenever they think proper. While, however, the American nation heaps duties upon the import of foreign machinery, thus increasing the cost of mill construction, and in other ways by her tariff arrangements artificially raising the cost of production, American manufactures will continue too high in price to compete with English goods in all but exceptional instances. America is a world in itself, and she would continue to prosper, tho in a less degree, if the old world disappeared. So long as her population increases in as great a proportion as her manufactures, so long will her manufacturing industries flourish ; but the time will come when her factories will turn out more clothing material than the Americans can wear. She will then feel her isolation." These conclusions must commend themselves to every impartial reader as true. But it would, nevertheless, be a most profitable thing if a national commission, fully commanding the confidence of the country, could thoroughly investigate this problem in all its details, and report.

Relation of the Iron and Steel Industries to the Tariff.—As the domestic manufacturers of iron and steel, at least of the primary forms of these articles, always have been, and now are, a most potential element in determining the nature of the tariff of

the United States, it will be interesting and perhaps profitable to ask the attention of the public to a line of fact and reasoning in the interests of those who use iron and steel as the
raw materials of their industry, and of the ultimate consumers
of these articles, who outnumber the primary workers in the
ratio of thousands to one.

And *first* it is to be noted that the system of protection
—meaning thereby the imposition of a duty upon a foreign product with a view of making it for a time more costly, and so
promoting or sustaining the business of making such product
within the limits of the United States—has ceased to protect
American labor in the iron-mines, iron and steel works, and rolling-mills of this country, if in truth it ever did so.   In proof of
this assertion, which to many will seem utterly audacious and
unwarranted, it may be stated that the census reports recently
made by Prof. Pumpelly in respect to iron-mining, disclose the
fact that there were in the census year 1880, 31,668 persons engaged in this branch of American industry, to whom aggregate
annual wages were paid of $9,538,117.   It further appears, from
the census investigations made by Mr. James M. Swank, that
there were also employed during the year 1880 in all the iron
and steel works of the United States, in converting ore into
pigs, bars, plates, ingots, and rails, 140,978 persons, whose annual
wages amounted to $55,476,785.   The whole number of persons
employed in these two departments of our iron and steel industries was therefore 172,646, and the sum of all the wages paid
them during the census year was $65,014,902.   Assuming the
force—made up mainly of adult men—to be employed three
hundred days in the year, their average earnings in the census
year, which was a year of great prosperity in the iron and steel
industries, amounted to $375 for each workman, or almost ex-
actly $1.25 per day ; a rate which every one knows is only a fair
average for the most ordinary labor in other employments, and
is much less than is paid on the average to workmen in machine-
shops and other branches of industry in which iron and steel
constitute a large part of the raw material.   (The average wages
for the most common labor in 1874 [see Young's " Labor and
Wages," pp. 739, 743] were $1.53 per day in New York, $1.58 in
Illinois, $1.75 in Michigan, $1.50 in Missouri.   For experienced

farm-labor the average per diem in the Western States ranged from $1.48 in Ohio to $1.75 in Michigan.) It is therefore a matter of absolute demonstration that "protection did not protect" the laborer in these departments (iron and steel) of our domestic industry during the census year; and further, that it is no advantage for him to be encouraged to remain in this kind of work, and for the sufficient reason that he can earn as high or higher wages in other employments of a more desirable and attractive kind. That there would be no difficulty in finding other employments, perhaps of a better kind (all things considered), than this work for this whole force of laborers in question, would seem to be proved by the circumstance that their aggregate number is less than one fifth of the number of immigrants who landed on our shores during the past year,—all of whom, certainly all of the more enterprising, appear to have speedily found employment; and it is probable that their average daily wages were not less than $1.25 per day.

Second. The work of the laborers in the iron mills and works of the United States during 1880 resulted in the production of 3,781,021 tons of pig metal, and its conversion, when mixed with foreign ore and domestic pig, into a proportionate quantity of finished bars, plates, ingots, and rails. For the year 1881 the American Iron and Steel Association reports that the product of pig-iron increased twenty-three per cent, or to a total of 4,641,564 tons ; and it is well known that this increased quantity was not sufficient to meet the demands for domestic or home consumption, and that large amounts of iron-ore and of iron and steel ingots, bars, and rails were imported from foreign countries.

Third. The American iron and steel manufacturers (the manufacturers of Bessemer steel excepted) almost unanimously and constantly represent that the manufacture of common iron—pigs, bars, and rails—has not been unusually profitable, or not more so than other branches of industry. On this point the American public have no direct and certain knowledge ; but it is not to be presumed that the iron-masters have put forth intentionally false statements. If, then, the average rate of earnings of the workmen in these departments of our domestic industry have only been equal to those of the most common labor outside the mines, the furnaces, and the mills; and if it be also true, as the iron-masters themselves allege, that there has been no realization of profits above the average in their business, it clearly follows that protection has ceased to protect either labor or capital in the industry under consideration, however it may have been in times past. And this being admitted, the conclusion is warranted that the excess of price, in consequence of protective duties, which the consumers of the United States have paid for iron and steel bars and rails over and above their competitors in other countries has been so much lost to the people of this country, either in useless transportation of ore and coal to furnaces which are misplaced, or in useless royalties to the owners of mining lands; or else the iron-masters of the United States are at this late period still representatives of an infant manufacture, which they are incapable of conducting for want of knowledge, and in which they ask to be sustained at public expense. The above general remarks as to profits may not, and probably do not, apply to very many iron and steel works that are well situated, especially to such as are west and south of the Alleghanies; for the testimony is conclusive that pig-iron has been made at many places in these localities at a cost—including all charges for royalties, for ore, for coal, for depreciation and wages—ranging from $12 to $15 per ton, and even less. One iron-master who recently appeared before the Tariff Commission at Nashville (Col. Shook) testified that the cost of the manufacture of pig-iron in Tennessee was $15 per ton. Near Birmingham, Alabama, the cost is represented as between $12 and $13; and at Chattanooga as between $11 and $12. Now such works as these, it must be apparent, cannot be protected and need no protection of any tariff of duties against foreign competitors; and simply for the reason that they enjoy so large a measure of protection in their distance from the sources of supply of British iron as to be entirely independent of all artificial encouragements. It sometimes occurs that iron is brought across the Atlantic at a nominal charge, but it may be assumed that the cost of bringing iron from the works of England and Scotland to the Atlantic ports of the United States is, on the average, about one pound sterling, or $5, per ton. Thence to further transport it either to the iron centre of Ohio or to Alabama will cost at least half a cent a ton per mile, or $3.50; and much more to the neighborhood of the iron-works of Missouri. In other words, the protection of distance which the iron mines and works west and south of the Alleghanies now enjoy is greater than the entire sum of wages paid for *making pig-iron in these works.* In fact, the cost of bringing the iron produced in the United States during the census year 1880 from Great Britain to the centre of population of the United States would have been at least $8.50 per ton, and at this rate would have amounted to more than one half the entire sum of the wages paid in all the iron-mines and iron and steel works of the United States for that year. In view, then, of this demonstrated failure of the attempt to protect either labor or capital in the iron-mines and iron-works of the United States by means of the imposition of heavy tariff taxes upon foreign imports of iron and steel, and the consequent large increase in the cost of such products, is it not clearly for our national advantage to entirely remove all such taxes in order that the people of the country may hence-forth be able to purchase iron and steel at prices which shall not be relatively much higher than the prices which are paid by our industrial competitors in other countries ; such taxes, further-more, being no longer needed for the purpose of insuring rev-enue? It is not to be denied that the prices of iron and steel, especially the prices of Bessemer steel, have been greatly re-duced in this country within a comparatively recent period. But the same reductions have taken place in other countries, and in even greater measure ; and it should not be overlooked that it is the prices which we pay at any given time for the materials which we use in our manufacturing industries which is of prime importance to us in considering what are to be our relations to the commerce and markets of the world,—which prices may be lower than they were ten, fifteen, or twenty years ago, both here and elsewhere, and yet be relatively much higher here than in any other countries. And of one other thing we may certainly feel assured, and that is if we, by our fiscal policy and taxes, keep up the prices of our raw materials, especially iron and steel, so that they continue to be relatively higher than the prices prevailing in other countries, we must abandon all hope of supplying the world to any great extent with the products of our labor, and the demand for the products of our industries will, as now, continue to be limited to the relatively small area of our territory.

In the above review the manufacture of Bessemer steel has been excepted. But the following is what an analysis of the census returns of 1880 tell us respecting the relations of the tariff to wages and product in this industry: Value of product (Bessemer and "open-hearth steel"), $55,805,210; tons of all kinds produced, 983,039; hands employed, 10,835; aggregate wages paid, $4,930,349. A little application of arithmetic will now show that the ratio of wages to returned value of product was only 9 per cent; and that the amount directly paid out in wages was but a trifle in excess of $5 per ton. And yet, mainly on the score of protecting labor, a tariff tax is imposed on the import of Bessemer-steel rails of $28 per ton.

So much for the present relations of the iron and steel industries of the United States to the existing tariff. It is proposed next to take a "look ahead" and endeavor to forecast what would happen if all the tariff taxes which now obstruct the importation of iron and steel from Great Britain into the United States were at once entirely removed; a proceeding which most people in the United States would probably regard as in the nature of an unmitigated national calamity. The present production of pig-iron in the United States is now nearly five millions of tons (4,641,000 tons in 1881), and in Great Britain (our chief competitor in supplying the commerce of the world) a little more than eight millions of tons (8,377,000 in 1881). The immediate effect of a removal of our tariff taxes on iron and steel imports would be a very heavy demand upon the iron-mines and iron-works of Great Britain for a large additional supply. (The American market at present absorbs about 30 per cent of the English, Belgian, and German export of iron; and of all the iron-producing countries of Europe the net export of none, with the exception of Great Britain, is very considerable. The production of pig-iron for the United Kingdom is reported by the "British Iron Trade Association," for the half year ending June 30, 1882, at 4,241,245 tons, and the consumption for the same time at 4,339,392, which was 496,271 tons in excess of the consumption for the corresponding period of 1881. The stock of pig-iron on hand in Great Britain on the 30th of June,

1882, was also reported as nearly 100,000 tons less than on the 30th of December, 1881.) If we could only maintain our product where it is (which we probably could in virtue of natural protection), without increasing it, and call upon Great Britain to supply the increase which we should need, year in and year out, over and above our present consumption—a consumption, which prices made relatively, if not absolutely cheaper, would inevitably increase—it would be impossible for the iron-mines and iron-works of Great Britain to respond to such a demand without instantly occasioning an effect; first, upon the prices of British iron in the state of pig, bar, and rail; second, upon the wages of those who work the British mines, furnaces, and rolling-mills; and third, upon the demand of Great Britain on this country for agricultural products, inasmuch as the iron-workers of Great Britain are even now as largely fed from the products of the prairies of the West as are the iron miners and workers of the United States: and in the case of Pennsylvania to an even greater extent, as the capacity of this latter State to feed her own working-people is much greater than the capacity of the iron districts of Great Britain in a like respect. Then in place of an artificial protection (uncertain in its bearing and effect), such as it is claimed that the laborers in the iron-mines and iron-works of this country now enjoy through our tariff, a natural protection would be established for them through the augmentation of the wages or earnings of their fellow-laborers abroad, without decreasing their own ; for it would be obviously impossible to diminish the wages which the American iron miners and workers now receive below the level of common labor outside of the works in which they are employed—which wages, as before shown, average only $1.25 per day, or less than the average wages which the farmers of the West pay the labor which successfully competes through its products with the poorest-paid labor of Europe and the world. Furthermore, when this additional demand had thus raised the prices of iron in Great Britain and increased the wages or earnings of the English operatives, the cost of iron to English consumers would be much greater and the relative advantages which the persons who use iron in Great Britain—the builders of machinery, steamships, etc.—now enjoy, would be done away.

The use of iron in this country would greatly and rapidly increase; we should at once realize and enjoy the enormous
natural advantages which we possess, growing out of the circumstance that our iron and coal mines are much more easily
worked and at a cost of much less labor, measured by day's or
hour's work, than the English mines can possibly be; and
through the speedy attainment of larger markets we should for
the first time turn to full practical account our acknowledged
skill in using iron and converting it into machinery, hardware,
agricultural tools and implements, and a vast variety of other
metal products which the world demands and in which supply
we yet have as a nation so very little share. Then would follow a
transfer of the control of the iron markets of the world from
Great Britain to the United States; and the transfer of the
control in the working of this imperial metal implies supremacy
in the world's commerce and an industrial aggrandizement of the
nation that the most enthusiastic of American orators have as
yet scarcely dreamed of. And furthermore, if in the readjustment of duties as proposed, any laborers engaged in the primary
production of iron and steel should temporarily find themselves
displaced from employment, and should prefer a continuance of
the same kind of work, the ranks of those who are the users of
iron and steel as raw materials will be readily opened to receive
them; inasmuch as the number of the latter, already far in
excess of the former, will not only all be wanted, but will also
be largely increased as soon as a full and unobstructed supply
of the raw·material of their industry is assured to them.[1]

[1] The circumstance that the present (December, 1882) capacity of the furnaces
and rolling-mills of the United States for producing iron and steel in their primary
forms is probably largely in excess of the present ability of the country to consume, and that trade in Pittsburgh and the great iron centres "is gloomy and dis-
appointing," is no argument against the policy here advocated of removing all
duties from the importation of iron and steel, but rather an argument of great
weight in its favor. Thus, the revival of business in 1878 and the subsequent
large extension of our railroad system created a large demand for iron and steel;
and the free supply of these articles being obstructed by tariff, their prices greatly and
abnormally advanced, thereby excessively and unnecessarily taxing all the other
industries of the country: Bessemer-steel rails, for example, rising from $42 per
ton in February. 1879, to $85 per ton in February, 1880, and pig-iron from an
average of $17⅝ per ton in 1878 to $28¼ per ton in 1880. The realization and
prospect of excessive profits next stimulated an unhealthy increase in the "plant"
or instrumentalities for production; and as production has gone on, supplies have

Is the picture thus presented overdrawn? The majority, not yet sufficiently educated to appreciate our capacity and readiness as a nation for industrial independence, and the strength and development which will inevitably attend and follow the emancipation of our industries from taxes and obstructions, will doubtless answer in the affirmative. But be this as it may, those who indulge in such forecastings of our possible industrial future, to be attained through a revision of our national fiscal policy, are surely not justly liable to the accusation of being the representatives of foreign interests, altho they may be to that of being enthusiasts. On the other hand, consider some points of a reverse picture.

The representatives of the iron-ore-mining interests in the United States have recently agreed to ask of Congress an increase in the duties imposed on the importation of foreign ores. *Per contra*, the domestic manufacturers of iron assert that the use of the foreign in conjunction with the American ores of iron is of the highest importance, inasmuch as the admixture improves the quality of the resulting product, obviates a necessity of importing the foreign ores worked up into higher forms,

rapidly increased, until, with the first check in business activity, they have become in excess of demand: all of which has induced in turn such a severe competition and reduction of prices that the manufacturer, on the one hand, now finds himself threatened with not merely a loss of profits but also of capital, and the laborer, on the other hand, with not merely a prospect of reduced wages, but also with an extensive limitation of his opportunity for labor. It has been intimated, and probably with truth, that the strikes in the iron-mills of the country during the past summer have proved a blessing to the mill-owners. But be this as it may, it is clear that, bad as the condition of the mill-owners now is, it would have been worse had it not been for the strikes. All this experience, however, is not new, but has been characteristic of the industry of the country—and more especially of the iron and steel industries—for the last thirty years, under the influence of frequent modifications of the tariff, and also of the war. What the people have gained as consumers at one time from extremely low prices they have more than compensated for at another by the payment of extremely high rates; and what in the way of high profits has accrued at one period to the manufacturers has been more than offset to him by periodical suspensions of industry, loss of all profits, and impairment of capital. That such experiences could be wholly avoided is not pretended; but it may be claimed that if Government was to cease to interfere through its fiscal policy with the natural course of production and exchange, the industrial course of affairs would be much more stable; and that any loss resulting from abandonment of protection would be as nothing in comparison with the destruction of capital and the waste and misapplication of labor that has been and is certain to be the result of a continuance of the existing policy.

and so, in fact, actually increases the demand and consumption of the domestic ores. And the experience of Great Britain, where every manufacturer is allowed to freely exercise his own judgment in respect to the management of his own business, powerfully reinforces this assertion; for the British iron-smelters, with a view of cheapening and improving their product, have long been in the habit of largely importing foreign ores, altho their domestic supply of other ores is unsurpassed in respect to either quality or quantity. The appeal of the owners of the American iron-mines for an increase of duties on the import of foreign ores, even tho the returns from their investments are not as profitable as could be desired, simply amounts, therefore, to the asking that our ability as a nation to cheapen the production of iron, with all the momentous consequences that would flow from such a result, shall be further obstructed and impaired. And altho, according to the principles which have heretofore characterized our protective legislation, it is most inconsistent for iron-smelters to oppose the petition of the iron-mine owners, the request of the latter is just as unreasonable as would be that of a small teamster to be allowed, for the furtherance of his own interests, to plant his horse and cart directly across the "Broadway" of our large cities to the great obstruction of the vast tide of larger interests that ebbs and flows through it. In short, if the full supply of foreign ore is any advantage to the American manufacturers of iron, the great interests of the country demand that they shall have it. On the other hand, if American mines, as is claimed, can furnish ores equally good and equally cheap, then protection is not needed. That *some* American iron-mines may suffer from the free import of foreign ores may be admitted; but that the domestic ore-mining interest in general is likely to be injured by such a policy, or needs any further protection than what naturally accrues to it from location—the cost of transportation—is not a reasonable supposition. And in support of this view attention is asked to the following items of evidences. An advertisement has recently been continuously and conspicuously published in one of the New York financial journals, of the organization of an American iron-ore company, which states that the company controls 5,000,000 tons of iron-ore, and that "contracts are offered for 300 tons per day on terms that will, on the completion of certain railway connections, net the company over $1 per ton, or $100,000 per annum " (40 per cent) on a total capital stock of $250,000. Again, the shipments of ore from the iron-mines in the vicinity of Lake Superior have been greater during the past year than ever before, and all the mines are reported as earning very large dividends. Tracts of land which a few years ago would not have commanded a dollar an acre are now worth millions. One hundred thousand dollars is said to have been refused during the past season for one sixteenth interest in the Quinnesic Mine (Michigan), which less than a year ago cost the owners $15,000. The moment the price of pig-iron rises from any circumstances, that moment the owners of the domestic iron-mines, freed in a degree from foreign competition, advance the price of ore. When the price of iron greatly advanced in the fall of 1879, the price of Lake Superior ore delivered at Cleveland, with cheap water transportation, rose to nearly the same price as that of pig-iron at Glasgow, Scotland. To the mine-owners this advance doubtless seemed a creation of national wealth ; but to the consumers of iron, who paid every dollar of such advance, the condition of things was somewhat different.

Again, the manufacturers of iron wire and "barbed iron fencing," whose interests are protected by patents to the extent of creating a monopoly of production, and whose products are especially in demand by the agriculturists of the country, also demand a continuation of the present duty on the importation of foreign competing (steel) wire of from 47 to 65 per cent. *Per contra*, the stock of the principal wire manufacturing company in the United States is scarce at 200—par 100—and pays regular dividends of 20 per cent per annum.

In unison with the ore-miners and wire-manufacturers, the manufacturers of spool-thread—a department of the cotton industry—are of the opinion that the protection of 74 to 78 per cent which they enjoy under the present tariff should also not be reduced. *Per contra*, consider the following statement of the profits of one of the principal thread-mills in the country, which recently appeared in the columns of the newspaper of the town where the mills are located :

"The amount of profits apportioned to the stockholders of the Willimantic Linen Company this year is $1,432,000, or ninety-five and one half per cent on the par value of January 1, 1882. The total profits of the stockholders for the past three years is $2,525,000, which is two hundred and two per cent on the par value of January 1, 1880."—*Willimantic (Conn.) Chronicle.*

Now as the general answer which will be made to the above statements and positions will be that the existing tariff cannot be materially reduced without reducing the wages of labor, and that one positive effect of the protective policy has been to secure high wages to the American laborer, it seems advisable, before further proceeding in this review of the relations of our industries to the tariff, to stop and ask attention to a brief exhibit of what an analysis of the returns of the recent census reveals to us on this topic. And first in respect to great primary manufactures of cotton, wool, silk, iron and steel, and the business of iron-ore mining: for the protection of each one of which, high-tariff taxes on the importation of all competitive products have long been imposed and maintained.

Class of Manufacture.	Hands Employed.	Average Annual Wages per Hand.
Cotton manufactures	185,822	$245 47
Silk and silk goods, etc.	31,337	291 88
Woollen manufactures of all classes	161,000	293 05
Hosiery and knit goods	28,328	230 53
Iron and steel	140,978	393 51
Iron-mining	31,337	301 19

Assuming 300 working days in the year, the average daily wages paid in the above industries would be approximately as follows: In the manufacture of cotton, 81 cents per day; silk and silk goods, 97 cents; wool, $1; iron and steel, $1.31; iron-ore mining, $1. If these deductions are not correct, the fault must be referred to the experts selected by the Census Bureau, who professed to make their several returns after careful investigation. If, however, they are correct, the claim that high protection insures high wages is proved to be without foundation; for the annual and daily averages for labor above given are less than the averages paid for labor in the great agricultural States of the West.

The following table next illustrates how wages rise in those industries which use textile fabrics and iron and steel in their primary forms as raw materials—industries which employ a very much larger number of laborers, and for the most part cannot be, or actually are not, protected by the tariff.

Class of Manufacture.	Hands Employed.	Average Annual Wages per Hand.
Agricultural implements....................	39.580	$388 06
Boots and shoes............................	138,819[1]	381 00
Foundries and machine-shops...............	145,795	454 18
Men's clothing............................	160,810[2]	286 00
Hardware[3]......................	4,034	424 74
Carpentering..	15,664	544 08
Furniture-makers..........................	19,656	470 75
Lumber, planing, etc.......................	3,739	458 53

The census statistics further show the percentages of labor, reckoned in wages, to the total value of the finished products of various industries, to be approximately as follows:

In the manufacture of wool............................		16 per cent.
"	"	" iron and steel....................	21 "
"	"	" cotton.........................	22 ".
"	"	" silk..........................	37 "
Iron-ore mining.....................................		41 "

If now the price of foreign fabrics, of cotton and wool, and of foreign iron and steel landed in the United States is increased by reason of freights, commissions, insurance, and packing to the extent of 5 per cent,—and if the above-specified articles are transported after landing to any considerable distance inland, it is at least this, and more,—then it follows that the American manufacturers of cotton and wool, and iron and steel in their primary forms could afford to pay their laborers some twenty-five per cent more than is paid by their foreign competitors and yet be on terms of equality with the latter so far as wages enter into and control the value of their products. Duties ranging from 30 to 50 per cent and upwards have, however, been given under the existing tariff, mainly on the claim that they were absolutely necessary to protect the American manufacturers against the advantages enjoyed by foreign manufacturers of similar products in the item of wages; but whether such claims have any justification in fact is a matter that may be safely left to the judgment of the reader.

[1] One fourth women.
[2] More than one half women and children.
[3] The analyses for hardware, carpentering, furniture, and lumber working are based on the statistics returned from certain of the leading cities of the United States and not from the whole country; the latter not being yet obtainable.

THE MOST RECENT PHASES OF THE TARIFF QUESTION.[1]

I.

THE second session of the last or Forty-seventh Congress
will undoubtedly stand in the fiscal and political history
of the United States as marking a transition-period in the sentiment of the country in respect to the tariff question of no little
economic and political importance. With the termination of
the war and its requirement for vast expenditures, it might naturally have been supposed that the whole of the vast and onerous system of taxation which the war made necessary would
have been promptly reconstructed with a view to the entire
abandonment or extensive reduction of no small number of
its burdens; and in the department of internal revenue this
was indeed done, but very slowly. But in the matter of taxes
upon imports, from which the largest proportion of the national
revenues, and the largest sums ever collected by any nation from
such sources, are derived, not only has there been no reduction
whatever in the average rates imposed during the war, but on
the contrary, and in the case of very many articles, the taxes
have been very largely increased. That such a course of fiscal
policy, or "*the maintenance of war-taxes in time of peace*," as it
has been fittingly termed, should not fail to encounter some
considerable measure of popular disapproval might also have
been naturally supposed ; for the popular mind, altho know-
ing little and caring less concerning economic matters, nevertheless moves pretty promptly and directly to the conclusion
that there is an intimate connection between high taxes and

[1] *Princeton Review, May,* 1883.

an increased cost of living and of production. But, singularly enough, this sentiment of disapproval has, until a very recent period, been comparatively limited. In the first place, the masses, finding it easy, through the great natural resources and rapid development of the country, to obtain employment and a living, and being also naturally disinclined to reason on such subjects, have either allowed themselves to remain indifferent or to be easily persuaded into the acceptance of any opinions or assumptions that might be plausibly urged upon them. While, in the second place, the so-called manufacturing interests of the country, accepting almost universally the proposition that the maintenance of high taxes upon the importation of nearly all foreign products, and the abandonment of all federal taxes upon all similar or competing domestic products, were essential to their prosperity, have through their intelligence, social position, and large command and use of money wielded an influence in behalf of their faith so irresistible, that the prediction has often been expressed that nothing could prevail against it until natural circumstances forced its representatives to radical differences of opinion among themselves.

The business of dissent from the tariff policy of the federal government since the war has therefore been mainly relegated (one meaning of which term is " to banish") to a comparatively few persons, and those mainly clear-headed and enthusiastic young men, who, as has always been the case in every other movement in the world's history for the extension of human liberty, have had but the minimum of personal grievance to complain of, but whose motive and inspiration, impelling to work and sacrifice for the cause they advocated, was simply the love of truth and right, for the truth and right's sake. To men whose opinions about the tariff are controlled mainly by their pocket interests, and indeed to all who have been educated to believe that government—which never has anything in the way of money or property but what it has previously taken from the people—can create national prosperity by arbitrarily taking the result of accumulated labor from one man and arbitrarily giving it to another, such motives appear absurd and incredible ; and in default of any other motives that would seem reasonable to those thus reasoning, the hypothesis of organized corruption and thorough disloyalty to American institutions has been resorted to, proclaimed, and extensively accepted. Hence the statements first made, it is believed, by Horace Greeley and H. C. Carey, and since positively repeated and enlarged upon by such men as W. D. Kelley, Cyrus Hamlin, president of Middlebury College, Vermont, John L. Hayes, late President of the Tariff Commission, and many other lesser lights, that the leaders of the cause of "free trade," "tariff for revenue only," and "free ships," and the repeal of our navigation laws, receive their inspiration and were bought up to do their work through "British gold;" and that organizations for the purpose of raising and disbursing funds for such purposes in the United States—as, for example, the Cobden Club—regularly existed and were successfully operated in Great Britain. Such statements and assertions up to the present time have seemed too silly to require anything in the way of positive challenge and denial; but when a recurrence to and a general use of them still constitute a marked phase of the current tariff discussion, and seem likely to continue, it may be well to here state, for the special benefit of those whose character and self-respect, in spite of most decided opinions and prejudices, will not allow them to deliberately falsify, first:

That the transmission on the part of any organization or individual in Great Britain or Europe to the United States of money or credit, to the extent of a single dollar, for the purpose of aiding any free trade or anti-protection movement in the latter country is not known to any American representative of such movement to have ever occurred; and the receipt of any such aid by any journal or organization advocating free trade in the United States, or by any person officially connected with such organization, is not only here unqualifiedly denied, but the ability on the part of any one to furnish a scintilla of evidence to the contrary is also here positively challenged and disputed. And secondly, as respects the Cobden Club, which is declared and extensively believed by protectionists to be a foreign propaganda of free trade of wonderful activity, and the organization through which large sums of money are constantly raised and disbursed for influencing public opinion in the United States, the following statements are further submitted. This club was founded in

1866 with the object of encouraging the growth and diffusion of those economic and political principles with which the name of Richard Cobden is associated, and which are also briefly but com. prehensively expressed in the motto which the club has adopted and caused to be engraved upon its seal; namely, "*Free Trade, Peace and Good Will among Nations.*" Altho the headquarters of the Cobden Club are in London, it enrolls among its members nearly all the leading economists and statesmen of Europe: as, for example, Gladstone, Bright, the Duke of Argyle, Sir John Lubbock, Sir Charles Dilke, Robert Giffen, Thomas Brassey, and James Caird, of England; Léon Say, Leroy Beaulieu, Jules Simon, Henri Cernuschi, and Maurice Block, of France; Schulze-Delitzsch and Karl Blind, of Germany; Emilio Castelar, of Spain; Frère Orban and M. Laveleye, of Belgium; Prof. Cossa, Quintine Sella, and Marco Minghetti, of Italy; and in the United States, Pres. Woolsey, Anderson, Gilman, and Gen. Walker; Geo. Bancroft, Edward Atkinson, C. F. Adams, Jacob D. Cox, H. W. Beecher, E. N. Horsford, E. P. Whipple, and Hugh McCulloch; while on the roll of deceased members are found the names of Baron Bunsen, Count Corsi, Léon Gambetta, Michel Chevalier, James A. Garfield, John Stuart Mill, L. F. S. Foster, Charles Sumner, H. W. Longfellow, R. W. Emerson, Samuel Bowles, W. C. Bryant, Francis Lieber, Isaac Sherman, Amasa Walker, Samuel Ruggles, Wm. Lloyd Garrison, and others: the name of any one of whom is sufficient proof that no organization in which it was voluntarily, continuously, and sympathetically enrolled, could be anything not in the highest degree honorable and open in all its transactions to public inspection. The receipts and expenditures of the Cobden Club are annually audited and published in detail in the leading journals of England; and its total income for the carrying out of its plans has never been as much in any one year as $15,000; with the single exception of 1881, when a special publication fund of $8860 was contributed, and of which $5140 was appropriated for the publication and distribution of works on " Systems of Land Tenure." From the regular receipts are defrayed the expenses of an annual dinner of the members; the salaries of a secretary and clerk; the expense of medals which the club annually awards for the best essays on any subject connected with political

economy by the students of various leading colleges in the
world (Harvard, Yale, and Williams, in the United States); and
the publication and distribution of a great variety of books and
tracts on many subjects, additional to those pertaining specially
to free trade.[1] When, therefore, Hon. W. D. Kelley, M. C., declared, in the political campaign of 1880, that the Cobden Club
had raised and transmitted to the United States more than a million of dollars for influencing the national election of that year;
and the Rev. Cyrus Hamlin, a minister of the gospel and president of a New England college, writes in the Journal of the
American Agricultural Association for November, 1882, that the
Cobden Club " *has expended vast sums during the last twelve or
fifteen years to incite our (American) farmers against the government and our manufacturers ;*" and that " millions of copies of an
appeal to American farmers were issued" (by it) " and distributed
all over the land," it is certain that these gentlemen, if they
claim to be men of honor, have placed themselves in a position
not a little embarrassing and dishonorable. For they either
knew or did not know whereof they affirmed. If they knew,
then they were guilty of uttering unqualified and intentional
falsehoods; and if they did not know, they used words without
meaning, and recklessly, if not intentionally, deceived their
hearers or readers.[2]

[1] The following is a more detailed exhibit of the income of the Cobden Club
since its organization, as derived from its official reports: For the seven years
from 1866 to 1873 the total income was £8204 ($41,020), or at the rate of $5857
per annum; 1878, £1529; 1879, £1825; 1880 (the year of the U. S. Presidential
election), £2557; and for 1881, £4163, of which £1028 were appropriated to the
publication of works on the subject of land-tenure. Among other works published or distributed by the Club during this same year, when, according to Judge
Kelley, a million of dollars was appropriated to the United States, were Caird's
" Landed Interest;" Maclehose's " Value of Political Economy;" Watterson's
" British Commerce;" " The Financial Reform Almanac;" Apjohn's " Cobden
and Bright;" Potter's " Workman's Views of Free Trade;" Krebs's " Working-
man on Reciprocity;" together with reports of meetings, lists of members, accounts, etc. etc.

[2] As further illustrating, notwithstanding the above exhibit, the extent to
which the Cobden Club has been effectually used as a "bogie" in the United
States for the raising of money and the controlling of votes in support of high
protection, attention is also asked to the following extract from the Report of the
American Iron and Steel Association for the year 1881: " During the Presidential and Congressional campaign of last year" (1880) "the Cobden Club of England

Recurring to the assertion before made, that the last session of the last or Forty-seventh Congress marks a transition-period of permanence and importance in the sentiment of the country on the tariff question, the following review of the situation would seem to forbid any other conclusion.

Nothing is more sensitive to changes in public opinion than the American politician, or more quick to respect them than the Federal Congress; and the circumstance that Congress at its last session devoted most of its time to a consideration of a reform of the tariff, and that the political party dominant in both Houses did not dare to adjourn without taking some action upon it, even tho such action, as it turned out to be, was little more than a pretence, is certain proof that the tariff, from a merely political point of view, cannot longer be treated, and as in former years, with political neglect and indifference.

Again, no one who has given the subject any attention has any doubt that the United States has at present more active capital, machinery, and labor engaged in the so-called work of manufacturing than is necessary to supply any present or immediate prospective demand for domestic consumption. And as general evidence confirmatory of this position, citation may be made, *first*, of the general and increasing complaint on the part of American manufacturers of *over-production ;* in connection with which attention is here asked to the very significant fact recently brought out by the N. Y. *Public*, namely, that while the domestic exchanges for the past year (1882) show a very marked increase as respects the manufacturing centres of the country, the exchanges at the great distributing centres on the other hand show a marked decrease, with accompanying heavy losses and shrinkage in business. *Second*, the interruption of great branches of domestic industry, of which examples are to be found in the recent suspension of the entire business of

threw off all disguise, and sought directly to influence the free expression of the popular will in many States by circulating large quantities of English-printed books and pamphlets which outrageously misrepresented the effects of our protection policy," etc. This association promptly undertook the work of counteracting this movement of the Cobden Club, and a series of protective tracts, embracing over half a million copies, was printed and circulated in the wake of the free-trade publications."

cotton manufacture in Philadelphia and vicinity; of the discontinuance in all or great part of the India-rubber and gunny-bagging manufacture; of the reduction of sugar-refining industry to about 60 per cent of its existing capacity; and the suspension or failure of some of the most important iron-furnaces and rolling-mills of the country. And *third*, the actual or attempted reduction of wages in almost every department of domestic manufacturing industry; the recent united effort for this end of the representatives of all the iron-works west of the Alleghanies being especially noteworthy.

Next, a large amount of evidence to the same effect of a more specific character, and in the highest degree interesting and instructive, has also recently been made public. Thus, during the past winter, a resolution was introduced into the Legislature of Massachusetts urging upon the representatives of that State in Congress "*the importance of reducing the national taxes and the propriety of abolishing as fast as possible (without too great injury to vested interests) the taxes upon imports, except so far as may be necessary for a revenue to meet the prudent and economical expenses of the government.*" Had such a resolution been introduced into this body five or ten years ago it would probably have been received with almost as much of surprise as a resolution in favor of the re-establishment of domestic slavery, and would probably have been as unceremoniously treated. And as it was, had the committee to whom the resolution was referred been governed solely by their private opinions, a majority, it is understood, would have summarily voted "leave to withdraw." But under the circumstances a full and respectful hearing, extending over some weeks, was granted to all interested. And to this hearing came, among others, Mr. Howard M. Newhall, one of the leading shoe-manufacturers of the famous Massachusetts shoe-manufacturing town of Lynn, who gave testimony of such a startling character that any discussion of the subject would be incomplete that failed to embody its nearly complete statement as reported.

"I have come before this Committee," said Mr. Newhall, "to present a few facts in regard to one specific branch of business interest—a protected shoe industry. The shoe industry is the most thoroughly American in its parts of any of our great industries. A few years before 1860 few would have dared to predict that a shoe could ever be made by machinery, or that in a quarter of a century there would be so many people employed in making shoes by machinery as to render the American market altogether too small for their industrial capacity. Yet such is the fact. In Lynn alone the capacity is three hundred thousand pairs of shoes per week, and Lynn is only one great representative of a great many shoe-manufacturing centres in New England, New York, Pennsylvania, and the West. This is its present capacity, but the power of enlarging this capacity is unlimited. This whole system could be duplicated and reduplicated if necessary within a short term of years. With such facilities it is very natural that the business should soon outgrow the home consumption. Where a few years ago it took nine months in each year to shoe this country, it now takes but six months, and, with the present increase of factories, a few years hence it can be done in less than that time. Of course the increase of capacity engenders competition among the manufacturers, and there is a constant incentive to underbid the market to secure trade. As in all trade, a low price (often quoted) "sets" the market, and in order to meet the market articles have to be made cheaper at the expense of the operatives. If the materials used to make a shoe go up in price, labor always has to go down. Strikes result, as that seems to be the only way the laborer can protect himself from the encroachment of the employer. In a general strike in a shoe-manufacturing centre the operatives often gain temporary advantage, but with a supply greater than demand it cannot long continue. A shoe-factory is what might be called "portable," and when a manufacturer cannot have his own way in one locality he goes where he can. When he finds he cannot make shoes cheap enough in some great centre, he finds some quiet country town where he starts a factory and is able to make shoes at less price. His city competitor is deprived of just so much work, and is obliged to ask of his employés a reduction in wages if they wish to save their work from going away. The general sequence of a strike, then, is the establishment of country factories, so called, and the sequence of country factories is a forced reduction in wages. Every time this programme has been repeated in the last few years it has left wages on a lower basis."

"Gentlemen, do not blame the manufacturer for trying to meet the market, or blame the operative for resisting a reduction in wages. It all goes to show that the supply is greater than the demand, and that our market is not large enough. Perhaps you may wonder how and where we are "protected" in our shoemaking. I will mention two or three articles specially, and speak of the others generally. Take, for instance, serges or lastings. The average duty on the serges or lastings used in the manufacture of shoes is 85 per cent. And how many factories do you think are protected by this enormous duty? I know of only two—one at Oswego, N. Y., the other at Woonsocket, R. I. I may be in error, but these are all which have been named to me, altho I have made diligent inquiry. As another instance, take that well-known article, French kid,

or, in fact, kid of any foreign make.   Kid requires a duty of 25 per cent
on the average.   French kid costs all the way from $18 to $45 per dozen
skins, according to the quality.   An average skin would cost about $30
per dozen, and each skin would cut about one pair of shoes.   Hence the
prospective penalty for wearing soft, pliable French kid shoes is sixty
cents before the process of making the shoe has begun.   This appeals to
our own pockets, but in its broader sense we are at just sixty cents' disadvantage in competition with the rest of the world in that grade of shoe.
The light, pliable glove-calf of foreign manufacture is taxed by a duty of
20 per cent.   I have selected the serges, kid, glove-calf, which perhaps
form a sufficient variety to illustrate the argument.   In the warm climates
where we must push our foreign shoe-trade, those of the inhabitants who
wear shoes require just these very kinds of shoes which have been mentioned.   American calf, goat, or grain is too heavy for use in warm countries, and if we are to compete with foreign manufacturers we need
every advantage of competition.   Cottons, nails, tacks, buttons, thread,
all have to be used in the make-up of a shoe, and they are protected.
The iron from which we make our machinery is protected.   If, as is face-
tiously said, we make shoes of paper, that is protected too.   In short, you
have paid a duty on nearly every component part of the shoe which you
are now wearing on your foot."

    " America is the home of the shoe-trade.   Almost every other large
manufacturing business was imported, and mechanics had to be taught by
men who were paid to come here and teach them.   But the Yankees invented their own shoe-machinery, and no one had to be imported to
teach them how to run it.   The best educated factory population in New
England is that found in your "shoe-towns."   They are thrifty, strive to
own their own homes, and represent the very best side of a working population."

    " Perhaps you may ask what may be the general opinion of the Lynn
shoe-manufacturers on any question looking toward a modification of the
tariff.   There has been but one organized effort to test their opinion, and
that a short time since, when an effort was made to increase the duty on
India skins from 15 per cent to 25 per cent.   A petition was sent to
Washington, very generally signed by the shoe-manufacturers, protesting
against any increase ; and from this we may judge that they are alive to
the fact that their next move is toward reduction.

    " A removal of duty from all articles used in the manufacture of a shoe
would be an advantage to employer and employed.   Why, up in Canada,
and in the provinces, they have been obliged to protect themselves from
American shoes by a duty of 25 per cent ; and even tho we are having
to pay a tariff on importation and exportation we are sending as many
shoes into Canada as ever.   This alone proves what our shoe-manufacturing industry is capable of achieving if it can have a chance.   There is no other
country knows how, or could make shoes as fast and as cheap as the
Yankees, and all we need is one end of the bargain.   If we are able to sell

our goods when protected and protected against, if half the disadvantage we now stagger under were removed, we could soon push ourselves into a place where the world's buyers could not afford to purchase from any other market."

During the year ending March 1, 1883, 62 new paper-mills have gone into operation, and 37 additional were in course of construction. The *Paper-Trade Journal* thus reports the opinions concerning the prospect ahead of certain leading members of this department of manufacturing industry : Wellington Smith, of Lee, Massachusetts, thinks the present supply of paper in the United States is in excess of the demand; that prices are lower than last year, and that his mills find it necessary to suspend one, two, or three days in the week in dull times, "giving the help something to live on and keeping the organization complete." But as the *Springfield Republican* in commenting on this state of affairs significantly remarks, "if this remedy is resorted to frequently, this condition is likely to become chronic and somebody projects a new mill to do the very work which ought to be done in the idle 'one, two, or three days' of the existing mills." William A. Russell, a leading paper-manufacturer and a representative of Massachusetts in Congress, says that low water has restricted production heretofore, but "when the old mills are turning out their full product, and this new product is placed upon the market, we are to see a crowded and restless time among manufacturers." He thinks that even the pulp-makers, "with 15 new pulp-mills started during the past year," "will find difficulty in marketing their pulp in the immediate future."

A comparatively few years since the India-rubber manufacturers operated their mills full time all the year through. Consumption within the last three years is said to have doubled, and to have attained a present annual value of $38,000,000. But the capacity of the mills in existence at the same time is also reported to be equal to supplying an annual domestic consumption of full $60,000,000; and there being no such demand, the manufacturers have gladly taken advantage of a "corner" in their raw material to almost entirely suspend production.

Gunny-cloth is the name given to a coarse textile used largely for cotton baling and other bagging, and manufactured from the coarse, cheap fibre of the butts, or lower part of the stalk of the plant that yields the so-called "jute" fibre. As the jute plant has thus far been successfully grown only in India, and as labor in that country is in most plentiful supply, at rates of wages which even in the much-talked-of "pauper countries" of Europe would be considered as insufficient, it would seem, reasoning *a priori*, utterly hopeless to expect that any manufacturer could ever successfully make gunny-cloth in the United States, even if he were not under the necessity of transporting his raw material twelve thousand miles, or half round the globe, and of paying a duty on its arrival of $6 per ton. And yet through the invention and application of machinery with which the hand-labor of India cannot compete [1] this has been done to such an extent that the United States now practically manufactures its own gunny-cloth, and the importation of this article from India, which was formerly very great, has become compar-

[1] The following story, which comes to the writer as strictly authentic, strikingly illustrates the nature and economic effect of this new application of machinery, and it also constitutes a demonstration of the falsity of the popular assertion and belief that it is the comparative rates of wages in different competing countries which determines the comparative cost of production and the necessity of tariff protection.

Some time since a gentleman, manifestly of oriental lineage, appealed for leave to inspect the operations of one of the large gunny-cloth manufactories in the vicinity of New York. He was courteously admitted, when the following conversation ensued:

Oriental—I have come all the way from Calcutta to find out why you Americans no longer import my bagging as you used to, but instead of it import the jute butts and make the bagging here; I don't understand it.

Manufacturer—Because we can manufacture cheaper here than you in Calcutta.

Oriental—How can that be? What does that weaver earn a day?

Manufacturer—About a dollar and a half. It is heavy work.

Oriental—Well, weavers in Calcutta work for less than a tenth part as much.

Manufacturer—Yes; but what does it cost you to weave your bagging per yard?

Oriental—About three cents.

Manufacturer—Well, that weaver's work costs half a cent a yard, and we can make a better article than the imported cloth with a less weight of fibre. That is the difference between our machinery and yours. Now do you see it?

Oriental—I see that I have come all the way from Calcutta to find out that I am a—fool not to have seen it before. Good-morning.

atively unimportant; the decline in imports of gunny-bagging having been from 18,800,000 lbs. in 1872 to 2,490,000 lbs. in 1882; and of gunny-cloth, not bagging, from 32,000,000 lbs. in 1867 to 226 lbs. in 1882. On the other hand, the importation of jute butts (the raw material) increased from 157,000 bales in 1874 to 320,174 in 1882. The success which attended the efforts of those who originally embarked in this manufacture was such that others have been rapidly tempted to engage in it, so that there are now about 30 manufactories of gunny-cloth and cotton bagging in the United States, with a reported capacity of producing 50,000,000 yards a year, or a quantity sufficient to bale a crop of cotton 2,000,000 bales larger than has as yet been produced. Under such circumstances the manufacturers are especially troubled with "over-production." The stock on hand is reported to be enormous : some mills have failed; others have shut down temporarily or permanently; while the sense of a general meeting of manufacturers recently convened in New York was to voluntarily close all their mills until the present stock on the domestic market is greatly reduced or exhausted.

Now these and many other similar illustrations which might be further adduced, did space suffice, demonstrate beyond all question that the present most urgent and most important question of the hour—a question that admits and will demand consideration alike from a political, economic, moral, and social standpoint—is, How shall an extension of markets for the products of our industries be attained? For in default of such a result our manufacturing operations cannot be continued with full activity without glutting the home market with their products ; which in turn must force a suspension of business, entail serious losses on employers, and restriction of opportunity for employment and reduction of wages to employés. And it is just this result and state of things which now characterizes the manufacturing industries of the country, and which, under our existing national fiscal policy, is certain to continue. Every manufacturer knows instinctively that if he could produce and sell with greater cheapness he could sell more largely, and so acquire larger markets for his products both at home and abroad. There is no limit to the consumption of desirable commodities, if the price of such commodities is brought within the ability to purchase of those who desire to consume. There can be, furthermore, no such thing as their overproduction, so long as any backs are bare, stomachs empty, and bodies cold; but there is such a thing as imperfect and faulty distribution of desirable products of labor, growing out of artificial or avoidable impediments such as taxes, selfishness, ignorance, and imperfect methods and instrumentalities of production.

But how shall the American manufacturer produce cheaper (or at least as cheap as his foreign competitor) in respect to many articles for which he has the greatest natural or acquired advantages, and so solve to a great extent the difficulties which now environ him? There are but two ways (it being taken for granted that he is not deficient in the invention and use of machinery).[1] He must have cheaper raw materials, the crude forms of the metals, coals, fibres, dye-stuffs, chemicals, unmanufactured wood, etc., or he must have cheaper wages, or labor.[2] But the former, a tariff like that recently enacted (which levies taxes for purposes other than revenue) *ordains that the American manufacturer shall not have ;* (as is strikingly illustrated, for example, in connection with the exhibit above given of the present condition of the domestic gunny-cloth manufacture, by the recent refusal of Congress to take off the duty on jute butts); so that there remains to him the only other alternative to a curtailment or suspension of business, namely, that of reduction of wages. And this is what the American manufacturing employer is now everywhere trying to effect, and what the employé everywhere is instinctively resisting. But what chance has the latter to succeed in this contest, with some six to seven hundred thousand new laborers coming into the country every year from other countries, while the whole number of laborers *primarily* engaged

---

[1] In view of reports of American consuls that large quantities of old woollen-machinery, which English manufacturers have discarded are continuously bought for the price of old metal and exported to the United States for manufacturing use, perhaps the assumption is not fully warranted.

[2] It would seem as if the talk of the necessity of having cheaper transportation in general was coming to an end when leading American railroads report that they can carry freight at half a cent a ton a mile and make a profit on the transaction; and when the cost of the ocean transport of fresh meat from the United States to England has recently been as low as one cent per pound, or, including insurance commissions, transport, and sale, not in excess of two cents per pound.

in all the manufacturing industries of the country is returned by
the last census at only 2,738,895 ? American workingmen ought,
therefore, to clearly understand (and as there is no logic so con-
vincing as scant wages and restricted opportunities for employment, it is only a question of time when they will understand)
that however it may have been in the past, when manufactures
were comparatively few, now that they are so numerous, if they
are to be kept in full operation they must produce more than
the country can possibly consume. *A high tariff*, under present
conditions, *therefore, necessarily means low wages.* Undoubtedly
some, whose prejudices and interests will not allow them to see
what they do not want to, may ridicule such a conclusion. But
there is no escape from it ; because a high tariff—under which
exemption from taxation is the exception—increases the cost of
all raw material, tools, and machinery; and to manufacture
cheaply, as before pointed out, the capitalist employer using
high-priced raw materials, tools, and machinery must reduce
wages, or stop through limitation of his market. And when the
masses of the American people do once understand this inevitable drift and result of our national fiscal policy, the tariff, instead of becoming a less important issue in American politics,
will become the question above all others predominant ; and
protection of the kind taught by the Pennsylvania school will
go down as rapidly as slavery before the uprising of the people,
and perhaps with a convulsion financial and commercial.

In no part of the country are opinions akin to those above
expressed, or an antagonism to the old-time notions about protection, more rapidly gaining ground, than in New England, especially in Massachusetts, as is illustrated by the evidence
respecting the condition of the shoe-manufacturing interests as
above given. And when one considers the special interests and
position of New England, the wonder is not that such a change
in public sentiment is now manifesting itself, but rather that it
has not come before. New England has no "raw materials" for
her manufacturing industries, using the term in the popular
sense. She has no home-supplies of coal, of the metals, of fibres,
of chemicals, and of dye-stuffs, and comparatively little lumber.
Nearly all of these essentials to successful manufacturing can be
obtained in many localities outside of her borders cheaper and

more readily than within her territory. Heretofore the skill and
intelligence of her people and her comparatively abundant capital have been to her a protection against these disadvantages.
But this protection is now rapidly disappearing. There are just
as good Yankees to-day outside of New England as within New
England. They have gone from her cold climate and sterile
soils to places where the raw material which they desire for
manufacturing production is cheaper ; and they have carried
with them their machinery and the knowledge and ability necessary to make the best use of it. These emigrants from the
place of their nativity do not propose to go back to New England to buy anything, which under the protection of the cost of
transportation and cheaper raw materials, they can afford to produce themselves ; and they mean to supply the localities in which
they have established themselves—the South, the valley of the
Mississippi, the Northwest, and the Pacific States—with the results of their local industries in these sections of the country.
Within the past month a wail has gone up from New England
cotton-manufacturers that unless the railroads reduce their South
and West bound freights they cannot compete in the manufacture
of the coarser cottons with other domestic competitors located
out of New England ; and every steamship which now sails out
of the ports of Charleston, Wilmington, and Savannah is in no
small part loaded with cotton fabrics in place, as formerly, with
cotton fibres exclusively.[1] Some three years ago ex-Gov.

[1] The following extract from a recent number of one of the most ultra high-
tariff journals of New England (the Boston *Traveller*) will be read with interest
in connection with this matter:

'Tho cotton manufacturing in the South is as yet in its infancy, it is
nevertheless becoming rapidly apparent that New England must not be too sure
of retaining a monopoly of this branch of manufacture. A sharp competition already exists, not only for the trade in sheetings in the cotton States, but Southern
cottons are now entering the markets of the Southwestern States, and the New
Englander finds himself confronted in all the leading markets of the Mississippi
valley with sheetings and shirtings in no way inferior in quality to those manufactured by himself, and which are offered at a less price than he, to make his
customary profit, can possibly afford. Instead of a possible competition twenty-
five years hence, the danger which threatens the New England manufacturer is
already imminent. . . . . The Southern mills are not yet producing the finer
qualities of goods, but, remembering the history of the last ten years, it is not safe
to assume that with the same machinery that is used in the North they will not
successfully do this within the next ten years."

Cheney of New Hampshire, in an address before a local association of cotton manufacturers, called attention to the fact
that when cotton-mills now burn down in New England they
are not rebuilt ; and at the present time, it is reported, that,
with one exception of an annex, there is not a single new foundation of a cotton-mill now going in.

There is much in the present and prospective industrial and
commercial condition of this country which is analogous to that
of England just prior to her decision to abandon the protective
policy, which she had maintained for centuries; and those who
have the time and opportunity will find much to interest and in-
struct in examining the history of this period, and especially the
speeches of Sir Robert Peel in the House of Commons and in the
spring of 1842. Sir Robert Peel, as is well known, was not one
of the original English free-traders, sympathizing at the outset with Cobden, Bright, and other leaders of the new movement,
but, on the contrary, was personally in antagonism with them,
and a comparatively late convert to liberal commercial opinions.
That the strong current of public sentiment in opposition to the
further continuance of the corn-laws, which was then everywhere
manifesting itself in England and even threatening revolution,
had something, perhaps very much, to do with influencing his
opinions in respect to the desirability of a change in the long-
established fiscal policy of his country, may be conceded ; but,
at the same time, Sir Robert Peel's whole life and character, and
especially his subsequent history, showed that while he ever
knew how and when as a statesman to conform to expediency,
he was too much of a man to allow expediency to ever become
a permanent and predominant basis for his public action; and
one therefore must seek for some other motive in explanation
of his conduct in radically and rapidly abandoning his long-
cherished protection opinions in the spring of 1842, and in the
undeviating support which he afterwards gave to the principles
of free trade. And this motive is thus set forth by his biog-
rapher, Thomas Doubleday, who, after remarking (see " Political
Life of Sir Robert Peel," vol. ii. p. 380) "that the arguments of
the apostles of free trade had made a deep impression upon the
mind of the minister," goes on to say that, " *with a population
then increasing at the morbid rate of about a million in the short*

space of three years, he (Sir Robert Peel) had manifestly become penetrated with the conviction that to find employment for the numbers that might in no long time demand it, and in a way not to be resisted, some large extension of foreign trade must in some way be created." And Bulwer, in his monograph of Peel's career as a statesman, speaks of his being impressed with the fact, which ought to be also pregnant, at this time especially, with meaning to the working men and women of the United States, *that the wages of the workman could not be made higher or more remunerative by making his food dearer.* In bringing forward his scheme for recasting the British tariff in May, 1842, Sir Robert Peel accordingly, while greatly simplifying the customs acts by abandoning the duties on many minor articles, sought more particularly to accomplish, and did accomplish, first, the cheapening of the living of the British people by abandoning or reducing the duties on imports of food ; and secondly, the cheapening of the cost of production to British manufacturers by entirely removing the duties on drugs and dye-stuffs and greatly diminishing the duties on the import of many other articles essential to manufacturing. And his great speech of the 10th of May, 1842, explaining and defending his new policy, abounds in practical illustrations which are almost identical with those which are now to be found in the present commercial and industrial experience of the United States. Thus, for example, in speaking on the subject of the then British duties on metals, he says :

" There is no part of the tariff in which we can make more important changes, than in that which relates to the reduction of duty on ores. Whether I speak of iron, lead, or copper, in my opinion great advantage to the commerce and manufactures of this country will result from permitting the entry of these important articles at a much more diminished rate of duty than at present. Let me take the case of copper. At present you cannot import and smelt foreign copper for internal use. You have greater advantages than any other country possesses with respect to coal, and you can apply that coal with great advantage to the smelting of foreign copper ; but when it is smelted you cannot make use of it for the purpose of home manufacture, and you send it to France and Belgium to be manufactured. What is the consequence ? Why, that those foreign countries can come into the markets of Europe, undersell you in copper, in bolts for the fastening and copper for the sheathing of ships, and in a variety of other articles made of copper and brass."

And he then further points out "that as ships can be fastened and coppered on the Continent at a much cheaper rate than in this country" (England), a very serious disadvantage in the way of the growth of British shipbuilding had been created.

To those familiar with the workings of our existing tariff it seems hardly necessary to point out that the United States in 1883 has almost exactly the same experience in respect to copper that Sir Robert Peel declared was proving so injurious to Great Britain in 1842 ; that is, we do not permit foreign ores of copper to be taken from Chili and other nations in exchange for our agricultural implements and textiles ; we do not allow such ores to be smelted with our coal and our labor, and in fact have actually destroyed great smelting establishments that flourished before the tariff of 1861 ; we have destroyed the shipping that formerly made such exchanges, and we give a bounty to foreign competitive copper-manufacturers by so shielding the proprietors of our rich mines from healthy competition, that the latter regularly sell the excess of their product over domestic requirement for a lesser price in foreign countries than they will sell in their own country.

Again, on the subject of oils, Sir Robert Peel, after pointing out that British manufacturing industry was then exposed to great disadvantages on account of the high prices of oils, more particularly spermaceti-oil, and that in consequence he proposed to greatly reduce the duties on their importation, went on to say :

" We shall then introduce the product of the American fisheries in competition with our own fisheries, and prevent the price of oil in this country from reaching an extravagant amount. I hope, sir, that I am not needlessly detaining the House, but I want to establish by proof a position, of the truth of which I feel confident, that the general result of this" (reduced) " tariff will be to give a new life and activity to commerce and to make a reduction of those charges which are now incurred by residence in this country. A very short time since the price of spermaceti-oil in this country was from £60 to £70 per ton, but lately it had risen to £95 and even £111 per ton ; and the manufacturer who required that oil had no alternative but to consume olive or other vegetable oils which did not answer his purpose so well, or pay an extravagant price as compared with the price of that oil in the United States. There are no oils that can be substituted for it without disadvantage, and yet we have to carry on a formidable rivalry with the United States in some branches of manufacture with the disadvantage of having to pay 8s. per gallon for oil which in America is sold for 4s. per gallon—a difference of 100 per cent."

So much, then, for one of the most recent and most important phases of the tariff question. An examination of it, such as in part has been here given, ought to abundantly satisfy us that the country has become too big to endure anything in the way of commercial and industrial restrictions except such as are absolutely necessary for the maintenance of the state. In fact the people of this country, more especially those of New England, would seem, from the evidence above submitted by the representatives of the Lynn shoe and other manufacturing interests to have come to a " parting of the ways" on the question of their future tariff policy. They may decide in favor of a continuance of such a policy as aims to protect their leading manufacturing interests by duly enhancing the cost of all the elements that enter into them, and learn through costly experience that such a decision means the fiercest of domestic competition, the limitation of markets, and the restriction of industrial growth. Or they may decide to favor a tariff which, while primarily levied " for revenue only," will at the same time discriminate in favor of and fully protect home industries by removing all unnecessary obstructions to their extension, and so gain for the country such control over the markets of the world as the skill and intelligence of its people fully entitle them to enter upon and possess.

In a subsequent article it is proposed to ask attention to other equally recent and no less important phases of the tariff question.

THE MOST RECENT PHASES OF THE TARIFF QUESTION.[1]

II.

IN the preceding number of this REVIEW (May, 1883) the assertion was made that our existing national fiscal or economic policy was so shrivelling up the manufacturing industries and trade of the country, and entailing so much of labor discontent and disturbance, that nothing could long divert the attention of the people from an earnest consideration of the tariff question, or prevent it from coming to the front, as a political issue of the first importance. In the two months which have now elapsed since the article referred to was written, much evidence additional to that then submitted in support of this position has accumulated; which in general may be summed up by saying, that continued failures, suspension of the work of production, and attempted reduction of wages on the part of manufacturers; strikes and resistance (rarely successful) on the part of employees; with a curtailment of the business of the country, and a reduction of profits on the transaction of the same to a degree most unsatisfactory,—have been and are now the most noticeable features of the situation; to which the further remark may be added, that one must be indeed sanguine who expects anything different in the *immediate* future, except as the result of one of those happy accidents, or " special providences," which on occasions of difficulty are said to always happen for the relief of infants, drunken men, and the United States.[2] The condition of one other great domestic industry,

[1] *Princeton Review, July*, 1883.

[2] When the maximum of industrial depression and commercial disturbance, arising from production artificially stimulated and in excess of current demand, is once reached, the recovery, in a country situated as is the United States, of necessity commences. The marvellous increase in our population alone causes

in addition to those previously noticed in detail, namely, that of the woollen manufacture, is, however, worthy of special attention. With the exception of the manufacture of iron and steel, this industry, more than any other, has now been protected in the United States for many years, by complex tariff provisions carefully devised for the purpose by representatives of the involved interests, and subsequently enacted without the slightest regard to either the interests of consumers, or of the state in respect to revenue. The result, so far as the *past* is concerned, is that no one of the domestic industries has been more subject to periods of extreme fluctuation, or has paid so small an average profit on the total capital invested, as has the woollen and worsted manufacture of this country since the enactment of the wool tariff of 1867 ; while, in regard to the present, there is almost no divergence of opinion " among the trade" that the woollen machinery and the production of woollens in the United States is very far in excess of any existing market requirements. Indeed, the estimate of some who assume to be qualified to speak is " that not over *fifty* per cent of the domestic manufacture of spring clothing and woollens for the seasons of 1882 and 1883 has really passed into consumption." It has, therefore, followed (to quote from a leading commercial review under date of June 6, 1883).

"that a heavy capital is locked up in old stock carried by clothiers and cloth jobbers, and that the spring clothing lately sold by the former has been forced on the market at less than the actual cost of manufacture."

consumption to rapidly gain upon production under such circumstances; until finally the community all at once realizes that supply has become unequal to the demand. Then those of the producers who have been able to keep their heads above water during the period of depression enjoy another season of remarkable prosperity; when others again rush into business in excess of any need, and the old experience is again repeated. Such has been the history of the industry of the country for the last twenty years under the influence of a high protective tariff, and such is most noticeably its present experience. To use a familiar expression, it is always " either high water or low water" with the business of the United States: no middle course and no stability. What the people gain as consumers at one time from low prices they more than compensate at another by the recurrence of extreme rates; and as producers, by periodic suspension of industry, reduction of wages, and depression of business. Meanwhile the loss to the country from the destruction of capital and the waste and misapplication of labor is something which no man can estimate.

Under such circumstances the woollen manufacturers of the United States, generally recognizing that there is to them no other prudent alternative to producing without orders, or at the best at infinitesimal profits, but to suspend operations, have begun to adopt this latter policy ; and a very large number of woollen-mills are already closed (nearly 800 sets of machinery reported idle, July 1), or working upon reduced time, and the progress of events is making it every day less and less a matter of choice to the manufacturer as to what course he will take.

So much, then, for one phase of the tariff question indicative of influences that are irresistibly working to compel changes in popular sentiment and a new " crystallization of political forces" on this subject.

Consideration is next asked to another phase of this question, which developed itself more conspicuously during the last session of Congress than ever before ; namely, the antagonism of different interests under the protective policy—an antagonism that bids fair to evolve more of bitterness and hatred than has ever been manifested by protectionists as a whole against the free-traders ; which from the necessity of the case must continue to intensify ; and which sooner or later will divide the protective party into hostile factions, and inevitably wreck the whole system which it advocates.[1]

It is evident that the representatives of many branches of domestic manufactures, more especially those engaged in the higher forms of production, are beginning to feel that their prosperity and even industrial existence is dependent upon a cheaper

---

[1] That this statement is fully warranted, attention is asked to the following extract from a letter reviewing the tariff legislation of the Forty-seventh Congress written by Senator John Sherman to the *Commercial-Gazette* of Cincinnati. He says :

"When the bill was reported to the Senate it was met by two kinds of opposition—one the blind party opposition of Democratic free-traders; the other (much more dangerous) the conflict of selfish and local interests, mainly on the part of manufacturers who regarded all articles which they purchased, as raw material, on which they wished the lowest possible rate of duty ; and their work as the finished article, on which they wished the highest rate of duty. In other words, what they wanted to buy they called raw material, and what they wanted to sell they wanted protected. It was a combination of the two kinds of opposition that made the trouble."

and better supply of their raw or crude materials, through a reduction or entire abrogation of the tariff taxes on the importation of such articles. That the attainment of such a result is most important to New England has already been pointed out.

But upon what principle of equity or consistency is protection through the agency of the tariff to be given to those who manufacture machinery, tools, hardware, and cutlery out of crude iron and steel, or who spin and weave wool, and the fibres of flax into cloth, and to be denied to the ore-miner, the iron smelter and forger, and the wool and flax grower ? Is not the laborer as much entitled to have the state protect him against the competition of the so-called pauper labor of Europe in the one case as in the other ? It seems almost needless to say that no answer in favor of such discrimination can be given that does not involve inconsistency and inequity. Nevertheless such discrimination in the levying of duties under the tariff has got to be made, if extended markets for our manufactured products are to be obtained through cheaper production. And the inevitable alternative in default of such discrimination is, that our industrial growth, and the sphere of opportunity for the employment of manufacturing labor, will be restricted to the comparatively limited and (in view of our capacities) wholly inadequate demands of an almost exclusively home market ; with a continued threat of business stagnation through excessive production to employers, and of reduction of wages to the employees.

Among the many illustrations which might be adduced in proof of the inevitable antagonism of protected interests that is, and is to be ; and how unquestionably protection destroys protection under a system like that now recognized in the United States, which attempts to protect every manufacturing industry, —the following, derived from the records of the Federal House of Representatives at the last session of Congress, is among the most curious and instructive.

The glass-bottle manufacturing interest, comparatively one of the smallest industries in the United States, and enjoying a protective duty on competitive imports of 35 per cent, asked to have this protection increased to such an extent that it would amount to near 100 per centum ad valorem. The representatives of this industry were, however, too wise to propose that any such increase should be incorporated into the statute in language sufficiently clear to be readily understood—the day for the enactment of 100-per-cent duties plain and simple, on the importation of articles of common use, having obviously passed; and they therefore, with a seeming absence of all guile, merely asked that specific rates be substituted for ad valorem, and fixed at 1½ cents per pound; the relative ad valorem of which none but experts could understand. But in opposition to this change appeared, some little time afterwards, the representatives of the great brewing interest of the United States— employing a capital of $91,208,000, while the whole common glass manufacture, a small proportion of which only is engaged in the manufacture of bottles, represents but $19,844,000 of invested capital; and in the course of the debate which ensued on the proposition to amend the tariff on bottles the following statements were submitted:

1st. That the proposed increase in duties would increase the price of beer-bottles to the extent of $2.13 per gross, and the cost of bottling to the extent of $14,807.86 for every 6000 barrels so treated; and that as there are brewers—individuals or firms—in the United States who now bottle over 100,000 barrels of beer annually, such manufacturers would, in the interest of the bottle-makers, be subject in consequence to a tax, in addition to what they now pay, of near $250,000 per annum. 2d. That the business of manufacturing beer—"ales" and "lagers"— in the United States has within recent years grown to enormous proportions; that the products of such manufacture are now beginning to be exported with success to Mexico, South America, Australia, and even to Europe; and that they can be exported safely only in bottles. 3d. That the increase of the tariff taxation on bottles to the extent asked by the bottle manufacturers, would tend to entirely break up and destroy this export business. And as evidence on this point a letter was submitted from the president of a single brewing association in Missouri, claiming to employ more labor and capital than any five bottle-making establishments in the United States, of which the following is an extract:

"While the present high duty of 35 per cent ad valorem is a great impediment to the exportation of American bottled beer, we have neverthe-

less managed to compete with some success with Europe for the trade of
Mexico, Central America, Sandwich Islands, and parts of Brazil and Australia, and the demand for the better American brands is constantly increasing. If there was no duty at all on bottles, as should be the case,
nearly the entire trade of the countries named, which is considerable,
could be diverted to the United States, where it properly belongs. We
have now to contend against this drawback of higher bottles than the European bottler pays. But a prohibitory tariff of 1¼ cents per pound would
result in driving out all American competition from such foreign lands
and damage the trade immensely."

Here, then, was clearly a case in which *not to discriminate* in
the imposition of duties in respect to different manufactures, and
not to deny, in the specific instance cited, the demands for any
additional protection, was to militate *against* the extension and
prosperity of one of the largest branches of our domestic industry ; against a most promising but incipient extension of our
foreign commerce, and in favor of a restricted market for one
of the leading products (barley) of our agriculture.

In the debate which took place on this proposition to increase the duties on bottles the members of the House of Representatives did not fail to see the importance of the point
involved, and accordingly, in two successive votes, *viva voce* and
by tellers, refused to increase the rates; but in the juggle of the
Committee of Conference the duty on bottles notwithstanding,
came out at 1 cent per pound, in place of the former rate of 35
per cent ad valorem, or was increased nearly 100 per cent;
and in the closing hours of the session, and with the cognizance
of only a very few members, the change was enacted into law.

Representatives of the Western beef and pork packing interests also appeared before Congress at its last session, and protested against further discriminations in the levying of duties
on imported salt, whereby benefits extended to the packers and
curers of fish in the Eastern sections of the country are not
equally given to the packers and curers of meats at the West.
This petition or remonstrance was almost unnoticed, but it is
nevertheless worth while to note how they presented their
case. After calling attention to the fact that during the year
1881, 133,024,447 pounds of foreign salt paid no revenue to the
government, it having been withdrawn from bond in accordance
with a provision of the act of 1866 that all salt used in the cur-

ing of fish shall be exempt from duty,—the assumption being
that much of the fish thus cured is sent to a foreign market,
where it competes with similar productions of those countries,—
the petitioners go on to say:

"The same argument" (*i.e.*, in favor of those who cure fish) "can be advanced in favor of the people of the balance of our country who continue
to pay duties on salt, for in the West and South large quantities of pork,
beef, and other products are annually cured with salt and sent to foreign
countries for a market, and are sold in competition with similar articles of
other countries. Why, therefore, should the products of one section of
the country be thus discriminated against, and those of another section be
encouraged and protected? Is this equity? is it justice?"

The curious state of things brought to light by the petition
presented to Congress at its last session by the Harrison Wire
Company of St. Louis ought also not to be passed unnoticed
in this exposition of newly developing tariff antagonisms. In
this petition it was represented that the company named was
engaged in the State of Missouri in the manufacture of wire for
fencing purposes; that their business was rapidly increasing in
volume, creating new and extensive opportunities for the employment of labor; and that their present production of wire
was nearly one hundred tons per day. It was further represented that the wire thus produced is manufactured from soft
steel, known to the trade as the Bessemer product; but that,
owing to the high price charged for this latter in this country,
the company had hitherto been compelled to purchase their
supplies in Europe; that recently it had been discovered that
ores out of which such steel could be easily and profitably produced by the so-called "basic process" existed in large quantities in Missouri, Alabama, and Tennessee; and that to take
advantage of such discovery the aid of foreign capital had
been sought and obtained. That the assignment of the right
to use the basic process had been also obtained from the
apparent owner thereof, and that suitable works, involving an
ultimate expenditure of five millions of dollars, had been
commenced, and would have been now completed, but for
legal proceedings instigated by the American Bessemer Steel
Company, avowedly for the purpose of preventing the Harrison Wire Company from proceeding with their new enter-

prise, and for the purpose of enabling the former company "to
keep up the price of its products" and "monopolize the iron and
steel business interests of the country." It was also set forth
in the petition, that the interference of the Bessemer Company
was based on a claim to have patents on this basic process, but
which process the Bessemer Company had not only never used
and did not desire to use, but also did not propose to allow any
one else to use outside of their own organization; and further,
that a suit commenced by the "Bessemer" against the "Harrison" Company for an infringement of patents was a pretence, inasmuch as, if the former did really own the patents (which is
disputed), there could be no actual infringement so long as the
new steel-works were incomplete and had not commenced
operations. "And thus it is," continues the petition, "that
Congress prevents foreign importation by a protective tariff,
and the patent-laws enable the Bessemer Company to prevent
all new competitive enterprises in this country." The Harrison
Company therefore prayed Congress for relief; to wit, by so
amending the tariff "as to prohibit the joint purchase by corporations of any patent for reducing iron-ore, as an act contrary
to public policy;" and also, "that if any such patent be now
owned under any purchase or pretended purchase," such owner
shall "be compelled to license all who desire to convert such
ores at a reasonable price." And "if they neglect or refuse" so
to do, they shall forfeit all rights under any patent, either foreign
or domestic." When this petition was first introduced, it was
no secret at Washington that its object was to force the Bessemer Company (mainly a Pennsylvania interest) to abandon its
"dog-in-the-manger" policy in respect to the Harrison Company
and other domestic manufacturers, through a threat of serious
tariff defection and revolt on the part of Western producers; and
that the political influence of the family of the president of the
Harrison Company was also to be invoked for the same end. But
be this as it may, as the petition after presentation was not made
the basis of any attempted legislative action, it is probable that
the object sought for was accomplished in another but not less
effective manner.

Again, in further illustration of the bitterness of feeling that
the policy of protection is certain to provoke among the ranks

of the protectionists, it is interesting to note that one of the most bitter, almost ferocious, exhibits of personal feeling that has ever been displayed during the whole twenty years of the present tariff controversy was embodied in a pamphlet distribu-ted to Congress at its last session ; in which Mr. Joseph Wharton, manufacturer of nickel in Pennsylvania, and a protectionist, at-tacked certain Connecticut plated-ware manufacturers, and the members of the Senate of the United States from Connecticut, all also and alike protectionists, because the latter desired and advocated a reduction of duties on nickel, which is a crude and raw material in the manufacture of plated ware, but which the former desired to produce, and through the maintenance of high duties to also monopolize and control the American market.   And as a specimen of this personal feeling, and also of the unity that pre-vails among these brothers in selfishness,—for self-interest and no other motive is the only ground of difference between the man who wants to make and monopolize, and the men who want to use nickel, as to how the government shall interfere in the mat-ter,—the following extracts from Mr. Wharton's pamphlet are here quoted :

"Senator Platt's constituents have nickel-ore quite similar to mine, and in apparent abundance, within a few miles of their German-silver works at Torrington, at Litchfield, and probably at other places in the Naugatuck Valley.   That Torrington ore was never successfully worked in Connecti-cut, whether because the brass and German-silver business paid the canny wooden-nutmeg men better, or whether their consciences forbade them to bloat themselves with the ungodly profits of the nickel manufacturer, his-tory does not inform us.   Let us believe it was piety."

And again:

" It is pitiful to think that the industries of our country should be at the mercy of legislators, some of whom are actually hostile and many of whom are so ignorant; to think that any lie of the busy agents of our national industrial enemies—mostly small barking creatures—should be believed, even when not understood, and that the statements of a fellow-citizen of known respectability should be disbelieved and cheapened, simply because he is a fellow-citizen.   It would be ludicrous if it were not lamentable to think that a tree bearing good fruit should be cut down by leg-islators" (*i.e.*, the Senators from Connecticut) " who know little more about the subject than a cow knows about Sunday. . . . . I have supported and aided the government more than it has supported and aided me.   I am one of the men who create and maintain the prosperity of the nation, and who enable it to survive even the affliction of wrong-headed and cranky legislators. We are the toiling oxen who make the nation's harvests, notwithstanding the gadflies." [1]

[1] Readers curious to know what was said on the other side by the "spoonmakers" of Connecticut and certain "actually hostile" and "so ignorant" legislators who spoke for them, will obtain this information from the following official report of a debate in the Senate of the United States, January 29, 1883; the subject under consideration being the duties on nickel:

"Mr. PLATT. Mr. President, nickel under the present law in the ore is 30 cents per pound, and nickel alloys are 20 cents per pound. Either duty is practically prohibitory. A single establishment in Connecticut uses of nickel annually three times the amount that has been imported into this country.

"Mr. INGALLS. Where is it mined in this country?

"Mr. PLATT. It is mined in one single mine near Lancaster, Pennsylvania, I think. When this duty was imposed of 30 cents on the ore and 20 cents on the alloy, nickel was worth from $2 to $2.50 or $2.75 a pound. A duty of 15 cents a pound to-day would be a higher ad-valorem duty than that imposed when nickel was from $2 to $2.75 a pound and the duty was really 20 cents per pound on the alloy.

"All this nickel, or three quarters of it, is consumed in Connecticut for the manufacture of German silver.

"It is said that this nickel mine is closed. It is simply closed not because it does not pay, but because at the present time there happens to be an overproduction, and the owner of it will not reduce the price. The price at the present time is about $1 to $1.05 a pound. It can be produced—I do not make this statement from my own knowledge, but I make it from representations made to me by persons who I think are entirely familiar with the subject—it can be produced in this country as cheap as it can abroad, owing to the fact that this ore here is more easily refined.

"Mr. BAYARD. What is the foreign price?

"Mr. PLATT. The foreign price is somewhere in the neighborhood of 70 cents at the present time. I believe that 15 cents per pound is more than a fair protective duty to the gentleman who produces this nickel. Certainly my constituents are very greatly interested in not having so high a rate of duty placed upon it as to unnecessarily enhance the cost of the article which they manufacture, and which is then taken in its third stage and worked into articles which go all over the country.

"Mr. SEWELL. I would ask the Senator from Connecticut if the manufacture of this article in this country has not reduced the price of the foreign article very largely?

"Mr. PLATT. The producer of nickel in this country produced nickel for a number of years at 50 cents, or from 50 to 70 cents a pound. He sold it from $2 to $2.50 and as high as $3 a pound, because there was a scarcity of it in the whole world. Recently a mine has been opened in New Caledonia which produces large quantities of nickel, and has thereby forced him to reduce the price, but I still believe he makes 100 per cent on every pound of nickel he produces.

It needs no gift of prophecy, therefore, to foretell what will happen if, with a view of promoting the interests of the greater industries of the country—those which employ the largest amounts of capital and the largest number of laborers—the old policy of attempting to protect everything is in any degree to be abandoned. It cannot fail to provoke the most violent antagonisms. And, to borrow an illustration from old Æsop, if any of the smaller protection monkeys should have their tails cut off— a work of necessity, if genuine protection of American industry by removal of burdens is ever to be entered upon—we may be sure that those experiencing such misfortune will be the most clamorous for the subjection of all the other monkeys to a like operation. For example, when the Senate at its last session, in recognition of a general and favorable public sentiment, largely reduced the duties on lumber, the indignation at such action, expressed both by action and word by at least one Senator specially representing the lumber interests, was almost ludicrous ; and notice was promptly served that unless such vote was rescinded active opposition would be made to the whole protective system, and more particularly to the maintenance of those duties in which New England was known to be specially interested. And before such threat, which would otherwise have undoubtedly been executed, the duties taken off pine lumber in the first instance were substantially restored, nearly every Senator from New England concurring. When the writer subsequently asked a Senator whose views, privately expressed, were in favor of the abolition of all duties upon lumber, why he voted for the retention of the duties, he received this reply : " It is

---

" Mr. SEWELL. Does the Senator from Connecticut say that the price of nickel is 75 cents a pound ?

" Mr. PLATT. That is stated by those persons who consume it.

" Mr. SEWELL. Mere hearsay.

" Mr. PLATT. It is not mere hearsay. There are eleven establishments in Connecticut engaged in the manufacture of German silver, all of whom depend upon this producer for the nickel. He has practically the control of the market in this country. They are very intelligent men; they are men who have examined this matter with the greatest care, and it is their statement that I make when I say that I believe Mr. Wharton can produce nickel at 50 cents a pound. I have never seen it denied by him. The statement has been made over and over again, and I do not think they intend to misrepresent him."

of no use for you to ask me this question. Without such a change of votes the interests of New England would have been slaughtered." But how unsatisfactory must be the industry of the country, or any section of it, whose prosperity depends upon the accidents of votes under such influences!

There are certain phases also of the tariff, or more precisely of the protective policy, involved in the so-called " silver question," which have not heretofore been generally recognized, but which it is well not to overlook in prospecting the future course of events—economic and political—in the United States. Notwithstanding all pretences and assertions to the contrary, the compulsory obligation imposed some years since by legislation on the Federal Treasury, and still continued, to purchase and coin silver, in disregard of any necessities or requirements of the business of the country, was never in any sense entitled to be regarded as a measure in the interest of the currency or of the bi-metallic problem, but on the other hand was from the very outset a measure of protection, pure and simple, for the benefit of a special industry, tho not in the usual form of a tariff enactment. Thus, with the reduction in the world's price for silver bullion consequent on the world's increased product of silver, and the disinclination everywhere manifested in all countries of high civilization and prices to use silver coinage, as too bulky and inconvenient for effecting exchanges, it became evident to the owners of silver-mines in the Southwest and on the Pacific that the market for their products was likely to be less profitable and certain than it would have been, had the old-time condition of affairs remained unaltered. And with the precedent and experience of legislation avowedly for protection under the tariff before them, what more natural than that the representatives of silver-mining should not only seek, but demand as a right, that government should interfere, and by means of additional taxation upon all other pursuits and industries of the country, make profitable to them a business which natural circumstances were tending to make less profitable or possibly wholly unremunerative. As tariff restrictions could not, however, help in this matter; as the price for silver throughout the world was irrespective of any question as to whether the labor entering into its production was "pauper" or affluent ; and as legislation in favor of an annual bounty of some twenty-four millions to be paid directly from the Federal Treasury to the silver producers was not likely to find favor with the public, the solution of the problem involved might have seemed at the outset to be not a little difficult. But happily and ingeniously all difficulties were overcome by apparently transferring the issue from the domain of protection and boun-ties to that of the currency, and this was accomplished by alleg-ing that the people were suffering from an insufficiency of silver coinage ; that the " gold-bugs," speculators and monopolists were everywhere hostile to the circulation of silver ; that the honor of the country required that the " dollar of the fathers" demoral-ized by a trick should be reinstated in its former position ; and finally that the solution of the vexed problem of bi-metalism would be greatly aided if the Federal Government would large-ly increase its coinage of silver and lend all its influence to force the same into circulation. And under such circumstances and pretences it was not difficult for the silver-mine interests to obtain a large measure of protection, by creating an extraordinary and wholly artificial but nevertheless a certain large additional mar-ket for their products, through an enactment that the Federal Treasury should regularly buy silver bullion, irrespective of all circumstances, to the extent of *two millions* of dollars per month, or twenty-four millions per annum, as a minimum. That the reasons put forth for the enactment of such a law were pretences and shams, as asserted, is made evident from the circumstances that now that the people have got all the " dollars of the fathers" in circulation that they want ; now that silver bullion and dollars are rapidly accumulating in the national treasury and remaining unused simply because no one wants any more of such material for currency ($61,000,000 of silver bullion, coined dollars and fractional currency being reported on hand June 1st, 1883) ; now that it is admitted that the existing coinage policy of the United States instead of aiding is greatly complicating and delaying the settlement of the bi-metallic cur-rency problem ; now, in short, that every object for which the coinage act of 1877 was ostensibly passed has been either ac-complished or proved to be beyond the province of legislation, the very men who were most anxious for the original enactment of the law are now most opposed to its repeal. And it ought to be further understood that the real reason why Congress refused at the last session to give heed to an almost general sentiment among business men that the further coinage and accumulation of silver by the Treasury should be stopped, was the open threat or intimation on the part of the Senators and Representatives of the silver-producing States, that in case of such action their support and votes could no longer be relied on for the mainte-nance of continued high duties under the tariff, on the ground that the principle and expediency of protection by the govern-ment being once admitted, there was no good reason for objection to one method of its application rather than another. Whether this threat will be made good, and a serious defection be so created in the ranks of the high-tariff party, by the repeal of the act for the continued purchase and useless accumulation of silver—a measure which the common-sense and necessities of the country will at no distant time compel—is a matter for the future to de-termine. But for the present it is sufficient to note that the sil-ver problem has become one of the new phases of the tariff ques-tion ; and to also call the attention of those who, apprehensive of financial disorder from the continuance of our present coinage policy, are solicitous for a change, that the issue before them involves a discussion of the principles of protection, and not in any rightful sense the principles of currency.

One further point in connection with this subject. In dis-cussing the question of the protective policy from the stand-point of expediency, which is claimed to be the only proper one from which the people of the United States can wisely consider the subject, the desirability of finding some actual and practi-cal cases in the everyday operations of production and exchange, in which the tests "*does protection really pay*" ? or "*how much does it specifically cost to protect*," could be fairly applied and clearly worked out, has always been acknowledged. The finding of such cases and their acceptance by all interested, as satisfac-tory, has, however, been thus far most difficult. But in this silver business it would seem as if there was sufficient evidence ready at hand, unimpeachable and clearly understandable, to allow of the making of an approximately fair estimate of the cost to the country, present and prospective, of the interference of the government, for the sake of artificially fostering and sustaining its industries, in at least one case, namely, that of silver-mining. And the items of such evidence may be summed up as follows:

1st. An annual present cost, defrayed by taxation, of $24,000,-000 for the purchase of bullion and its conversion into coin, which is not only not needed, but which the people seek to avoid using. 2d. A present annual loss of interest on some sixty millions of silver coin idly hoarded in the vaults of the Treasury, which at an estimate of three per cent would represent $1,800,-000 per annum; a no very large sum in the accounts of a nation, but which nevertheless represents all the profits, assumed at twenty cents per bushel, on the growing by somebody of 900,000 bushels of wheat. 3d. The loss contingent on the present withdrawing from the channels of domestic trade or foreign commerce of some sixty millions in value of an industrial product of the country, and the movement and sale of which in the open market and in accordance with natural laws would be no less desirable and beneficial than the movement and sale of an equal value in bushels of wheat, bales of cotton, tons of lead, or yards of cloth. 4th. The loss contingent on the future sale of surplus silver by the government at a discount from the prices at which it was originally purchased, a result which would seem to be an inevitable alternative in the future to a compulsory use of a fluctuating depreciated currency. 5th. The immense loss to the business and commerce of the country through the derangement and depreciation of the currency, which nearly all who have carefully studied the subject are agreed must result from any long continuance of the present silver coinage policy—a loss which cannot be forecast in figures smaller than hundreds of millions—and all this to protect an industry enjoying natural advantages of an exceptional character, and the value of the total product of which for the year 1881 was only $43,000,000.[1]

[1] There is one other matter of curious interest connected with this silver experiment to which attention may be also called. The mint is required to purchase each month at least $2,000,000 worth of silver bullion for the standard dollar. It is obvious that these purchases are effected from the proceeds of a like amount of Federal taxation. But these dollars are in turn coined by the government at a large profit; the profit from this coinage alone for the year 1881–2 having amounted to $3,438,829. A pertinent question which now suggests itself is, Does not this profit represent a further tax? Thus, to state the case in detail, the

It would seem as if sufficient had now been said to fully
prove the assertions which have been made the basis of this discussion ; namely, that the tariff question before the country is
rapidly assuming new phases, that public opinion in respect to
it is in a transition state, and that its introduction into politics
is unavoidable.

government purchases 84 cents worth of silver bullion and makes it into a coin of
a nominal value of $1, and in paying it out obtains a dollar's worth of commodi-
ties.   Is not here an indirect tax of 16 cents for every dollar issued ?   Were silver
alone the currency, a rise in prices would remedy this, as all values would be
measured by the standard silver dollar.   But at present, silver is not even the
predominant element in the currency; and as the gold dollar is the standard,
prices do not rise.   In short, can the government at any time and in any manner
obtain any money from the people except through the agency of a gift, a tax, or
confiscation?

THE "FOREIGN COMPETITIVE PAUPER LABOR " ARGUMENT FOR PROTECTION.[1]

TO all who bestow any attention on the course of public events, it must be evident that the so-called *"Foreign Competitive Pauper Labor"* argument is hereafter to be more than ever relied upon to defend and sustain the cause of protection in the United States, and that the advocates and believers in protection regard such argument as not only all-sufficient for this purpose, but also as wholly unanswerable. Or, to state the case more plainly and in detail, the claim is set up in warrant and justification of a continued high-tariff policy, that the difference in wages in favor of competitive foreign producers constitutes a good and sufficient reason why compensating protective duties should be levied on their resulting products when imported into this country; and the assertion is further constantly and conjointly made, that unless such duties continue to be levied, the American manufacturer will be unable to withstand foreign competition; that our workshops and factories will be closed, and our workmen and their families made dependent on public charity. It stands to reason, therefore, that the issue here involved can be second to none in importance to which the attention of the people of the United States can now be directed ; and further, that the accusation, which the position of the advocates of protection inferentially but necessarily make against all those who favor an abatement of the present tariff is so serious, as to rightfully subject the latter, if true, to the brand of unmitigated public scorn and infamy. But is it true ? And with a view of helping the public in some degree to intelligently determine for themselves whether it is or not, it is here proposed to attempt to review the whole matter, and present the facts in

[1] *Princeton Review.*

133

the case, as clearly and impartially as is possible for one who
frankly acknowledges at the outset that he enters upon the discussion with a profound conviction that the assertions and implied accusations of the protectionists in the matter have not
only nothing whatever of a substantial basis to rest upon, but
that the continuance of the policy they advocate will inevitably
and rapidly produce the very result they deprecate : and indeed
has already done so, to a very considerable extent. Before
doing so, however, it may profit to ask attention to certain incidents connected with the subject of an historical interest.
Thus, in a little essay recently published (1883) by Mr. Taussig
of Harvard University,—not in advocacy of either free trade or
protection, but as a contribution to economic history,—it is
shown that during the first half of the period of the existence of
the United States as a nation the demand for protection and
the claim that it was necessary was based almost exclusively
upon the "infant industry" argument, or the asserted necessity
of fostering domestic industries in their incipiency, the eventual
cheapening of the resulting products being the chief advantage
that it was proposed to compass; and that the pauper labor
argument never put in an appearance. But about the year 1840
it began to be seen that American manufactures could no longer
consistently claim protection on the ground of being infant industries, and that a new position must be taken ; and then for
the first time, says Mr. Taussig, the claim "that American labor
should be protected from the competition of less highly-paid
foreign labor" was brought forward, and has ever since "remained
the chief consideration impressed upon the popular mind in connection with the advocacy of a tariff for protection."

Recurring next to the subject more immediately under discussion, let it be assumed, for the sake of argument, that all that the
advocates of protection assert concerning the absolutely and (as
compared with the United States) the relatively low wages paid
for labor in the different departments of foreign industry is in all
respects correct ; and next let it further be granted, that any real
reduction in the standard of wages, and consequently of living, in
the United States is most undesirable—and then what of it ?
Does it necessarily follow, as all advocates of protection invariably
assume and assert, that the maintenance of a high tariff on for-

eign importations will prevent or contribute to prevent the reduction of the wages of American labor and their assimilation
to the so-called pauper-labor rates of foreign countries? Or, on
the contrary, is it not the real truth, that while "protection"
has never exerted anything more than a temporary influence in
enhancing wages, it is now, in virtue of influences clearly and
unmistakably referable to its policy, directly and powerfully
operating in a manner exactly the reverse of what is popularly
believed—or, in other words, to reduce the wages of labor in this
country, and cause them to approximate to the European standard? Here again is the issue involved restated clearly and
plainly; and as it is not for the interest of a single man or woman in the United States to ignore it or be misinformed, let us
therefore reason about it.

Wages in the United States are, as a general rule, unquestionably higher than in Europe; and mainly for the following
reason. Owing to our great natural advantages, a given amount
of labor, intelligently applied, will here yield a greater or better
result than in almost any other country. It has always been so,
ever since the first settlements within our territory, and has
been the main cause of the tide of immigration that for the last
two hundred years has flowed hitherward. Hamilton, in his celebrated report on manufactures, made before any tariff on the
imports of foreign merchandise into the United States was enacted, notices the fact that wages for similar employments were
as a rule higher in this country than in Europe; but he considered this as no real obstacle in the way of our successful establishment of domestic manufactures, for he says "the undertakers"
—meaning thereby the manufacturers—"can afford to pay
them." And that this assertion embodies a general truth would
seem to follow from the following considerations:

Wages are labor's share of product, and in every healthy business are ultimately paid out of product. No employer of labor
can continue for any great length of time to pay high wages
unless his product is large. If it is not, and he attempts it, it is
only a question of time when his affairs will be wound up by the
sheriff. Or, on the other hand, if a high rate of wages continues
to be permanently paid in any industry and in any country, it is
in itself proof positive that the product of labor is large, that the

laborer is entitled to a generous share of it, and that the employer can afford to give it him.   And if to-morrow our tariff
was swept out of existence, this natural advantage which, supposing the same skill and intelligence, is the sole advantage
which the American laborer has over his foreign competitor,
would not be diminished to the extent of a fraction of an iota.
Consider, for example, the American agriculturist.   He pays
higher wages than his foreign competitor. In fact, the differences
between the wages paid in agriculture in the United States and
Europe are greater than in any other form of industry.   The
tariff cannot help him, but by increasing the cost of all his instrumentalities of production, greatly injures him.   With a surplus product in excess of any home demand to be disposed of,
no amount of other domestic industry can determine his prices.
How then can he undersell all the other nations, and at the same
time greatly prosper individually ?   Simply because of his natural
advantages of sun, soil, and climate, aided by cheap transportation and the use of ingenious machinery, which combined give
him a greater product in return for his labor than can be obtained by the laborers in similar competitive industries in any
other country.   What has he to ask of government other than
it will interfere with him to the least possible extent?

In further illustration, compare the condition of Switzerland
with that of the United States. No people are more industrious,
frugal and moral than the Swiss.   They are the Yankees of the
Old World.   No one talks in Switzerland of abridging the hours
of labor in the interest of the laborer ; but whenever the hand
finds anything to do, it begins to do it with the rising of the sun,
and keeps doing with all its might until not "the going down
thereof," but until the darkness of the night makes further
effort impracticable.   But notwithstanding all this hard work
and frugal living, Switzerland and her people are poor: wages
are low, and the comforts and luxuries attainable by the masses
are comparatively few.   On the other hand, the people of the
United States, working fewer hours and less industriously than
the Swiss, and living as a rule wastefully and uneconomically,
are as a whole, the richest people on the face of the globe.   What
is the explanation of this seeming paradox ?   There is but one.
Nature has been niggardly in her bounties to Switzerland ; and

lavish to the United States; with the result, that while the smallest product, in proportion to the labor and capital applied, is the law of production in the former country, the largest product at the smallest cost is the law for the latter. In short, great resources and large product are natural concomitants; and under such circumstances there is only one thing, under a government that affords adequate protection to life and property, which can prevent capital and labor from securing large rewards, *i.e.*, profits and wages—and that is the diversion of their products from the channels in which they would naturally flow, by destructive taxation; to which may be added this further corollary, that all taxation is destructive which is excessive and not restricted to the legitimate requirements of the State.

Take another case in point. Wages in England, in every industry, are much higher than in the continental states of Europe. In the cotton-manufacturing industries they are from 30 to 50 per cent higher than in France, Belgium, and Germany; and an English cotton operative receives more wages in a week than an operative similarly employed in Russia can earn in a month.

Now which of these countries has the cheapest labor? The question may be answered by asking in return: Does England seek protection against the competition of the continental states or is it the continental states that demand protection against England?—and by the further statement of fact, namely, that just in proportion as the wages in any country decrease, the demand as a general rule in these same countries for protection to domestic industries increases, as well as the dread of British competition. In short, instead of high industrial remuneration being evidence of high cost of production in this country, it is direct evidence of a low cost of production; and in place of being an argument in favor of the necessity of protection, it is a demonstration that none is needed. Furthermore, all experience shows that as the *per capita* results of production become greater, the profits of capital always tend to a less share of the product; and that this must be so will be apparent if one reflects that the more effective the capital, the lesser the proportion which the capitalist will need (and under competition can take) to make good interest upon his investment. Investigations made by Mr. Edward Atkinson show that, taking the experience of Massachusetts as a basis for reasoning, "ninety parts in every hundred of product are divided among those who do daily work for their daily bread in that State; and that ten parts in every hundred are the utmost that can ever be set aside for the maintenance or increase of capital or wealth." As the product increases, labor therefore, in the absence of disturbing causes, must get a larger share—or in other words, wages will rise; or, to put the case differently, large wages can only come from abundance, and not from scarcity.

High wages, then, are the normal result of low cost, and low cost is the normal result in turn of intelligence, conjoined with good machinery, applied to great resources for production. Wages in the United States, then, are and ought to be high, because here are the above conditions in a pre-eminent degree.[1]

[1] Mr. Edwin Chadwick, the distinguished English economist, in a recent essay on "Employers' Liability for Accidents to Workpeople," furnishes the following very interesting illustrations, drawn from British industrial experiences, confirmatory of the above propositions:

"A coal-cutting machine," he says, "has been invented, by which one man and a boy will do better and more safely the work of twenty colliers; that is to say, at present in thick seams. I some time ago asked a large colliery owner whether he knew of the machine, and doubted that it would do the work. He did know of it, and did not doubt it would work; but they got on as they did, and change was troublesome. Recently I asked him whether they, the coal-owners, were not sufficiently pressed to have recourse to the machine. 'No, I do not think we are,' was the answer. 'I dare say that the Yankees will use it first, and then we shall follow them.' In Nottingham, the introduction of more complex and more costly machines for the manufacture of lace has, while economizing labor, augmented wages to the extent of over 100 per cent. I asked a manufacturer of lace whether this large machine could not be worked at the common lower wages by any of the workers of the old machine? 'Yes, it might,' was the answer, 'but the capital invested in the new machinery is very large, and if from drunkenness or misconduct anything happened to the machine, the consequence would be very serious.' Instead of taking any man out of the streets, as might be done with the low-priced machine, he (the employer) found it necessary to go abroad and look for one of better condition, and for such a one higher wages must be given."

Mr. Chadwick quotes an observation made to him by Sir Joseph Whitworth, the eminent English mechanical engineer and inventor, that "he cannot *afford* to have his machines worked with cheap and poor labor; and also states that the English shoe manufacturers, who have recently introduced the ingenious American shoe-manufacturing machinery, tell him that it paid them the best to work these machines with wages that are at least double those which were paid to the shoemakers under the old hand system.

But passing from these general conclusions, which may not command the assent of the reader without some careful reflection, it is proposed to next ask attention to the present industrial condition of the country, and to the action of certain influences on wages, the profits of capital, and the demand for domestic labor, which would seem to require to be merely pointed out to command universal recognition and acceptance.

The daily course of events is fast educating our people up to a comprehension of the fact, which economists have long been predicting, that owing to our great natural resources, our rapidly increasing population, the increased use and product of machinery and the energy of our people, the power of domestic production continually tends to be, and in most departments of industry is, far in excess of the power of domestic consumption. In the case of agriculture the fact is so obvious that no confirmatory evidence is necessary; but if any is needed, it is all-sufficient to call attention to the enormous surplus of food and cotton which we now export to other countries, and to the circumstance that these exports during the last ten years have increased out of all proportion to any increase of our home pop-

"At the beginning of this century the cost of spinning a pound of yarn (No. 40) was a shilling, and the wages divided amongst the workers—men, women and children—did not average more than 4s. 6d. a week, or 13s. 6d. per week per family of three. Recently, the cost of spinning a pound of yarn was three half-pence ; but the wages have advanced to 40s. per week. In a paper by M. Poulin, a manufacturer at Rheims, France, it appears that in the wool manufacture there, the progress of wages and machinery have been similar. In 1816 the wages were 1f. 50c. per diem ; they are now 5f. The price of weaving a metre of merino cloth was then 16f. ; it is now 1f. 45c."

"I might at considerable extent adduce the experience of Lancashire, that as a rule the pressure of manufacturing distress has stimulated the adoption of labor-saving machinery and putting more and more capital or machinery under the same hands, *at increased wages*, attended by reduced costs of production, by extended consumption at reduced prices, and restored and augmented profits of capital."

"Finally," concludes Mr. Chadwick, "it may be noted that whilst all this progress has been made, population, which should have diminished, has been largely increased by the progress of labor-saving machinery. At the same time the profits of capital have largely diminished. At the present time capital is being driven to subsist on very small profits, and the quickened turn over of large capital. Of late, a poor pinched and distressed capitalist would only get for a loan of £1000 ($5000) of his capital (accummulated labor) for one day one shilling, or a third of the *improved* day's wages of a spinner."

ulation. And in respect to our so-called manufacturing industries it is only necessary to refer to general complaint that business, tho large (as it necessarily must be to supply the needs of a nation of fifty-six millions), is, through excessive competition, conducted with little profit; that a very large percentage of our manufactures, and notably those of iron, cotton, and wool, which enjoy high protection, have suspended or curtailed their operations; that' manufacturers in certain lines of the two last-named articles especially have only been able to dispose of their surplus stocks by forced sales at auction and at prices less than the cost of production; that failures and fires (the latter the inevitable indicator and concomitant of bad times) are increasing at a rapid and alarming rate; that the wages of manufacturing operatives almost everywhere throughout the country are undergoing extensive and as the manufacturers claim, enforced reductions; that the opportunities for employment are conjointly becoming limited; and finally, that artisans especially imported from foreign countries to work in certain employments (*c.g.*, glass-making) in the United States are returning to Europe, with a view of bettering their condition.[1]

The situation is extraordinary and anomalous, but only such as might naturally be expected from the circumstances. It needs but a superficial glance at our tables of exports to see that, comparatively speaking, we have but little other than the

---

[1] The following opinions concerning the present condition of the iron and steel industries of the United States have been communicated to the *New York Tribune* by Andrew Carnegie, the well-known iron manufacturer of Pennsylvania, under date of September 24, 1883:

" Much as I regret to say it, I believe that matters will grow worse for some months before manufacturing interests can reach a profitable business. A much more decided curtailment of production must take place before there can be any improvement. This will be brought about naturally by the prevalence of such ruinous prices as will compel manufacturers to stop producing goods in advance of the country's needs. But as great loss is entailed by curtailment of production, the works are kept running to their full capacity, altho prices have fallen to figures which leave even those manufacturers who have unusually favorable facilities little or no profit, and entail a positive loss upon the average manufacturer. I think the wages paid at the (iron) mills on the seaboard of the United States to-day are about as low as men can be expected to take. In the West, notwithstanding a recent agreement of the men to accept a reduction of 30 per cent, it now seems probable, from the very unsatisfactory outlook, that they will have to be asked to work for still less."

domestic market, and not the whole of that, for our vast and varied manufactured product—the ratio of exports for the years 1878–80 being only 12.5 of manufactured to 87.5 of unmanufactured commodities, or $102,246,000 of the former to $721,700,000 of the latter. And to make up even this beggarly 12 per cent it was necessary to count in lumber, coal, and leather as manufactured exports. Now it simply stands to reason that if the manufacturing industries of the United States are to be mainly limited to the requirements of a domestic market, that their growth must be also limited, and far below their normal capacity and tendencies; and if, under such limitations, or arrest of industrial growth, we are to have poured in upon us annually from half a million to seven hundred thousand immigrants,—mainly laborers in the prime of life,—and an annual increase of our population from natural causes of about 3 per cent per annum, it would seem also clear that there must be extensive reductions· in the wages of American laborers; for with two, three, or more sellers of labor for every one buyer, the buyer will fix the price; and the price which the buyer or American employer will strive to fix, and indeed the price which his necessities will compel him to fix, if he is going to extend his operations and avoid producing at a loss, will be such as will enable him to produce equally cheap with his foreign competitor. A continuation of the present national fiscal policy, or in other words a continuation of our present high-tariff policy, inevitably means, therefore, low wages, and the degradation and impoverishment of the masses, or ensures the very results which it is claimed the protective policy is certain to avert. And there is no need further of adopting in any degree, in regard to such a conclusion, this line of prophecy, for the results in question have in a large degree already come, and in the absence of reform, have come to stay.[1]

---

[1] The extent, however, to which many of even the most intelligent of American citizens fail to recognize the condition of affairs into which as a nation we are drifting, finds a striking illustration in the following reported extract of a recent speech by Hon. J. B. Foraker, one of the candidates for Governor in the State of Ohio, during the recent political canvass: "The laborer," he says, "in this country is a part of the governing power. He is a voter. He has a voice in the government. Aside, therefore, from all humanitarian reasons, we want him to have a chance for self-elevation. We want him to eat meat and be comfortable.

The main reason why American manufacturers cannot dispose of their surplus products by exportation and sale of the same in foreign markets, admits of a ready understanding, if one will only keep in view and reflect upon the following facts : 1st, from 80 to 90 per cent of all our manufactures exist because they must as a condition of our civilization, and because no foreign products of like kind can be imported. Any one may abundantly satisfy himself of this by analyzing the history or origin of the bulk of the commodities that pass him on the streets of any busy community, or are exposed for sale at the marts of trade ; 2d, possibly from 10 to 20 per cent are in a greater or less degree subject to foreign competition ; 3d, in the effort to protect this 10 to 20 per cent, through the agency of taxation and restrictions on exchanges, the cost of all the products of our entire industry is enhanced to such an extent

And for this reason it is that we say if we cannot go into the markets of the world without being subjected to an unjust and degrading competition, we will make ourselves independent of those markets by making markets of our own. Instead of sending our raw cotton across the ocean, to be there manufactured and sent back to us, we will have cotton mills here. We will mine our own coal, develop our own minerals, manufacture our own iron and steel, build our own railroads with our own products, and thus have home markets and domestic commerce." Now it is not the intent of the writer to say anything discourteous of a man of such high character as Judge Foraker, but it is nevertheless true, that if the above remarks are rightfully attributed to him, he certainly had very little idea of what he was talking about; for the trouble of to-day with our industry and labor is that as a nation we have too exclusively the very home markets he thinks so desirable, and are producing more than we can ourselves consume. We export at present more than three fifths of our annual product of raw cotton. Suppose, instead of sending this enormous quantity "across the ocean," we erect mills, as proposed, and spin it ourselves. What will then be done with the product of cloth in excess of domestic want? It must be sold abroad, if sold at all ; and if sold abroad, the people who buy must pay for it in turn with the products of their labor, for they have nothing else to buy with. But this means foreign commerce and international trade, which Judge Foraker thinks we can profitably get along without. Again, we raise annually many millions of bushels of cereals in excess of any possible demand for domestic consumption ; and unless this excess can be sold abroad, it will either not be raised, or, if raised, will rot on the ground ; and what, under such a condition of affairs, would be the avenues of employment open to laborers in mining coal, smelting iron, or building railroads and agricultural machinery? In short, the system which Judge Foraker proposes is the Chinese system of inclusion and exclusion, which the Chinese are preparing to abandon ; and his remedy more of the hair of the same dog that has already sorely bitten us.

that exports only exist in cases where our natural advantages for production are so great as to overcome the increase of cost thus artificially and unnaturally created.[1] And as confirmatory evidence, if not absolute demonstration, of the truth of this statement, attention is here asked to the results of an investigation in the last Report (1883) of the Massachusetts " Bureau of Labor Statistics," which altho constituting a contribution to economic science of surpassing interest, and of such a nature as ought to startle every fair-minded American citizen who has been educated to believe that our present high protective policy really works for the benefit of domestic labor and capital, has thus far, very curiously, almost entirely escaped public attention. In this report a very careful analysis is made of the comparative condition of 2240 manufacturing establishments in Massachusetts, representing 21 different industries and 207,798 employees, for the years 1875 and 1880 respectively ; the elements of the analy-

---

[1] The following tables and estimates, deduced from the census of 1880, will afford approximately correct data for estimating the method in which the burden of the taxation imposed to maintain the protective policy of the United States distributes itself among population, occupations, and professions :

OCCUPATIONS OF THE PEOPLE OF THE UNITED STATES IN 1880.

Agriculture.	7,670,493
Professional and personal service	4,074,238
Trade and transportation..	1,810,256
Manufacturing, mechanical, and mining industries	3,837,112
Total	17,392,099
Proportion engaged in agriculture who may possibly be subjected to foreign competition in some manner— mainly the growers of sugar and of rice, and of wool possibly, to a very small extent, about 5 per cent, or	400,000
Proportion engaged in manufacturing, mechanical, and mining industries, who can be in part but not wholly subjected to foreign competition — large estimate based on calculation	837,112
Total	1,237,112
Proportion that are heavily taxed, and placed at a disadvantage in agriculture, manufactures, mechanical pursuits, and in mining, by the protective system...	16,154,989
Proportion in whose favor the protective system is invoked, but whose wages are not lower than in other employments	1,237,112

sis being the census returns made to the Federal and State Governments respecting capital, laborers, value of stock used and of product, cost of management, profits, etc., in the years specified, which are acknowledged to be as reliable as any such returns possibly can be, and as probably superior to any similar statistics ever before collected. The 2240 establishments also employed 53 per cent of the invested capital, paid 58 per cent of wages, used 57 per cent of the stock, and produced 57 per cent of the entire manufactures of the State. Premising further that Massachusetts practically produces none of the stock or raw material which its manufacturers use, but buys almost everything from beyond her borders, the investigation shows that the stock— metals, fibres, leather, coal, lumber, chemicals, and the like—used in manufacturing in that State in 1880, cost 11.52 per cent more than it did in 1875 ; and that the manufacturers, as the report expresses it, " counterbalanced " this result by reducing the wages of their employees during the period involved to the extent, on an average, of 4.35 per cent, and by submitting to a reduction of their net profit of 7.19 per cent. Now, when it is remembered that the prices of manufacturers' raw materials have notably declined in all foreign competitive countries during the period covered by the Massachusetts analysis; that the wages of foreign competitive labor during the same time have also very generally advanced ; and that, apart from possible differences in the wages of labor, Massachusetts industries, in comparison with foreign industries, are not only not subjected to any special disabilities, but on the contrary enjoy many advantages—it seems clear that the extraordinary results under consideration cannot be referred to any other agency than that of our present national fiscal policy, which, as above pointed out, does by excessive taxation and restriction of exchanges inevitably enhance the cost of all manufactured commodities and their elements. And if other evidence in support of this conclusion were needed, it is so abundant that the only difficulty attendant is to decide what to present; as, for example, the fact brought out before the Massachusetts Legislature at its last session (1883), that in respect to certain shoes, for which there might naturally be a large domestic demand to supply the requirements of tropical countries, the cost of the Massachusetts-made shoes is enhanced to

the extent of 60 cents per pair before the manufacture even
begins, by reason of the taxes on their constituent materials;
that cordage manufactured in New York of imported materials
(which the country cannot produce) can be, and actually is,
through a rebate of duties, sent to China and Brazil and sold
there for the equipment of foreign ships, cheaper than an American ship-owner can buy it within one mile of the factory where
it is made; and that, for the same reason, salmon packed in tin
on the Columbia River can be transported by rail and sold
cheaper to the people of New Brunswick for food than the people of Maine, many miles farther east, can buy it. Indeed,
were it not joking on a serious subject, there could be no more
fitting comment on the situation than to recall the lines of
" Truthful James" when he says:

> " Then I looked up at Nye,
>   And he gazed upon me ;
>   And he rose with a sigh,
>   And said, ' Can this be?
> We are ruined by Chinese (foreign) cheap labor !' "

It is not overlooked in connection with this discussion that
the complaint of overproduction, restricted markets, and no
profits in business, by reason of excessive competition, is at
this time general in all commercial countries, and especially in
Great Britain, where protection as an element of disturbance is
wanting; and that, therefore, the reference here made of the
existing unsatisfactory state of affairs in the United States to
our national fiscal policy may seem to not a few to be unsound
both in respect to facts and logic. That there have been great
disturbances in the work of production and exchange of most
countries in recent years, and, taking the world throughout,
most notably since 1873, and that these disturbances still continue, is not to be denied. And the explanation of it is referable, in the opinion of the writer, in a very large degree to a
class of agencies which have not thus far received the attention
from economists and publicists which they merit ; namely, the
wonderful changes which through invention and discovery have
recently taken place in the world's method of doing its work of
production and distribution. These changes have been accompanied with immense losses of capital and great disturbances of

labor, in which the United States has participated and suffered
in common with other countries. That their ultimate outcome,
however, is to be good, cannot be doubted; for by an economic
law, which Mr. Atkinson, of Boston, more than others, has
recognized and formulated, all material progress is affected
through the destruction of capital by invention and discovery,
and that the rapidity of such destruction is the best indicator
of the rapidity of progress.[1] But in the readjustment by nations of their industries to the new circumstances, which is still
going on and is yet very far from complete, the "law of the
survival of the fittest" is going to fully assert itself; and in this
struggle the United States, by reason of possessing as no other
nation does, the conditions for the cheapest production of the
great staple commodities of the world's consumption, ought
to prove itself the fittest, and dominate in " manufactures" as it
now dominates in respect to the production of cotton and food
products.   Why such a result has not yet been attained; why
in the readjustment of industries to the new conditions, the
United States suffers disproportionately, or even as much as
her chief industrial competitor, Great Britain; and why under
the present national fiscal policy there is little chance for improvement—finds a sufficient explanation and answer in the
results of the Massachusetts industrial investigation before referred to, even without taking into account a vast amount of
other corresponding and confirmatory evidence.[2]

[1] Every man who is trying to make some new labor-saving invention or discovery is trying at the same time to practically destroy the value of previously
accumulated labor or capital.   If an invention could be made to-morrow which,
at no greater cost, could spin or weave ten per cent more of cotton fibre in a
given time than is now practicable, all the existing cotton machinery of the world,
now representing hundreds of millions of dollars of expenditure, would be worth
little more than old metal.   By the discovery within the last decade of a method
of manufacturing the coloring principle of madder (the principal coloring material used in printing calicoes), three or four factories in Germany and England
employing but a few hundred men were substituted for hundreds of thousands
of acres of land and thousands of laborers which had been before devoted to the
cultivation of the madder plant.   So also the construction of the Suez Canal is
said to have practically rendered worthless over 2,000,000 tons of British shipping which, built for the India trade *via* the Cape of Good Hope and not fitted
for the canal, was no longer wanted.

[2] A recent writer in the British *Boot and Shoe Journal*, after noticing the
testimony given before the Massachusetts Legislature last winter, to the effect

Coming back now more directly to the "pauper-labor" argument: there is no question that there is a great amount of poorly paid, half-starved labor in Europe and other countries. But what, let us inquire, is its true relation, from a purely practical, business point of view, to the laborers and industries of the United States? Apart from agriculture, in the sphere of which industry we have no formidable competitors, inasmuch as we can profitably undersell the products of the poorest paid labor in the world,—the peasants of Russia and Hungary, the fellahs of Egypt, and the ryots of India,—the dreaded pauper of foreign countries is engaged mainly in handicraft, as contradistinguished from machinery manufacturing; as, for example, in the manufacture of pottery, where the laborer works almost exactly as did his predecessor four thousand years ago; or in the case of silk-ribbon weavers, whom a recent correspondent of the New York *Tribune* describes as operating their hand-looms in poor, ill-ventilated cottages, and in the same rooms in which the operatives eat and sleep. And apart from pottery and silk, a great variety of other products manufactured or produced under similar conditions might be mentioned. In the case of Europe, the people who work at these handicrafts live for the most part in the most densely populated districts, where all natural advantages and opportunities for employment have long ago been exhausted, and where the moral inertia consequent on lack of intelligence or means is an almost insuperable obstacle in the way of any attempt on the part of the laborer to improve his situation by engaging in other pursuits or by emigration. Under such circumstances wages are undoubtedly very low, and the protectionist, in view of this fact,

that the existing capital and labor at present engaged in the manufacture of shoes in the United States is sufficient, if fully employed for nine months, to supply any current market demand for the entire year, the recent failures in the shoe industry, and the general tendency to a reduction of wages in this and every other branch of industry in the United States, thus pertinently comments on the situation: "One may here [England] ask, Where are the advantages and disadvantages of protection to the shoe trade? We have in this country [England] certainly not so much trade as could be done, but, nevertheless, we have a trade which exists all the year round; we have in addition a considerable export trade, and the wages of our workmen have advanced rather than declined. Our cousins across the Atlantic have six or eight months' home trade, no export, and a falling labor market. Surely the comparison should be deterrent enough."

asks us, with a sort of "now-I-have-got-you air," how can we, apart from the protection afforded by the tariff, enter into successful competition with them, except by bringing down the wages of our laborers to a level with the wages of these paupers? But, in the name of common-sense, why should we as a nation desire to attempt any such competition? What possible reason or inducement is there for wanting to introduce these handicraft industries into this country, and of attempting to keep them alive by means of enormous taxes levied under the tariff upon the whole people,—as, for example, 60 per cent upon silks, and from 60 to 100 per cent on earthenware and crockery,—when we can buy all we want of these products with a very small part of the excess of our cotton and grain; and which excess, it ought to be especially borne in mind, if not sent out of the country and exchanged for some products of foreign labor, will either not be raised, or if raised, will rot in the ground? The main thing which pauper laborers in Europe and everywhere else want is food ; food beyond everything else, for they are starving. And when it is proclaimed, with real or feigned fright and horror, by political orators and partisans, that these people are willing to work for fifteen or twenty cents per day, the proclamation means that they are willing to give the results of each and every day of their hard and often disagreeable and degrading labor, in making things which the American agriculturist wants and cannot advantageously produce himself, for one fourth of a bushel of wheat, one half a bushel of corn, two pounds of beef, or three of pork or lard, products which represent but a fraction of a day's labor in the United States. For this is the basis on which the pauper laborer of foreign countries, working for fifteen to twenty cents per day, is going to exchange with us, if he exchanges at all. Certainly it would seem that there is nothing which the agricultural interest of the United States, which represents directly or indirectly three fourths of our entire population, could do to profit itself more than to encourage such exchanges.

Consider next the relation of this same bugbear of foreign competitive pauper labor to such of our manufacturing industries as rely mainly on machinery for the work of production. In regard to a majority of these, there can be no doubt that their representative manufacturers would be able to defy the competition of the world if the burden of taxation was removed, to the extent that it is in Great Britain, from the materials which enter into their products, and from tools and machinery, and from many of the commodities which are essential to the living and comfort of their employees, and the continuance of which is no longer needed to meet any necessities of the state for revenue. Where the use of machinery—especially of a complex kind—which is the kind mainly used in the manufacture of the world's great staple products, and in the invention and application of which the United States especially excels—forms an important factor in the work of production, the cost of the wages paid to the people who work such machinery forms no criterion of the cost of the goods which are the resulting product. In all such cases " it is the operative that earns the highest wages who compasses the lowest cost of production ;" and whoever doubts or fails to comprehend these propositions has not yet grasped the A B C of the subject. Thus, for example, when the product of one day's labor in the manufacture of cotton cloth in the United States, properly apportioned and with the aid of machinery, is equivalent to the product of at least twenty days' labor for a like purpose in China, Central America, and other semi-civilized countries (as is the case), it is a matter of very little consequence whether the laborers who grow the cotton in Texas or spin and weave it in New England receive a greater or less number of dollars per week for their wages; for the question as to who shall command the markets of such countries turns up other and entirely different considerations. To-day the poorest paid labor in the world, namely, that of the natives of India, will be glad to work for twelve and a half cents per day, making bagging (gunny-cloth) to bale American cotton out of the fibre of the jute ; but the American manufacturer, paying from seven to ten times as much per day to women operatives, can make a better article so much cheaper, that the Indian producer has been practically driven from the field of competition in this country. And yet, so long as the Federal Government continues to levy a tax of six dollars per ton on the fibre which the American manufacturer uses there is very little chance for the latter to sell the results of his ingenious machinery and highly paid labor in any other than his own country; and so a large number of the American bagging mills are now idle, and the home market is glutted with their unsold products. The case of the miserably paid women and children in the "black country" of England has recently been cited by a correspondent of the N. Y. *Tribune* as a fearful example of what the working men and women of the United States would be subjected to if they should undertake to make nails in the absence of a high protective tariff on the importation of nails, when the truth is that the logic is all the other way, and it is the English laborer who needs to be protected against the American, and not the American against the English pauper; inasmuch as the latter, if he will persist in making nails by hand, has got to compete against machines of American invention which can make more nails in one hour than the paupers working by hand can make in a day, and at less than a tenth of the expense. To which it may be added, that the operatives who work the American machines receive almost the highest wages paid in the United States in any department of mechanical industry.

One of the most novel and interesting illustrations, which the writer has recently met with, of the absurdity and fallacy of much of the current averment of the necessity for protection for such a country as the United States against the competitive pauper labor of foreign countries, is given in Senior's " Conversations and Journals in Egypt," (London, 1882). Mr. Senior was an English lawyer and economist of high standing, who some years ago visited Egypt in company with a celebrated British engineer, Mr. McLean, and in the course of their travels the two visited the Pyramids ; and while on the ground speculated concerning the cost and the amount of labor entering into these great structures. " I asked Mr. McLean," writes Mr. Senior (pp. 63, 64), " for what he could reproduce the largest of them on a spot in the immediate neighborhood, as in their case, of a quarry. He said, roughly estimating their contents at 80,000,000 cubic feet, and the cost at 3d. (six cents) per cubic foot, for a million sterling. It appears that their contents are 88,000,000 cubic feet. The cost, therefore, would be £62,500 more—in all, £1,062,500" (or $5,310,000). McLEAN: " There would not be the least difficulty in the performance, and with 25,000 men I could do it in one year; with 2500 men in ten years and turn out a much better article." SENIOR: "For what could you build a pyramid in England?" MCLEAN: " I cannot answer that question without knowing what I should have to pay for the stone —that is, for permission to extract it. Let me have the use of the quarry for nothing, and I think a pyramid could be built nearly as cheaply in England as in Egypt. It is true that labor is four times as dear in England as in Egypt, as our laborers receive three shillings a day where the Egyptians receive a sixpence, and our men do only two thirds more work; but our skill and our mechanical contrivances nearly make up the difference."

Now if pyramids were an article of international trade, *i.e.*, of demand and supply, and the question of wages was to be held to be determinative of what country should furnish them, it would seem impossible for the English laborer to engage in the pyramid business without being largely protected against the pauper labor of Egypt, when the real truth would be that it was the Egyptian pauper, working for sixpence a day and finding himself, that needed large protection against the comparatively high-priced Englishman, and that even then he could only supply a comparatively restricted demand of his own local market for pyramids.

Further evidence to the same effect might be adduced to almost any extent ; but enough, it is believed, has been said to abundantly prove, that instead of fearing the competition of foreign pauper laborers, who are paupers mainly because of the absence of natural advantages and a lack of the ownership and use of machinery, we ought rather to welcome it and recognize that there is no way in which as a nation we can so rapidly and certainly enrich ourselves as by exchanging the products of our skill and machinery, representing but a comparatively small amount of labor, with the products of the so-called foreign pauper laborers, representing a comparatively large amount of labor.

I.

THE term " political economy" has had many, and to some extent discordant, definitions. As a department of knowledge all will, however, probably agree that its object is to endeavor to learn from the experience of mankind the conditions for the production, accumulation, and distribution of wealth (using the term " wealth" in the sense of abundance of all material good, and the results which flow from such abundance), and to deduce from such conditions the rules or principles which, when adopted as the guide for human action, will best determine and facilitate progress in this same direction for the future. Again, some deny that political economy is entitled to be called a science. But be this as it may, all will probably further agree that, in common with political, mental, and moral philosophy, it is not an exact science in the sense that the physical sciences are so considered ; inasmuch as it is founded on the results of human action, which vary greatly under different conditions and influences, and the record of which is rarely so complete and unquestionable as to compel universal and unqualified acceptance ; whereas the natural laws constituting the basis of the physical sciences are so universal and unvariable, and so well defined and accepted, that deductions can be made from them with the utmost certainty. Under such circumstances, it would seem that the most important contribution which could be made to the history and progress of political economy would be a full and unquestionable record of the results of a large and complete experience in respect to any one of the subjects which are acknowledged to be embraced within its sphere of inquiry and consideration ; and such a contribution, it is believed, can now be made in the record of the recent experience of the Government of the United States in obtaining revenue through taxa-

[1] *Princeton Review.*

tion of the domestic manufacture and sale of distilled spirits. This record it is now proposed to make more completely than has ever before been attempted ; and as the personal experiences of the writer as a former official of the Government largely intrusted with the supervision of this department of the national revenues forms a not unimportant part of the record, no further apology, it is thought, will be needed for making the narration to some extent autobiographical in its character.

As the manufacture of distilled spirits in some form exists, and always has existed, among all civilized nations, and as the use of the article is always constant and extensive, generally immoderate, and largely voluntary and as a matter of pure luxury, nearly all governments have come to regard it as an eminently proper and productive source for the obtaining of revenue through the agency of taxation. Such taxation accordingly forms an essential feature of the fiscal systems of most of the European States ; but in three only—Great Britain, France, and Russia—are the present taxes so large and productive as to call for any particular notice. Thus, in Great Britain the taxation of distilled spirits is (1884) at the rate of 10s. ($2.50) per imperial proof-gallon [1] of $277\frac{270}{1000}$ cubic inches; which would be equivalent to 7s. 4d. ($1.83) on the *wine-gallon* of 231 cubic inches, which is adopted as the American standard. It is also to be noted in this connection that the first cost of British spirits ranges, according to the price of grain from which they are distilled, from 1s. 6d. (37½ cents) to 2s. (50 cents) per *imperial* proof-gallon ; while the first cost of the American product ranges from 17 to 24 cents per wine-gallon ; thus making the excise on British spirits range from five to six and a half times the first cost of production ; while a tax of $2 on the wine-gallon of proof-spirits, as formerly imposed in the United States, was equivalent to from eight to twelve times their first cost. The revenue collected from distilled spirits under the excise in Great Britain for the fiscal year 1883 (apart from licenses for the sale of the same) was £14,211,490 ($71,057,450), as compared with £14,273,786 in 1882 and £14,393,572 in 1881. The amount which accrued in addition to the British revenue during the year 1883 from spirit

---

[1] By proof gallon is understood a mixture of equal parts of pure alcohol and water.

distillers', dealers', and publicans' licenses was £1,598,803
($7,991,015), as compared with £1,601,985 from the same sources
in 1882 and £1,570,955 in 1881. From 1660, the year when
taxes on domestic distilled spirits were granted "by Parliament
to Charles II. and his successors forever, as full compensation"
for loss of payments previously "due by landholders to the
crown," down to and including the receipts of the year 1883,
the amount of revenue that the British Exchequer has obtained
from this single department of excise or internal taxation has
been estimated at the enormous sum of £614,994,896, or
$3,074,974,480. (See "Financial Reform Almanac," London,
1884).

In France the budget for 1876 estimates the receipts of internal revenue from the tax on liquors at 364,190,000 francs, or
$72,858,000.

In Russia the manufacture and sale of distilled spirits is a
strict government monopoly,—the government in the first instance selling the privilege of dealing in the article ; and secondly, reserving to itself the right of distilling all domestic
liquors, and supplying the same to dealers at a present rate of
about one dollar (gold) per gallon. The aggregate consumption
of the common distilled spirits of Russia (termed "*vodki*") is
very great, and of the entire income of the government from
ordinary sources more than one third is believed to be derived
from the manufacture and sale of domestic liquors. In the
budget for 1872 the net receipts were estimated at £61,899,000,
of which £21,500,000 ($107,500,000) were credited to excise
taxes on spirits and beer.

The first attempt of the United States to obtain revenue
through the taxation of domestic distilled spirits was authorized by the first Congress under the Constitution, and under
a law that went into operation in 1791. Altho the rate
of taxation imposed was comparatively moderate,—ranging
from *nine* to *twenty-five* cents per gallon, according to the
strength of the spirits, with an abatement of two cents per
gallon for cash payments,—and altho the necessities of the new
Government for revenue were most imperative, the enactment
of this law provoked great opposition and resistance ; and in
1794 the counties of Western Pennsylvania rose in insurrection

against its enforcement. A proclamation by President Washington commanding the insurgents to disarm and disperse was in the first instance entirely disregarded; and it was not until an armed force, collected from the militia of the other States, had marched to the centre of the disturbed district and had arrested the ringleaders that the authority of the Federal Government was restored. As further illustrating the very serious character of this insurrection, it may be noted, that the cost of its suppression was one and a half millions of dollars, and that at a time when the aggregate annual expenditures of the Federal Government for all ordinary purposes were only about four millions of dollars. The amount of distilled spirits produced in the United States at the time of the enactment of the tax-law of 1791 was estimated by Alexander Hamilton, then Secretary of the Treasury, at 6,500,000 gallons, of which 3,500,000 gallons was believed to be the product of the distillation of foreign materials,—mainly molasses, imported largely by New England from the West Indies for the manufacture of rum,—and of which product from 300,000 to 500,000 gallons were sent annually at that time from the same section of country to Africa for the purchase of slaves.[1] Allowing 6,000,000 of gallons for domestic consumption, the per capita consumption of distilled spirits in the United States during this period must have been about one and a half gallons (1.52).

Upon the accession of Mr. Jefferson to the Presidency in 1800, and upon his recommendation, the obnoxious spirit-tax, in common with all other internal-revenue taxes, was repealed. In 1813, as the result of the war with Great Britain, it became necessary for the Federal Government to again resort to the collection of an internal revenue, and of the system then enacted the taxation of domestic distilled spirits through the agency of licenses for distilleries formed a part. With the close of the war, however, all these taxes were again and soon repealed, and from 1818–22 to 1862, or for a period of more than forty years,

[1] Official documents show that from 1804 to 1807 inclusive 202 cargoes of negro slaves were brought into Charleston, S. C. Of these slaves 3914 were sold for account of persons residing in Bristol, R. I.; 3488 for Newport, R. I.; 556 for Providence, R. I.; 280 for Warren, R. I.; 200 for Boston, Mass.; and 250 for Hartford, Conn. This was, it will be observed, at only one port in the South, and during a period of only four years.

the Federal Government levied no *direct* taxes upon any process or result of domestic industry, nor any excise, stamp, or
income taxes, nor any direct taxes upon real property; the expenses of a simple and economic administration, and the payment of the interest and principal of a small public debt,—never
in excess at any one time of twenty-one millions,—being defrayed
almost entirely by indirect taxes, levied in the form of a light
tariff on the importation of foreign goods and merchandise.

It was then with such antecedents, and under such conditions in respect to taxation, that the nation found itself, in the
spring of 1861, suddenly and unexpectedly involved in a gigantic civil war, in which its very existence was threatened by the
uprising of at least a third of its population against the legitimate and regularly constituted authorities. The most urgent and
important requirement of the Federal Government at the outset
was for money. Men in excess of any immediate necessity vol-
unteered for service in the army; but to equip and supply even
such as were needed required a large expenditure, and for defraying it there was, on the part of the Government, neither
money, credit, nor any adequate system of raising money by
taxation. Furthermore, as the necessities of the Government
developed and became more urgent, there also developed on
the part of Congress and the Federal officials a most remarkable
timidity and muddle of ideas respecting the financial situation.
From the very outset all direct or internal taxation was avoided;
there having been an apprehension on the part of Congress that,
inasmuch as the existing generation had never been accustomed
to it, and as all machinery for assessment and collection was
wholly wanting, its adoption would create discontent and
thereby interfere with the vigorous prosecution of hostilities. It
would be foreign to the purpose of this special discussion to
here notice the various substitutes for obtaining revenue that
were resorted to by the Federal Government in addition to the
increase of the tariff on imports,—such as loans from the banks,
the issue of Treasury notes payable on demand, the apportion-
ment of a direct tax among the States, and an income-tax of 3
per cent on the excess of all incomes over $800; the first to take
effect eight and the latter ten months after the date of enactment;—and it is sufficient to say that it was not until July, 1862,

or nearly fifteen months after the outbreak of the war, that any
systematic scheme for internal taxation was devised and put
into operation. And of this scheme, as might naturally have been
anticipated, the taxation of the domestic manufacture and sale
of distilled spirits constituted a leading feature.

For a period of nearly a half-century previous, the manufacture
of spirits in the United States, as already stated, had been free
from all specific taxation or supervision by either the national or
State governments; and being produced mainly from Indian
corn, at places adjacent to the localities where this cereal was
cultivated, and to a large extent also from corn that was damaged
and so otherwise unmarketable, was afforded at a very low price ;
the average market-price in New York for the four years next
preceding 1862 having been about 23 cents per proof-gallon, with
a minimum price during the same time of 14 cents per gallon.
In Cincinnati the market-price of whiskey for August, 1861, was
commercially reported as " closing dull " at 13 cents per gallon.
The price of alcohol in New York during the period above
noted ranged from 40 to 60 cents per gallon.   Under such circumstances, the consumption of distilled spirits in the United
States previous to the war, for a great variety of purposes,
had become enormous ; affording a practical illustration of the
curious varying relations between prices and consumption, and
also of what may be considered in the light of an axiom in political economy, namely, that practically there is almost no limit
to the consumption of any useful commodity, provided that
through a reduction of cost or price it is brought within the purchasing power of those who desire to consume.   Thus, for the
year ending June, 1860, the product of distilled spirits in the
United States, as returned by the Census, was 89,308,581 gallons (proof-spirit); or including alcohol, 90,412,581 gallons (as
compared with a present taxed product and consumption in
Great Britain of about thirty millions of gallons) ; and this aggregate, subsequent investigations proved, was considerably less,
rather than in excess of, the actual production.   The maximum quantity of domestic distilled spirits exported in any one
year previous to the war was never in excess of 3,000,000 of gallons; so that the annual consumption of domestic spirits in the
United States in 1860, for all purposes, was at the rate of nearly

three gallons for every man, woman, and child of the population.

It would be an error, however, to assume that all of this immense production of spirits was used for intoxicating purposes or in the way of stimulants, inasmuch as the extreme cheapness of proof-spirits and of alcohol in the United States at the period under consideration occasioned their employment in large quantities for various purposes which were absolutely or almost unknown in Europe, where the price of these same products, through the fiscal necessities of the various governments, has always been made so artificially high as to greatly limit their industrial application. Thus one of these employments, peculiar to the United States at this time, was the manufacture of a cheap illuminating agent known as "burning-fluid," composed of one part of rectified spirits of turpentine mixed with from four to five parts of alcohol, each gallon of alcohol thus used requiring 1.88 gallons of proof-spirits for its manufacture. The use of this preparation in the United States in 1860, in places where coal-gas was not available, was all but universal, and necessitated a production and consumption of at least twenty-five millions of gallons of proof-spirits per annum, which in turn would have required the production and use of from ten to twelve millions of bushels of corn. And so extensive was the scale on which its manufacture was conducted, that in Cincinnati alone the amount of alcohol required every twenty-four hours for this industry was equivalent to the distillate of 12,000 bushels of corn. Here, then, had been gradually created a new, peculiar, and large market, for one of the staple products of American agriculture, and also for the peculiar product—turpentine—of mainly one agricultural State, North Carolina. The excessive cheapness of alcohol also led to its most extensive use for fuel in manufacturing, and in domestic culinary operations; for bathing and cleaning; for the manufacture of varnishes, vinegar, imitation wines, flavoring extracts, perfumery, patent medicines, white-lead, percussion caps, hats, photographs, tobacco, and a great variety of other purposes. It is also to be noted as a curious part of this history that nearly all preparations, washes, and dyes for the hair, which at that time in other countries—as now almost universally—were prepared almost exclusively on a basis of fats or oils or some non-spirituous liquids, were in the United States then composed almost wholly on a basis of alcohol, the comparative difference in the price of this article in the United States and Europe giving an entirely different composition to products of large consumption intended to effect a common object. The transcript of the sales of a single distillery and rectifying establishment in New York City, put in as evidence before the U. S. Revenue Commission of 1865, showed sales in a single year of 19,040 gallons of alcohol in one case, and 12,657 in another, to two manufacturers of different popular hair washes and tonics. From the same firm a manufacturer of an "extract of sarsaparilla" bought in one year 81,300 gallons; and another manufacturer who made a "pain-killer," 41,195 gallons. A single firm of patent-medicine proprietors in Massachusetts testified their consumption of distilled spirits to have averaged one hundred thousand gallons per annum ; while another in Western New York, engaged simply in the manufacture of a horse-medicine, reported a consumption, prior to the imposition of internal-revenue taxation, of upwards of 50,000 gallons of proof-spirits annually. Individual hair-dressers in the large cities also testified that the use of 400 gallons of alcohol (equal to 750 gallons of proof-spirits) yearly in their local business was not an unusual circumstance.

For the manufacture of imitation wines the demand for distilled spirits in the United States prior to 1864 was also very large ; four firms in the city of New York reporting a consumption of 225,000 gallons of pure spirits for this purpose during the year 1863. Large quantities of neutral or pure spirits were also used at the time in the United States for the "fortifying" of cider, to prevent or retard acidification—especially in the case of cider intended for export to tropical countries, to the Southern States, or to the Pacific. One distiller in Western New York reported a regular sale, during the year 1862, of eight thousand gallons per month for this purpose exclusively.

The first tax imposed by Congress on distilled spirits of domestic production was 20 cents per proof-gallon, and went into effect on the 1st of July, 1862. This tax continued in force until March 7th, 1864, when the rate was advanced to

60 cents per gallon. On the 1st of July, less than four months subsequently, the rate was again raised to $1.50 per gallon, and on the 1st of January, 1865, six months later, it was further and finally advanced to $2 per gallon. In addition to these specific taxes heavy additional taxes on the mixing, compounding, and wholesale and retail dealing in spirits were also imposed in the way of licenses.

The immediate effect of this imposition and rapid increase of internal taxes upon distilled spirits was a series of industrial and commercial phenomena, more remarkable than anything of the kind before recorded in economic history; and yet so completely was the attention of the American people engrossed at this time in other and greater events—events affecting their very existence as a nation—that the results referred to did not so much as create a ripple in public opinion, and were barely adverted to, if noticed at all, in the columns of the public press. In short, the influence of these taxes was to entirely and rapidly revolutionize great branches of domestic industry, and in some instances to utterly destroy them. Thus, for example, the manufacture of burning-fluid entirely ceased, inasmuch as the rise in the price of alcohol from 40 cents to $4 and upwards per gallon, together with the cessation of the supply of turpentine from North Carolina,—then a State in rebellion,—rapidly converted it from the cheapest to the dearest of all illuminating agents. Here, also, very curiously, the public did not experience any great inconvenience by reason of this change; for by one of those happy and unexpected occurrences, almost in the nature of accidents, which have so often characterized the history of the United States, and which some are pleased to regard as "special providences," it so happened that the discovery of vast and natural supplies of petroleum in Pennsylvania, and the practical application of its distillates for illuminating purposes, was almost coincident in point of time with the compulsory disuse of burning-fluid; while the fact that the new material possessed great advantages in point of cheapness and effect over the old caused the change in popular use to be effected voluntarily and with great rapidity.[1] As a further illustration of the

[1] The first company organized to supply petroleum in the United States was in 1854; but it was not until 1861-2 that the product began to constitute an im-

compensations which invariably attend the losses immediately contingent upon industrial progress, and through the disuse of old products, methods, and machinery, it may be stated that, altho the manufacture of burning-fluid ceased, the business of collecting, preparing, and exporting petroleum rapidly became one of the most important in the country; while the demand at home and abroad for the lamps and their appurtenances devised and adapted in the United States for the use of the distillates of petroleum was alone sufficient to employ the entire manu-facturing capacity of all the glass-works of the country for a term equivalent to two entire years.

Druggists and pharmaceutists in the United States estimated the reduction in the use of alcohol in their general business, consequent upon its increased cost from taxation, at from one third to one half. The popular hair preparations into which alcohol entered largely as a constituent vanished from the market ; and manufacturers of patent medicines and cosmetics generally abandoned their old preparations and adopted new ones. The manufacturer of horse-medicines, who used 50,000 gallons of spirits in 1863, wofully testified in 1865 that his business was destroyed. Varnish-makers, who, when alcohol could be purchased at from 50 to 60 cents per gallon, used it in large quantities, were of necessity compelled to entirely or in a great degree abandon its use when the price rose to $4 per gallon and upward ; and yet special investigation showed that the quantity of varnish manufactured was not correspondingly reduced ; inasmuch as the manufacturers at once substituted other and cheaper solvents for their gums, especially the naphthas or light distillates of petroleum which were then opportunely seeking uses and a market. Within a comparatively few years, also, the continued high price of alcohol has led the manufacturers of quinine to substitute the distillates of petroleum as a solvent for the alkaloids in the cinchona barks; and with such success that it is doubtful whether the old processes would be again

portant article of commerce; and it was some considerable time later before its distillates were made sufficiently cheap and good to induce anything like general use. The average price of burning-fluid from 1856 to 1861 was from 45 to 65 cents per gallon. The average price of refined petroleum in 1863 was 51 cents ; and the domestic consumption about 500,000 barrels.

adopted, even if alcohol could again be afforded at its former prices. The manufacturers of hats, who had before used a composition of gum-shellac dissolved in alcohol almost exclusively for stiffening the hat "bodies" or "foundations," and were thus large consumers of alcohol, were compelled to abandon its use, and for a time were subjected to no little inconvenience. But even here substitutes were soon found; and in addition the use of cloth as a material for hats, in the place of felt and silk plush, was largely introduced and became popular. The manufacture of vinegar from whiskey, by reason of the great advance in the price of distilled spirits, was also in a large degree broken up; and this in turn had the effect to destroy a large export business of this article, as well as to increase the market-price of pickles to the extent of from *one third* to *one half;* and also to seriously affect the manufacture and cost of white-lead, and occasion extensive importations of this article from other countries.

The business of fortifying cider for movement or export to the Pacific coast and to the tropics, before referred to, as well as the manufacture of imitation wines and of cheap perfumery, was likewise very seriously interfered with or destroyed, as was also the business of manufacturing the fluid extracts of the medicinal principles of plants; and it was represented to the Revenue Commission by members of the American Pharmaceutical Association that there was a marked tendency throughout the country on the part of physicians and others to abandon the use of alcoholic extracts and fall back upon the old custom of employing crude drugs, decoctions, and syrups as substitutes; and further, that there was an attempt to keep down the price to the consumer of many officinal preparations which absolutely required the use of alcohol, by putting them up at less than their proper officinal strength; thus inflicting a sanitary injury upon the whole community. Finally, in all branches of the industrial arts, where the continued use of distilled spirits was indispensable, and no cheaper substitute could be found, the utmost economy in its use was everywhere practised.

Another curious incident connected with this history was that the curators of the leading museums of the country—anatomical or natural history—attached to institutions of learning, memorialized Congress to the effect that, owing to the high price of alcohol, they could not afford to make good the waste of this substance (by evaporation and leakage) as employed by them for scientific purposes; and that in consequence many important collections were becoming greatly impaired in value, and the progress of scientific discovery and research greatly impeded. And Congress, recognizing the desirability of giving relief in respect to this matter, empowered the Secretary of the Treasury to grant permits to incorporated American institutions of learning to withdraw spirits from bond in specified quantities for scientific purposes without payment thereon of the internal-revenue taxes.

It seems desirable to state here that the facts as above detailed, as well as some others to be presented hereafter, were the results of the investigations of a Commission authorized by Congress in the winter of 1865 for the purpose of inquiring into the condition and sources of the national revenue, and the best methods of raising revenue for the Federal Government by taxation, with full power to summon witnesses and take testimony; and that of this Commission the writer was the chairman. It will be interesting also at this point to diverge somewhat from the thread of this history and consider what information is available concerning the present and past consumption of distilled spirits in the United States for drinking purposes; and also to some extent the experience of other countries in respect to the same matter.

Previous to the imposition of internal taxes by the Federal Government in 1862, raw or common whiskey was retailed freely throughout the country at from *seven* to *fifteen* cents per quart, or from twenty-five to fifty cents per gallon. At these low prices, it was within the ability of every laborer to indulge freely, and this ability was largely taken advantage of, especially at the close of a week or at the periodical settlement of wages. It was also a very general custom in many parts of the country for agriculturists to buy whiskey by the barrel, for the use of their farming help, and to use it freely as a beverage during the season of harvesting. In short, previous to 1860 a man could undoubtedly get drunk in the United States with a less expenditure of money than in any part of the civilized world.

But it may well be doubted whether, with these increased facilities, drunkenness increased in the United States in any greater ratio, or more rapidily, than in other countries, where the facilities for obtaining intoxicating liquors were notably less. On the contrary, the obtainable evidence is all the other way. Thus at the time of the formation of the constitution, or more precisely in 1790, the domestic production and consumption of distilled spirits in the United States, as before stated, was about 6,000,000 of gallons per annum ; which, with the then population of 3,929,000, would be in the ratio of about one and a half gallons per capita. As there were at that time in the country no industrial establishments or processes requiring an extensive employment of alcohol, it is probable that nearly the whole domestic production of this article was then used for drinking purposes ; a conclusion which finds support in the circumstance that at the time referred to, and for many years thereafter, almost every county, and indeed almost every town, had its little distillery of spirits from fruits or grain ; the market for the products of which, in the absence of facilities for cheap transportation, must of necessity have been largely local. At the time of the whiskey insurrection in 1794, the number of distilleries in Pennsylvania alone was reported at 5000. Furthermore, at this time everybody drank, socially and in public, privately and at home ; men and women, young and old, the clergymen and their parishioners, farmers and their laborers. The last half-century has, however, through the agitation of the temperance question, the general progress of civilization and refinement, and the extensive introduction and use of the malt liquors, not only worked a change in the social habits of Americans,—a change little understood by the present generation,—but has also unquestionably largely decreased the average consumption of distilled spirits in the country. From 1790 to 1840 the Census returns in regard to production are entitled to but little respect ; but the whole weight of evidence is to the effect that the number of distilleries and their products steadily increased during this period, and fully kept pace with the population. In 1840 the Census returned the annual domestic product of distilled liquors at from 40,000,000 to 50,000,000 gallons. The population at that time was 17,069,000 ; while in 1880, with a popula-

tion of 50,155,000, the Internal Revenue Bureau was only able
to take cognizance for assessment and tax-collection of an annual production of 62,132,000 gallons of proof-spirits, or 9,000,-
000 gallons less than in 1870, when the population was 12,000,-
000 smaller. (But this notable increase in 1870, as compared
with 1880, and a larger population, is undoubtedly referable to a
greatly increased consumption of spirits for industrial purposes,
consequent upon a reduction in price and taxation of near fifty
per cent.) For the year 1883, with an aggregate population of
approximately 56,000,000, the number of gallons of proof-
spirits of all kinds on which the internal-revenue tax was paid
was returned at 76,762,063 ; but a considerable part of this product undoubtedly represented spirits which paid the tax and
were taken out of bond by necessity, through the expiration of
the permissible bonded period, and not by reason of any increased coincident demand on the part of the public for consumption. For the year 1883 the quantity of spirits produced
and deposited in the distillery warehouses was 74,013,303 gallons, as compared with a similar production and deposit for the
year 1882 of 105,853,161. And the extent to which production
had exceeded any legitimate demand for domestic consumption
is indicated by the circumstance that the taxable product remaining in the bonded warehouses on the 30th of June, 1883,
after all demands for domestic consumption had been supplied,
amounted to the large aggregate of 80,499,993 gallons. That
the Federal authorities do not succeed in collecting the tax on
all the distilled spirits annually produced in the United States
is absolutely certain ; but making a large allowance for evasions,
and supposing the present annual consumption for all purposes
to aggregate as high as even eighty millions of proof-gallons, it follows that while the population of the country has increased nearly
three-fold, the amount of spirits distilled for domestic consumption in the same period, under influence of increased price through
taxation and other agencies, has probably not more than doubled.
The evidence, therefore, is conclusive of a diminished consumption, comparing 1840 with the results of 1880 and 1883. But this
is not all. The use of alcohol in the arts and manufactures has
enormously increased since 1840. Whole trades in which it is
largely used have since come into existence ; and altho the

amount now so consumed is absolutely and comparatively less than in 1860, when distilled spirits were untaxed, yet the quantity so used for industrial purposes is still large, and every gallon so applied reduces the proportion which can be used for stimulants. If we assume the present annual consumption of domestic distilled spirits in the United States to be about 70,000,000 gallons; and about twelve per cent, or 8,400,000 gallons, of this amount be used for industrial or scientific purposes, or is lost by leakage and other casualties,[1] then the use of domestic spirits for drink in this country must be at present at the rate of about 1.10 gallons per capita annually for the entire population. To this must also be added the consumption of foreign or imported spirits—the amount of which exclusive of wines is not, however, very considerable, less than a million and a half of proof-gallons having been imported during the fiscal year 1882–3. But adding this amount to the consumption of domestic distilled spirits before assumed, the total consumption of spirits—wine, cider, and fermented liquors excepted —by the population of the United States, would therefore appear to be at present at the rate of about 1.14 gallons per capita. During the same year the importation of wines was returned at 6,187,520 gallons in casks and 195,957 dozen bottles. The consumption of champagnes and other sparkling wines of foreign production would seem to be on the increase in the United States; the value of the importations for 1883 being re-

---

[1] The amount of leakage allowed during the fiscal year 1883 by the Government, on domestic distilled spirits withdrawn from warehouse, was 2,291,013 gallons, in addition to 184,770 gallons lost by casualty, theft, etc. During the same year 28,725 gallons of alcohol were withdrawn from warehouse free of tax for the use of colleges and institutions of learning, and 22,359 also for the use of the United States.

In 1882 the Internal Revenue Bureau estimated the amount of alcohol annually used in the arts and manufactures in the United States to be equal to 4,269,978 proof-gallons. This estimate was not, however, founded on returns from all the collection districts in the country, and on its face was based on little other than absurd guesses; country districts of Tennessee, for example, being assigned a consumption of from 13,000 to 19,000 gallons, while the annual consumption of the 22d District of Pennsylvania, which comprises the city of Pittsburg, was put down at only 260 gallons, with the subjoined opinion that this quantity would not be likely to be increased if the tax on distilled spirits were to be entirely removed.

turned at $4,603,722, as compared with a similar valuation of $3,028,309 in 1882 and of $2,883,668 in 1881.

In Great Britain, where, owing to a rigid enforcement of their excise laws, the domestic production and consumption of distilled spirits is more accurately known than in any other country except, possibly, Russia, the amount of revenue collected from the direct tax on this article for the year ending March, 1883, was £14,211,490, or $71,057,450; indicating an annual consumption (exclusive of spirits allowed to be used for industrial purposes after having been made unfit for drinking purposes by mixing with naphtha or wood-spirit) of 28,422,980 imperial gallons. As compared with the preceding year, 1881–2, there was a decrease in consumption of 294,270 gallons in England, and of 46,254 in Scotland; while in Ireland, notwithstanding an estimated decrease of population, there was an increased consumption of 245,667 gallons.

The consumption per capita in Great Britain at different periods of the various beverages which are there made subject to taxation is shown in the following table derived from the "Report of the [British] Commissioners of Inland Revenue" for 1882–3.

	1852.	1862.	1872.	1882.
British spirits, gallons per head.	.916	.644	.844	.809
Duty increased in 1860.				
Foreign and colonial spirits, gallons per head....	.187	.177	.285	.236
Duty reduced in 1860.				
Foreign wines, gallons per head	.262	.335	.530	.409
Duty reduced in 1860.				
Beer, barrels per head.........................	.608	.661	.885	.766
Tea, pounds per head.........................	2.140	2.694	4.014	4.679
Duty reduced from 2s. 2¼d. to 6d. per pound.				
Coffee, pounds per head	1.274	1.108	.994	.906
Cocoa, pounds per head......	.123	.134	.247	.339

It appears, therefore, from the above table, that the increase of duty on British spirits has been followed by decreased consumption, while in the case of foreign spirits and wines, and tea, a diminution of duty has been followed by a large increase of consumption, tea being the most notable example; and also that the present per-capita consumption of strong spirituous liquors, domestic and foreign, in Great Britain and the United States—1.04 and 1.14 gallons respectively—is not materially different. It must, however, be borne in mind, in considering this subject, that malt liquors are used in the place of spirits to a much greater extent in Great Britain than in the United States. Thus for the year 1880 the British consumption of beer is stated by Mr. William Hoyle, an English specialist on this subject, to have amounted to 905,088,978 gallons, costing £67,881,678. The tables of the "Financial Reform Almanac" for 1884 give the per-capita consumption of beer in Great Britain as 27.8 gallons in 1881 and 27.6 in 1882. For the year 1882 the official estimate (see table above given) of the domestic consumption of malt liquors was .766 of a barrel per capita. In the United States, on the other hand, where the manufacture and sale of malt liquors is also made subject to a tax, and is so brought under the supervision of the Federal Government, the number of barrels of such liquors returned as manufactured during the fiscal year 1882-3 was 17,757,886; which quantity in turn, reckoning 31 gallons to the barrel, would represent 550,494,000 gallons. Adding 1,500,000 gallons to represent the excess of imports over exports of malt liquors, the consumption of such liquors by the people of the United States for the year 1883 would, therefore, appear to have been at the rate of nine and seven tenths (9.68) gallons per capita, as compared with a per-capita consumption in Great Britain for the same period of 27.6 gallons. If allowance be now made, as there should be, for the quantity of spirit contained in this excess of fermented liquors produced and consumed in Great Britain over and above the amount of similar liquors consumed in the United States, then the per-capita estimate of the consumption of spirits in the former country would have to be fixed at a somewhat greater figure than the ratio of 1.04 above given.

From the above facts and experiences the following deductions of general interest are warranted. First, that the consumption of distilled spirits and fermented liquors in Great Britain is not increasing in proportion to the increase of population, but is absolutely decreasing. Thus, with taxation remaining unchanged, the British revenue from duties on imported spirits has declined from £6,141,336 in 1876 to £5,331,561 in 1879, and to £4,365,383 in 1883, or at an average rate of about $1,250,000 per annum. In the case of the excise the decline has been somewhat smaller, but nevertheless most significant; namely, from £15,154,327 in 1876 to £14,211,490 in 1883, or at an average of $670,000 per annum. For the year 1883 the British revenue from beer was also less by £269,000 ($1,445,000) than had been anticipated. Commenting on these results, the British Commissioners of the Inland Revenue in their report for 1883 say:

> "The decrease in the consumption [of spirits] in England and Scotland appears comparatively small, but it becomes more significant of altered habits when considered with the natural increase which must have taken place in the population. There cannot be any doubt that in some localities the spread of temperance principles has already caused a marked diminution in the consumption of intoxicating liquors, and the tendency is still increasing; . . . . the past year having been, apparently, one of unusual progress in this direction."

The decrease in the revenue from beer for the year 1883 the Commissioners attribute to some extent to the influence of temperance societies, but especially to the failure of the hop-crops throughout the world, which increased the price of hops from an average of £6 10s. to above £22 per hundred-weight.

Commenting on this falling-off of the imperial revenues from wine and spirit taxes, the Chancellor of the Exchequer, in his budget statement for 1883, stated that in comparison with the receipts from these sources in 1874–5, and allowing for the increase of population, the product for 1883 ought to have amounted to £24,840,000; whereas it was, with the same rates, but £19,840,000; or in other words, he showed that the domestic consumption of wine and spirits during the period under consideration "had fallen off to an amount represented by five millions of duty, and, including the beer duties, the three had fallen off to an amount represented by 3d. on the income-tax." During the same period the population of the kingdom had increased not less than 4,000,000.

The notable decrease in the consumption of foreign wines in Great Britain since 1874–5, indicated by the decrease in the receipts of revenue from the duties imposed on their import (£1,789,855 in 1874, as compared with £1,293,833 in 1883, representing in quantity a change from about 18,500,000 to 14,000,000 gallons), finds concurrent support in the testimony of social experience. "Something of this falling-off," says *All the Year Round*, "is due, perhaps, to a distaste for wine as a beverage, brought about by a general deterioration in quality, and by the enormous adulteration of which wine is the subject. But there is also a change in the social habits of the wealthier classes. Instead of the popping of champagne-corks we have the fizzing of mineral waters. The hospitable suppers where wine and wit flowed freely are things of the past ; the balls of other days, when the fair dancers refreshed themselves so freely with sparkling wines, are succeeded by parties, where nothing is provided beyond tea and lemonade."

Commenting also on these reductions in the receipts of the British national revenues from the taxes on liquors, the London *Standard* says :

"The change indicated by them in the social habits of our population is enormous. Some of these were mentioned by Mr. Caine in his address to the Central Temperance Association. Thus, to take a single instance, commercial travellers who, only fifteen years ago, were called upon to pay at hotels for a bottle of wine whether they drank it or not—being charged in consideration of this usage only a shilling for their dinner—are charged now three shillings for that meal, but are not expected to order anything for 'the good of the house.' It is to be feared that in most great commercial cities, furnished as they are with their wine 'shades' and subterranean drinking-saloons, there is still a good deal too much tippling at odd hours. But, on the whole, no one can shut his eyes to the fact that there exists a strong and growing public opinion against drunkenness even among those who are less rigidly abstemious than might be desirable. For the first time in the history of this country, intoxication, irrespective of the social level on which it may be seen, carries with it a lasting stigma. The whole tendency of the day is opposed to excessive drinking. The temperance movement is not only making a great number of teetotallers, but influencing those who are not abstainers greatly to decrease the amount they take. At the great majority of dinner-parties the quantity of wine taken after the ladies have left the room is very small ; and if Thackeray were to rewrite Chapter X. in his 'Book of Snobs,' he would represent Captain Rag and Ensign Famish as ordering a 'lemon-squash' in the small hours, rather than a sixth glass of whiskey-punch."

But the points of interest in connection with this matter are not yet exhausted. It has long been the aim of the Chancellors of the British Exchequer to obtain the largest possible revenue from spirituous liquors, to the assumed concurrent relief of all other forms of business and commodities from taxation ; and the proportion of the annual revenues of the United Kingdom derived of late years from these sources is probably not recognized by the public, or even by economists and financiers generally. For the period 1859 to 1865 the proportion of the tax revenue of Great Britain derived from spirituous liquors was in the ratio of 37½ per cent to 62 from all other sources. From 1869 to 1873 the ratio was 46 from the former to 53 from the latter; while from 1874–5 to 1879–80, 51 per cent of all British taxes, except the income-tax, was levied on liquors, and 49 per cent on all other sources. But since 1880 there has been a reaction, and in 1882 the proportion had changed to 47 from liquors and 53 from other sources. The British Exchequer is therefore confronted with a new problem, namely, What provision is to be made if this decrease of revenue from a decrease in the consumption of spirituous liquors by the British public is to continue? Such a continued decrease being not improbable, there are but two courses open, new taxes or diminished expenditures; and the latter, in view of the Eastern complications of Great Britain, does not seem to be possible. But for the present it is not a little curious to find that Ireland comes to the rescue, and by increasing her consumption of whiskey to the extent, even with a diminished population, of 245,667 gallons in the single year 1883, helps relieve from financial difficulties the treasury of her Saxon oppressor.

Commenting on this reduction in the consumption of spirits in Great Britain, its causes and effects on the social condition of the mass of the British people, Mr. Gladstone in his budget speech in April, 1882, said :

"If this diminution of consumption is going on, and if a main cause of this diminution is the foundation of those valuable and useful institutions known all over the country—I believe, in all the great towns or in most of them, and even in many country places—as coffee and cocoa houses, we ought to see a large increase of revenue, at least, from other sources. But that increase we do not find. That is a curious fact. I am not going to include tea, because tea, after all, is not much used in these public places. The revenue derived in 1867–8 jointly—I will not give all the details—from chicory, cocoa, and coffee, was £523,000. The revenue derived from the same sources in 1874-5 had fallen to £310,000; but then, in the first place, the movement adverse to alcoholic liquors had not then commenced, and, in the second place, a very large reduction had been made on the coffee duty, which in 1867 yielded £390,000; but it was reduced in 1872 from 3*d*. to 1½*d*. per pound, and in 1874 it only yielded £207,000. But while this great movement adverse to alcohol, which has been so eminently favorable to both coffee and chicory, has been at work since 1874-5, it has not produced the slightest rally in the revenue from coffee, but, on the contrary, during the last seven years there has been a further diminution on coffee. In 1874 the coffee duty was £207,000; in 1881 it was only £189,000; and altho the chicory duty had been slightly increased, it only increased by £8000, and did not make up the whole difference. The cocoa duty had increased somewhat, from £40,000 to £46,000; but the joint yield of these three articles, which in 1874 was £310,000, was only £306,000 in 1881. When we turn to tea the case is very different. There it is not in the tea houses, but the domestic use of tea that is advancing at such a rate that there you have a powerful champion able to encounter alcoholic drink in a fair field and to throw it in fair fight. The revenue on tea, which in 1867 was £3,350,000, had risen in 1874 to £3,875,000 and in 1881 to £4,200,000. The increase of the population during that period of 14 years was 4,900,000. But there was no corresponding augmentation in the revenue from coffee and chicory. One other circumstance in connection with this state of facts and with the great diminution in alcoholic drinks I have ventured to lay before the committee; for certainly I do not hesitate to say that I think we can trace the operation of this diminution in the use of alcoholic drinks precisely where we should wish to trace it—that is, in the augmented savings of the people. I will show what are these savings as far as they come under the cognizance of the government, and I hope that forms a very small portion of those savings, but at the same time for the purposes of comparison it is perfectly effectual. I look first to the old savings banks. In 1846 their deposits were 31¾ millions. In 1861 they had risen to 41½ millions; in 1867, owing to the competition of the Post-Office savings banks, which paid a considerably lower rate of interest, they had fallen to 36½ millions. Since that time they have been advancing, not rapidly, but steadily. In 1874 they were 41¼ millions; in 1881 they were £44,175,000, showing an annual increment of about £350,000. The Post-Office savings banks, as the committee are aware, were founded in 1861. They have advanced on the whole very steadily. Even the most unfavorable state of circumstances among the laboring classes has never done more than reduce, not inconsiderably, but still not vitally, not the amount of the deposits, but the yearly increment of the deposits. The ordinary increment of the deposits in the Post-Office savings banks has been from £1,600,000 to £1,800,000. In the first decade the lowest amount for any year is £1,533,000, and the highest £1,926,000. The lowest year in the

second decade was 1879, when there was great distress and want of employment; but even in that year the deposits were £1,600,000. In the highest
of the prosperity years, 1872, the savings were £2,293,000, and for 1881-2,
with a great diminution of means on the part of the laboring population,
they have risen to £3,189,000. I think that shows that, whatever other
effects this diminution of the duty on spirits is producing, it is clearly associated with the gradual extension of more saving habits among the
people."

Another point of interest established by the records of recent experience is a very remarkable increase in the production
and consumption of malt liquors in the United States. In 1863
the estimated production of all malt liquors was estimated at
about 2,000,000 barrels of 31 gallons each, or 60,000,000 gallons.
In 1880 the production actually assessed for revenue by the
Federal Government was 13,347,110 barrels; 1881, 14,311,028;
and in 1883, 17,757,892, or 550,494,000 gallons, reckoning 31 gallons to the barrel. The increase of beer production and consumption in the United States since 1863 has been, therefore,
in a far greater proportion than the increase in population.
How far it has served to diminish the vice of drunkenness in its
most vicious form by supplanting the consumption of the
stronger spirituous liquors for the purposes of drink and
stimulants has not yet been shown by any statistics, and it may
be difficult to do so with any high degree of accuracy; but such
a supposition is, to say the least, extremely probable, and is
claimed by the representative brewers of the United States to
be almost in the nature of a self-evident fact. The President of
the American Brewers' Association, in his address before the
annual meeting in 1883, commented upon it as follows:

" A more remarkable revolution in the habits and customs of a people,
nor a longer stride in the path of temperance by the substitution of a
healthful and invigorating drink, nutritive and but slightly stimulant, for
the fiery spirits whose consumption is so apt to lead to excess, is not to be
found in the history of the world."

Attention should here also be called to a most significant and
notable circumstance in connection with this matter; and that is
that while the number of persons who take out licenses under the
internal revenue to retail liquors in the different States and Ter-

ritories is continually increasing—163,523 in 1879-80; 170,640 in 1880-81; 168,770 in 1881-82; and 187,871 in 1883—the number of those who take out similar liquor licenses in those States where prohibition has been engrafted on the constitution or placed upon the statute-book appears to increase in an equal or greater proportion. Thus, in the State of Maine the number of such licenses in 1880 was 757; in 1881, 820; in 1882, 918; and in 1883, 1054. In Kansas there were 1132 in 1881; 1460 in 1882; and 1898 in 1883. In New Hampshire there were 747 in 1880 and 1066 in 1883. Iowa, 3965 in 1880; 4104 in 1882; and 5001 in 1883. Vermont, on the other hand, shows a decrease from 508 in 1880 to 454 in 1883. As illicit dealing in malt liquors, by reason of their bulkiness, is more difficult than in the case of spirits, it would seem as if one effect of prohibition of all retail sales of all liquors must be to discriminate against beer and in favor of whiskey drinking; but record of licenses for the sale of malt liquors in the prohibition States does not show a decrease, but rather a marked increase, in the number granted.

The aggregate exportation of American beer, altho increasing, is as yet very insignificant in comparison with the domestic production; the export in 1883 having been 220,792 gallons in casks and 215,938 dozen bottles, as compared with 61,661 gallons in casks and 3633 dozen bottles in 1875. Most of the beer exported finds its market in Mexico, Central America, the West Indies, Colombia, Venezuela, Brazil, Japan, and the Sandwich Islands.

The statistics of the Dominion of Canada indicate a comparative consumption of distilled spirits largely in excess of that in the United States, approximating two gallons per capita; a conclusion which perhaps ought not to be regarded as surprising, when consideration is given to the proportion of the population of the Dominion engaged in a rigorous climate in rough, out-of-door employments, as fishing and lumbering, in which the consumption of spirits is regarded almost in the light of a necessity.

Recently published French statistics indicate a marked increase in the consumption of alcoholic liquors in France within the last fifty years, and that the present annual rate is about three fourths of a gallon (3 litres = 3.15 quarts) per capita. The present annual per-capita consumption of wine in France is estimated at about 30 gallons (120 litres). The departments of France which consume the most spirituous liquors are those which produce no wines; and in the departments where wine is largely produced cases of "delirium tremens" are acknowledged to be rare.

II.

WITH a view of making as complete as possible the curious record of the experience of the United States in taxing distilled spirits, especially in that department of the subject which relates to the influence of this tax on other industries, it is proposed to here turn back and ask attention to an example of no little economic interest and importance which inadvertently was not noticed in its proper connection in the preceding article, and which illustrates in a remarkable manner the subtle, diffusive, and often remote and unexpected influence of a tax, especially when the same is imposed on the processes rather than the final results of industry.

Before the tax was levied upon distilled spirits in 1862, a large (and probably the largest) proportion of the vinegar used in the United States was made from this product, rather than, as was popularly supposed, from the juice of apples and grapes; the process of manufacture being substantially to add yeast to alcohol (low proof-spirits) largely diluted with water, and allow the mixture to trickle slowly through a cask filled with shavings of beech-wood. In this way the alcoholic liquor is caused to present an immensely extended surface to the action of the air, when oxidation takes place so rapidly that very frequently by the time the liquor has reached the bottom of the cask it no longer contains any alcohol, but is entirely converted into vinegar. Experience has also shown that vinegar thus manufactured and with care is always purer and a better preservative of animal and vegetable food than vinegar manufactured from the juices of fruits, inasmuch as the latter always contain putresci-

ble constituents which are rarely fully eliminated by the process of fermentation ; and further, that when the use of distilled
spirits at their first cost of production is permissible for the
preparation of vinegar, the product can be sold at a much
cheaper rate than any other competing article: and the desirability of cheapness and purity in the supply of this commodity
at once becomes evident, when it is remembered that the largest
consumption of vinegar in every community is for the pickling
(preservation) of meats, fish, and vegetables. All this business
the war-taxation at once and almost completely broke up. On
the other hand, the manufacture of cider—which was not
specially taxed—received a great stimulus. New orchards were
set out, new nurseries were called into existence, additional
cider-mills were demanded in every apple-section of the country,
and thousands of dollars were invested in this industry where
but a small sum had formerly sufficed. The old fashioned press
also gave place to improved and expensive machinery, and expensive buildings were erected for conducting the business on a
most extensive scale. According to a statement submitted to
Congress in 1882 by the " Cider-Vinegar Makers' Association,"
the number of persons engaged in cider and cider-vinegar
making in the United States at that time was between ten
and twelve thousand, and the amount of capital invested as
aggregating into millions. As the amount of available cider
and wine produced in the most favorable fruit-years is, however,
never sufficient to supply the demand of the country for vinegar,
other and cheaper materials for its manufacture were sought for
and found, but always at the sacrifice of the purity and health-
fulness of the resulting product. Great hopes were for a time
entertained that a fermented syrup made from glucose, or
starch-sugar, would answer, and this material soon came into
extensive use; but the vinegar made from it was found to
soon putrefy, and its use, after occasioning great losses to pick-
lers and the community, was abandoned. Unscrupulous manufacturers also made use of mineral acids for the manufacture of
factitious vinegar; and as some evidence of the extent to which
such fabrications came into general use, it may be stated that
in 1877 the Board of Health of the District of Columbia con-
demned five car-loads of so-called vinegar sent to Washington

from Chicago, analysis showing that the same was little other than dilute sulphuric acid; the board further reporting that the sample analyzed formed part of an invoice of a thousand barrels which had been brought to that city for sale and consumption as vinegar.

Under such circumstances, Congress in 1879 made it lawful for manufacturers of vinegar to separate by a so-called vaporizing process the alcoholic element of an ordinary distiller's "mash," and condense the same in water in such a way as to form a weak mixture, suitable for making vinegar, and yet not salable as spirits. But the moment this was done, fresh industrial antagonisms arose. Vinegar manufactured from distilled spirits again made its appearance on the market, and in such quantities and at such prices that the cider-vinegar makers claimed it would be no longer possible for them to continue their business. The latter accordingly, as was to have been expected, speedily organized themselves into a National Protective Cider-Makers' Association, and demanded of Congress, through petitions and deputations, that the permission granted to vaporize alcohol and use it in the manner described for the manufacture of vinegar should be at once repealed, alleging that the consequence of refusal would be to destroy many millions of dollars of capital which the original tax-law had caused to be invested, and (with less of truth) that the fruit-production of the country would be checked, and the manufacture and sale of deleterious compounds to serve as vinegar be encouraged. Very curiously, also, the distillers actively co-operated as allies of the cider-vinegar makers in asking for a repeal of the new law, alleging a fear that it would encourage illicit distillation and consequent frauds on the revenue. That there were some reasons for such apprehensions could not well be doubted; but the real motive influencing the distillers undoubtedly was, the fear of losing a limited market for their products which had come to them through a revival to some extent of the manufacture of spirit-vinegar, in consequence of the reduction of the tax on proof-spirits in 1868 from $2 per proof-gallon to 50 cents, with subsequent changes to 70 and 90 cents in 1872 and 1875 respectively. And the antagonisms thus inaugurated still exist, and continue to occupy the attention of the committees of Congress in a greater or less degree at almost every session ; the whole history affording a most striking illustration of the unnatural, unpatriotic, and false view that has come to be almost universally taken under the leading free representative government of the earth of the great function of taxation. The distiller, for example, in the case in question, asking to have returned to him what he regards as an alienated right, namely, to levy contribution on every one who desires to use alcohol in any shape ; the cider-maker, that the tax may be so fixed as will prevent competition and thereby enable him to exact a larger profit on the sale of his product ; and, finally, the spirit-vinegar maker claiming that as he alone occupies a humanitarian standpoint, because his product alone is cheap and always healthful, therefore that the law should be especially framed to promote and encourage his business ;—each and all speaking, as is proper, for their own interests ; each and all, as is not proper, ever ready to promote their interests by fictitious pleas and averments ; while no one (or but rarely) appears on behalf of the consumers, who are the great mass of the people, in whose interests, it is popularly claimed, all laws are enacted. Furthermore, none of the disastrous consequences which it was confidently predicted would ensue if Congress failed to withdraw from the spirit-vinegar makers the permission to use vaporized spirits have apparently occurred as the result of such failure. The regular business of producing distilled spirits goes on as usual. Farmers have not ceased to plant and care for their orchards ; cider continues to be manufactured in increasing quantities when the seasons are propitious ; while the general public have abundant opportunities to supply themselves with whatever vinegar they may desire at lower prices than have prevailed since the breaking out of the war in 1860. The Commissioner of Internal Revenue alone seems warranted in complaining that through the use of the vaporizing process the facilities for illicit distillation are increased, and probably taken advantage of, to a considerable extent. Finally, if to any it may seem that this history has been stated in greater detail than is expedient, it may be replied that no more important contributions can, in the opinion of the writer, be made to economic science than just such records of practical experience ; for it is mainly through the force and teaching of such examples that the masses can be induced to acknowledge the truth and make the application of abstract principles.

One of the topics to which the attention of the Revenue Commission of 1865 was given, was the influence of the greatly increased cost of distilled spirits in the United States, through the war-taxation, on their demand for drinking purposes; and the testimony of a large number of persons from all sections of the loyal States—manufacturers and dealers in liquors, United States revenue officials and others—was taken in reference to this matter. The opinions expressed were almost unanimously to the effect that no change in consumption was noted by retailers until after the tax was raised above 60 cents per gallon; but that when the tax was increased to $2 the reduction for a time in consumption, especially in the thinly settled sections of the country, was very noticeable. With the increase of taxes on whiskey there was also an immediate and very marked increase in the consumption of beer, the price of which was not enhanced by taxation to a corresponding extent with that of spirits. Thus in 1864, with an internal-revenue tax of $1 per barrel, the assessment was paid on an equivalent of 2,223,000 barrels; in 1865 on 3,657,000; in 1866 on 5,115,000; in 1867 on 3,819,000; while in 1883 the number, as before stated, was 17,757,892 barrels.

On the other hand, the testimony of leading retail and package dealers in liquors in many of the *large* towns and cities was generally to the effect that their business *in the aggregate* was not diminished by the high rates of taxes imposed on spirits; but at the same time all admitted that the demand for the so-called "foreign" or "imported" liquors (upon which the tariff rates had been raised to a greater extent than the taxes on domestic spirits) largely diminished; and also that this loss was fully made good by an increased sale of American whiskey. In fact, the great increase at this time in the price of foreign liquors greatly promoted the sale and use of whiskey in the northern and eastern sections of the country, and seems to have nationalized this liquor as a beverage, and also the term "Bourbon," which then for the first time was, in common parlance (as it ever since has been), generally given to every variety of American whiskey. One prominent retail liquor-dealer of New York testified before the Commission in 1865 that where during the preceding two years he had lost a sale of *four* gallons of "foreign" (?) brandy, he had in the same time gained a sale of twelve gallons of American whiskey. There was also a general agreement among the witnesses that one noticeable effect of the greatly increased cost of spirits through taxation was an increase of adulteration of the cheap liquors that were retailed, thus debasing the quality of the article that was consumed by the habitually intemperate or the physically exhausted among the poor. One practical illustration in proof of this (contained in a memorial presented to Congress by the American Wine and Spirit Society) was, that in 1860, when gin was selling, duty paid, in New York, at 65 cents per gallon, the retailer charged 6 cents a glass; and that the retail price continued the same when the wholesale price had subsequently advanced to $3.25 per gallon.

Previous to the war and the taxes, the cheap liquors bought by the masses in the United States for stimulant or intoxication were not much adulterated, because there was nothing much cheaper than the crude proof-spirit itself (costing from 14 to 23 cents per gallon wholesale) which could be used as a material for adulteration. At the same time, nothing could be much more deleterious than the American raw spirits (whiskeys) from which the so-called fusel-oil (amylic alcohol), which is the invariable accompaniment of its distillation, has not been removed by redistillation or by oxidation through standing and atmospheric exposure.[1]

Some reliable testimony was also taken illustrative of the specific consumption of distilled spirits in the United States before the war. Thus, according to the opinion of those best conversant with the trade, the quantity of proof spirits required to meet the demands of New York City and its immedi-

---

[1] While fusel-oil, in itself, is so deleterious that the inhalation of its vapor, even in minute quantity, is very dangerous, there can be no doubt that it is almost completely removed from spirits through what is technically called "ageing," or atmospheric oxidation and moderately high temperatures. Under such circumstances the fusel-oil appears to be naturally converted into innoxious ethers, which give to wines and liquors their delicate "bouquet," or flavor, which is so much prized and is so agreeable.

ate vicinity in 1862 was from 800 to 1000 barrels daily, or from twelve to fifteen millions of gallons per annum. Of this amount one half was set down as directly consumed for drink; while the balance, having been converted into alcohol, pure spirits, imitation liquors, medicinal preparations and the like, found a market elsewhere. According to the testimony of the then Superintendent of Police, the number of places where spirituous liquors were sold at retail in New York City in 1862 was upwards of 8000; and that the quantity sold over the bars of some of the largest hotels, restaurants, and drinking-saloons was equivalent in each case to a barrel of fifty gallons daily.

The results of investigations made some years ago in England, and communicated in a paper read before the Statistical Society by the Rev. Dawson Burns in 1875,[1] were to the effect, that increased taxation upon spirits in Great Britain, and a consequent increase in their price, had always resulted in restricted consumption; that the lowering of the rate had, on the other hand, stimulated consumption; and that seasons of manufacturing and commercial prosperity and development virtually operated as a reduction of the rate and of the price. Mr. Burns, in the paper referred to, also brings out this further interesting fact; namely, that in 1861 Mr. Gladstone, with a view of inducing a popular consumption of light wines, and in accordance with the popular theory that light wines, if cheap, would readily enter into consumption, and by helping to drive out the stronger liquors would assist in the work of promoting popular sobriety, largely reduced the duties on imported wines, i.e., from 5s. $9\frac{3}{10}$d. to 1s. per gallon on wines containing less than 26 per cent of proof-spirits, and 50 per cent on wines more highly alcoholic but not exceeding 42 per cent of proof-spirits. The result was a refutation, in a degree, of the popular theory. The importation and use of imported wines, as was expected, largely increased; and altho a taste for the French clarets was partially excited among the British public, the consumption of the stronger wines of Spain and Portugal—the sherries and the

---

[1] "The Consumption of Intoxicating Liquors at various periods as affected by the rates of duty imposed upon them," by the Rev. Dawson Burns, M.A., Metropolitan Superintendent of the United Kingdom Alliance. (*Journal of the Statistical Society of London*, vol. xxxviii. 1875.)

ports—was stimulated in a much greater degree. In the debate, however, which followed the reading of this paper, the drift of opinion expressed was, that the conclusion of Mr. Burns, that high duties as a rule reduced the consumption of spirits in England, was not sustained; and it was pointed out by Dr. Farr and others that the consumption of intoxicating liquors in Great Britain was affected far more by the prosperity of the country and the rates of wages than by the duties which had at different times been imposed upon them. And the late Mr. Dudley Baxter, especially, whose knowledge and judgment of economic matters are entitled to great respect, maintained that, as regards the upper and middle classes of Great Britain, Mr. Gladstone's legislation in respect to wines had been of most decided advantage to the cause of temperance; and that this, together with the spread and cheapening, by his measures, of tea and coffee, had been one of the most effectual agencies that had been adopted in the country for many years for the furtherance of the object which the advocates of temperance had at heart. But be this as it may, the whole evidence from the experience of the United States is, that if the great and rapid increase in the price of distilled spirits, after the year 1863, through Federal taxation, did for a time and to some extent operate to diminish their popular consumption, the effect was but temporary. And such a result, when the habits and character of the people of the United States are taken into consideration, ought not to have been unexpected; and it is to be observed, furthermore, that it accords entirely with the experience of Great Britain, as accepted by her leading economists and expressed in the debate above noticed. For such is the degree of material abundance in the United States, and so easy has it been for the masses of its people to obtain what they want in the nature of food-supplies, that they are notoriously extravagant and not given to economy in the use of all such materials;[1]

---

[1] The following example in the way of confirmatory evidence on this point, which has come to the knowledge of the writer while the present article was in the course of preparation, is so interesting that he cannot forbear submitting it to the reader.

During the past year, the price of sugars, all over the world, owing to an increase of production has been lower than at any previous time in the history of commerce; and, in accordance with a well-recognized economic law or axiom,

and a rise of price operates less in restricting consumption than
in almost any other country.   And as illustrative of this matter,
it is interesting to note the difference in the methods by which
liquors are retailed in the United States and England respectively.   Thus in the former, when a drink of distilled spirits is
called for at a public bar, the bottle or decanter is set before the
customer and he helps himself ; in the latter, on the contrary,
every quantity of spirits retailed is measured by the seller. and
accurately proportioned to the price to be received by him.   This
custom prevails universally in Great Britain—in the leading hotels
and club-houses as well as with the smallest and lowest retailers ;
and hence the original signification of the term " dram-shop," i.e.,
a place where liquor is sold by the fluid drachm or other measure,
but which in the United States has become so perverted in
meaning as to now signify a place where one can drink without
any exact measure, or have as much strong liquor for a common
price as the average consumer would ordinarily desire for one
act of drinking.   Besides, as remarked by Mr. Burns in his paper
above referred to, industrial prosperity and full employment of
the masses virtually operate as a reduction of the tax and the
price of spirits; and such employment and industrial activity
existed in the United States in a high degree from the latter
years of the war down to the era of business and financial dis-

consumption has also noticeably increased.   In the United States this increase is
estimated as high as from 10 to 15 per cent; and, very curiously, has manifested
itself in a greater proportionate demand for the lower grades of refined white
sugars, rather than, as might naturally have been expected, for the best qualities of
refined yellow sugars, which are cheaper.   This circumstance attracting the attention of one of the great refiners in the United States, he sought an explanation of it from one of his most intelligent workmen, and in answer received the
following reply: " There is no difficulty, sir, in explaining it.   I give my wife,
for instance, every Monday morning fifty cents to buy sugar for the family for a
week, as I have always done; and she buys the same quantity as before: but
the same money now gives us the same quantity of white sugar that it once did
of the yellow."   Or in other words, the wife. being the judge of the interests and
desires of the family. preferred to take her share of the advantage resulting from
the fall in the price of this essential article of household consumption in an increase in quality (which, by the way, was more apparent to the eye than the taste).
rather than in the form of a larger quantity, for the same price, of the grade which
had before been satisfactory; or than the same quantity and quality as before, and
applied the resulting saving to the purchase of something additional or to an
increase of the family reserve in the savings-bank.

turbance and paralysis in 1873. During all this period, accordingly, the aggregate drinking consumption of distilled and fermented liquors in the United States went on steadily increasing, or at least keeping pace with the increase of population. With the advent of bad times in this latter year, some diminution in the popular use of these commodities might naturally have been expected; and during the years 1873 and '74 there seems to have been some decrease, or at least no increase; the decrease manifesting itself rather in the consumption of fermented liquors than of distilled spirits: the receipts of internal revenue from the former, from the tax of $1 per barrel, declining from $8,910,-823 in 1873 to $8,880,829 in 1874, and $8,743,744 in 1876; while the population continued to increase. But subsequent to 1875-6, and especially on the recurrence of national prosperity in 1878-9, the aggregate consumption of spirits and beer in the United States rapidly increased; the internal-revenue receipts from distilled spirits—tax remaining the same—increasing from $56,-426,000 in 1875-6 to $69,893,000 in 1882-3; and of fermented liquors from $9,571,000 in 1875-6 to $16,153,920 in 1882-3: which increments, it will be noted, are in much greater ratio than any concurrent increase in population.

It is interesting to here also note the changes which have taken place during the period under consideration in the importation of champagne, a form of spirituous liquor almost exclusively consumed by the more wealthy portion of our population. In 1870 the importation was returned at 2,106,000 quarts and 906,788 pints. In 1874, the year following the commencement of the long commercial and industrial depression, the importation was 1,615,000 quarts, a decrease of 491,000; and 1,688,000 pints, an increase of 782,000. In 1878 the importation was 837,000 quarts, a decrease, as compared with 1874, of 778,000; and 1,185,000 pints, a decrease of 500,000. In 1880, national prosperity having returned, the importation was 1,351,000 quarts, an increase, as compared with 1878, of 514,000; and 1,784,000 pints, an increase of 599,000. For the fiscal year 1883 the importations of champagnes were returned at 2,506,092 quarts and 3,927,372 pints or less; a very large increase over the importations of any former years.

Finally, considering all the evidence available on this matter of the production and consumption of distilled and fermented liquors in the United States and other countries, one cannot resist the impression of the small apparent effect which specific agencies—legislative, societary, and personal—produce in restrict. ing their consumption as stimulants or for intoxicating purposes. Excepting, possibly, the recent experience of Great Britain and certain exceptional periods, the aggregate everywhere goes on increasing : no matter whether the prices be high or low, in bad times as well as in good : in the *latter* because the masses have the means to indulge their appetites, and in the *former* because they think there is a need of stimulants to counteract the tendency of the times to mental depression.   The most remarkable illustration to the contrary is probably to be found in the results of the labors of Father Mathew in behalf of temperance in Ireland in the years 1838–40.   Under his influence, the consumption of distilled spirits in Ireland, as indicated by the revenue returns, fell off more than 40 per cent, and did not materially increase for many years thereafter.   Now, however, the *per capita* consumption of Ireland, with a greatly reduced population, is about the same as it was prior to the temperance agitation in 1838 ; thus indicating that the influence of Father Mathew, tho resulting in great immediate good, has not been permanent.   It is also to be noted that the reduction in the consumption of distilled spirits in Ireland which followed Father Mathew's work was accompanied by a notably increased consumption of tea and malt liquors.   On the other hand, and as matter of encouragement to any friends of temperance who may feel a sense of discouragement at the results of these investigations, the fact before noticed should be recalled, that while the production and consumption of *distilled spirits* in the United States continually increase and appear very large in the aggregate, the *comparative* consumption is undoubtedly much less than it was forty years ago,—unquestionably very much less than it was at the commencement of the present century,—and does not at present tend to increase, but rather to decrease ; and that what is true of the United States appears to be also true of Great Britain.   All available evidence, furthermore, is to the effect that with the increase of civilization, of facilities for intercommunication, and general consuming power,

7

the increased consumption of distilled spirits—taking a term of years for comparison—has not been by any means as great as has happened in respect to other commodities of common consumption. Thus, while, according to Mr. Leone Levi, the British economist, the consumption per head of the British people from 1866 to 1877 of bacon and hams increased 277 per cent, of wheat 94 per cent, of sugar 57 per cent, and of tea 32 per cent, the consumption of spirits increased only 21 per cent. A similar conclusion is reached by comparing the estimated *per capita* consumption of certain articles of daily consumption by the population of the city of London in 1843 and 1865. Thus, in respect to sugar, the increase during this period was from 16.5 lbs. to 41.1 lbs.; of tea, from 1.4 lbs. to 3.2 lbs.; of cocoa, from 0.09 lb. to 1.1 lbs.; and of spirits, from 0.87 gallon to only 0.89 gallon. Evidence to the same effect, even more striking and confirmatory, was also presented by Robert Giffen, Esq., President of the Statistical Society of London, in his inaugural address delivered in November, 1883; from which appeared that the proportion of various imported and excisable commodities retained for home consumption had increased per head of the total population of Great Britain during the period from 1840 to 1881 as follows: bacon and hams, from 0.01 lb. to 13.93 lbs.; butter, 1.05 to 6.36; raw sugar, 15.20 to 58.92; rice, 0.90 to 16.32; tobacco, 0.86 to 1.41 : while the *per capita* increase in the consumption of spirits had been from 0.97 gallon to only 1.08 gallons.

The statistics of German consumption are also reported to lead to similar conclusions.

It has been a somewhat popular opinion that the great increase in the price of alcoholic liquors, through taxation, since 1863 has induced and increased the consumption of opium and other drugs in the United States, as substitutes for spirits. Of this there is no positive proof. There has been a marked increase in the importations of *crude* opium into the United States, and in the importation and domestic manufacture of morphia, the principal derivative of opium, since 1860, but not greater than what would seem to be warranted by the increase of population. In 1860 the importations of crude opium were returned at 119,525 lbs., and in 1866 at 180,852 lbs.; and these facts would indicate some basis for the belief of an abnormal use of this drug during the years of the war. In 1869 the importation fell off to 90,997 lbs., but increased in 1875 to 188,238 lbs., in 1880 to 243,211 lbs., and fell off in 1883 to 229,012 lbs. Supposing the entire opium importation into the United States for the past year (1883) to be exclusively used for domestic consumption, certainly this amount is not large for 53,000,000 people. But all of this import was not so used; inasmuch as there is some export of opium and its derivatives from the United States to the West Indies and Central and South America; in all which countries the comparative consumption of opium is much greater, and the comparative consumption of spirits much less, than in the United States: an illustration of what is now accepted as a cosmic law, that the use of intoxicating liquors is to a certain extent dependent on climate. Medical experts have very generally come to regard the danger in respect to opium consumption in the United States to be at present almost wholly confined to the use of morphia; there being an undoubted tendency among persons affected with nervous ailments,—more especially women,—when they feel depressed from various causes, and in need of some stimulant, to resort to this drug, which, altho most costly, does not affect the breath like alcohol and can be easily carried and concealed about the person.

On the other hand, the importation of opium specially prepared for smoking purposes, which did not exist in 1865, has in latter years increased enormously; rising from 12,554 lbs. in 1871 to 77,196 lbs. in 1880, and 298,153 lbs. in 1883; paying in the latter year a customs revenue of nearly two millions of dollars. The preparation of opium for smoking finds its way into the country mainly through the port of San Francisco, and its consumption has hitherto been supposed to be almost wholly restricted to Chinese residents; but the circumstance that the increase of import has been of late in a ratio so far in excess of any ratio of increase in Chinese immigration suggests a probability that the vice of opium-smoking is finding favor and adoption with the native American.

Attempts have been made from time to time to estimate the annual cost to consumers in the United States and other countries of distilled and fermented liquors used for the purpose of drink. At the best, these estimates, no matter how carefully prepared, can but be regarded as approximately accurate, as the necessary data for forming an opinion cannot be obtained with exactness. The following statements and inferences respecting the cost of such consumption in the United States may, however, be of some value and interest.

Assuming the present (1883) consumption of distilled spirits for drinking purposes at about 60,000,000 proof-gallons per annum,[1] the original or *first* cost of this quantity at 25 cents per gallon would be only $15,000,000. (The average price of proof-spirits in Cincinnati, exclusive of the tax, for the year 1882 was 24.9 cents; for 1883, 23.8 cents.) Adding the internal-revenue tax of 90 cents per gallon ($54,000,000) and all the additional taxes which the Federal Government imposes on the whole business of producing and vending distilled spirits, i.e. licenses, etc. ($6,410,764), and the first cost would become further augmented to $75,410,764. (The census return of the value of the entire product of distilled liquors in the country for 1880 was $41,063,000.) The returned value of the imports of spirits, of imitations thereof, and of champagne for 1883 was $6,906,900, on which the duties collected were $5,593,869; making the aggregate first cost of such importations $12,500,769, and the total first cost of the entire distilled spirit and imported champagne consumption of the United States for the fiscal year of 1883 $87,911,533: of which large sum, $66,004,633 accrues to the internal revenue. It will thus be seen that the Government is the largest partner, and has by far the largest interest, in this business.

The next question of interest and importance is, To what extent is this aggregate of first market-price or cost, and of the accompanying taxation, increased in the process of distribution?

---

[1] The number of gallons of proof-spirits on which the internal-revenue tax was paid for the year 1883 was 76,762,063, of which 75.508,785 gallons were distilled from grain, molasses, etc., and 1.253.278 gallons from fruit. Of this aggregate, 7 561.171 gallons were withdrawn from warehouse under the form of alcohol; which would represent in turn about 14,400,000 gallons of proof-spirits, and indicate a larger consumption of spirits for industrial and pharmaceutical purposes than was assumed on page 166 of the first article of this series.

The drift of opinion on the part of those who have discussed this subject in Great Britain appears to be that it is about doubled. If we assume this to be the case in the United States, then the ultimate cost to the consumer of the distilled-spirit and champagne consumption in this country from the year 1883 would be $175,823,066.

It may here also be mentioned that the value of the still wines imported into the United States during the fiscal year 1883 (duties included) was returned at $8,827,000.

The present (1884) domestic production and consumption of fermented liquors—ale, lager-beer, etc.—is probably about 18,500,-000 barrels, of an average capacity of 31 gallons each ; or an aggregate of 573,500,000 gallons. At an assumed valuation in the hands of the manufacturer at $6 per barrel, the resulting aggregate would be $111,000,000. (The returned census valuation of the malt-liquor product of the United States for 1880 was $101,088,-000.) The internal-revenue tax of $1 per barrel ($18,500,000), and an allowance of an equal sum to cover expenses and profits of distribution to the retailers, would further increase this original cost as above assumed to $148,000,000. If sold (retailed) to the consumer at double this sum, the final aggregate figures would be $296,000,000. For the year 1883 the value of the importations of ale, beer, and porter—duties included—was returned at $1,657,178, which to the ultimate consumer may be assumed to represent an expenditure of at least $3,000,000.

We have then, on the basis of the above figures and estimates, a present direct annual expenditure on the part of consumers in the United States of $175,823,000 for distilled spirits (domestic and imported) and of champagne, but exclusive of all still wines ; and of $299,000,000 for fermented liquors of domestic and foreign production ; or a total annual aggregate of $474,823,-000. This result is much less than the estimates that have been heretofore made, and which have obtained much credence on the part of the public ; and they are also less in comparison, as will be directly shown, than the estimates of the cost of similar consumption generally accepted as correct for Great Britain. The main element of uncertainty pertaining to all these calculations is in respect to the extent to which the original or first cost of the various liquors is enhanced in price on their way to

the ultimate consumers; and here, in the absence of much defi-
nite evidence, there is an opportunity for great latitude of
opinion. It is obvious that the price paid for drink varies
greatly according to the circumstances under which it is obtained; the man buying each glass from a public retailer necessarily paying much more per gallon than the one who takes it
from a cask or bottle at home;[1] and to accurately ascertain how
final consumption is apportioned in these respects in a nation
of 55,000,000 is clearly an impossibility. It will also be noted
that the above aggregate does not include any estimate of
the cost of the annual consumption of domestic or foreign
wines other than champagne.

But assuming $474,000,000 as the minimum annual cost to
the consumers of distilled and fermented liquors in the United
States at the present time, it will be interesting to compare
this amount with the returned value, according to the census of
1880, of the annual product of certain other leading commodities.
Thus, the returned valuation of cotton manufacturers for 1880
was $210,000,000; of woollen goods, $160,000,000; of boots and
shoes, $196,000,000; of agricultural implements, $68,000,000;
of men and women's clothing, $241,000,000; of iron and steel,
$296,000,000; and of lumber planed and sawed, $270,000,000.
The amount of expenditures for public schools in the whole
country, including building and all other expenditures, for 1880,
was also returned at $79,339,814.

This same subject has also attracted much attention of late
years in Great Britain; and the results of its investigation have
been presented in several elaborate papers to the Statistical
and other economic and scientific societies. The general conclu-

---

[1] Popular estimates of the cost of distilled and fermented liquors to consumers
which have obtained extensive circulation and acceptance fix the retail price of
the former at from $3.78 to $6 per gallon, and of the latter at from $16 to $20
per barrel, or from 50 to 67 cents per gallon.

One ingenious writer has given the following estimate of the number of
drinks represented by the present annual consumption of distilled spirits in the
United States: "Each gallon contains fifty average drinks; which multiplied by
the total number of gallons consumed for drinking purposes (assumed at 60,000,-
000 for 1883) would give 3,000,000,000 drinks; which would be at the rate of over
54 drinks per annum for each man, woman, and child of the present population,
estimated at 55,000,000."

sions which seem to be accepted as approximately accurate are: that the amount paid for the production and distribution of alcohol in its several forms of spirits, beer, and wines in Great Britain for the year 1880 was from £120,000,000 ($600,000,000) to £130,000,000 ($650,000,000), or a sum nearly double the whole land-rental of the United Kingdom. The actual cost of the production of the raw materials used in the aggregate manufacture of these several products has been estimated at about £25,000,000, or $125,000,000, and the original cost of the home products and imports (including the expense of manufacturing, but not that of retailing and distribution) at about £42,000,000 ($210,000,000). According to an estimate presented to the Statistical Society of London, April, 1882, by Mr. Stephen Bourne, the number of persons employed in producing the raw materials out of which the alcoholic products annually consumed in Great Britain are in turn manufactured must approximate 300,000 in number; and that nearly 600,000 people (workers) additional are employed in the subsequent and contingent manufacturing and dispensing processes; or a total of near 900,000 persons "whose occupation it is to provide the liquor consumed in the land." Mr. William Hoyle, an English investigator, who for many years has made this subject a specialty for discussion and investigation, and who publishes an annual report and estimates, in a recent communication to the London *Times* fixes the expenditure of the British people for the year 1883 on intoxicating liquors at $627,386,505, a decrease of $3,870,420 as compared with 1882. Accepting these conclusions respecting the annual direct expenditure of the British people for alcoholic liquors, the estimates above given of the present annual expenditure of the United States for like purposes would seem by comparison, as before stated, to be too small. But, on the other hand, it should be borne in mind that the present wholesale market-price of crude spirits in the United States, inclusive of the tax, is less than half that charged in Great Britain; and that the estimates of expenditure for the United States as above given do not include the cost of the consumption of domestic wines: so that, if allowance is made for these differences, the estimates for the two countries, as above given, will very closely approximate. But again, it is to be remembered that the population of the United States is at present almost one third larger than that of Great Britain. In the face of such antagonism of results, there would seem therefore but one thing that could be said in explanation ; and that is, that the latitude of opinion existing, and which, in the absence of authentic data, is fully permissible, of the extent to which the wholesale cost of distilled and fermented liquors is increased in the process of retail distribution, warrants, without any imputation of inaccuracy, a very great discrepancy of conclusion as to the aggregate final cost of spirit consumption.

III.

WE come next to a consideration of the most interesting and novel phase of this history; namely, the financial results and moral influences which have followed the attempt of the United States to obtain a large revenue through the imposition of high taxes on distilled spirits.

The first tax imposed by Congress after the outbreak of the war, namely, under the act of July 1, 1862, was 20 cents per proof-gallon, or at the rate of fully 100 per cent on the then cost of the article taxed. The revenue derived from the same for the fiscal year ending July 1, 1863, exclusive of the revenue derived from licenses for the manufacture, rectification, and sale of spirits,[2] was $3,229,941, indicating a production of 16,149,950 gallons, as compared with a production returned under the census of 1860, three years previous, of 90,000,000 gallons.

The tax of 20 cents continued in force until March 7, 1864, when the rate was advanced to 60 cents per gallon. The rev-

---

[1] *Princeton Review.*

[2] In addition to the tax directly imposed on the distilled spirit, the United States from the first imposed a number of other collateral taxes, i.e., license-fees, permits, etc., on the business of producing, refining, and vending of spirits, all of which, altho assessed and collected independently, are included under a general return of aggregate revenue from distilled spirits. Thus the total revenue returned as collected in any one year is always considerably greater than the receipts from the direct tax on the spirit itself. These annual aggregates since the first imposition of the tax have been as follows: 1863, $5,176,520; 1864, $30 329.149; 1865. $18,731,422; 1866, $33,268,171; 1867, $33,542.695; 1868, $18,655,630; 1869. $45,071,230; 1870, $55,606,094; 1871, $46,-281,848; 1872, $49,475,516; 1873. $52,099,371; 1874, $49,444,089; 1875, $52,-081,991; 1876, $56,426,000; 1877, $57,469,000; 1878. $50 420,815; 1879, $52,570,-284; 1880, $61,185,508; 1881, $67,153,974; 1882, $69,873,408; 1883, $74,368,775.

enue derived under these two rates for the fiscal year ending June 30, 1864, was $28,431,798, and the number of gallons returned as having been assessed was 85,295,391.

On the 1st of July, 1864, the tax on distilled spirits was further raised to $1.50 per proof-gallon, and by the same act it was further provided that the tax on and after February 1, 1865, should be $2 per gallon. When Congress reassembled, however, on the succeeding December, the time when the $2 rate was made to take effect was changed from the 1st of February, 1865, to the preceding 1st of January. The revenue which was collected under these two rates for the fiscal year ending June 30, 1865, was only $15,995,000. For the fiscal year ending June 30, 1866,—the first full year under the $2 tax,—the receipts were $29,198,578 (exclusive of $283,409 derived from spirits distilled from fruits), the assessment being on 14,599,000 gallons.

With these curious figures before us, let us next inquire somewhat more in detail into the course of events of which they are the exponents. From the very commencement of the war, until its issues became certain, and indeed for a considerable period thereafter, the attention of the Government was so engrossed with current military events, foreign relations, the operations of the Treasury in respect to the most complicated and gigantic system of finance and taxation that the world has ever known, and later with the problems of the reconstruction of the Union, that the efforts made to prevent, detect, and punish frauds in respect to the revenues were almost absolutely of no account. Indeed it may be further alleged with truth that the spirit and working of the revenue statutes were to a very great degree in the direction of the encouragement of fraud and speculation. And while there was also during all these times an immense amount of patriotism on the surface, it rarely with the producing and commercial part of the community struck in so deep as to prevent them from taking prompt advantage of any necessities or neglect of the Government, to benefit their individual and material interests. Thus, going back to the rates of taxation on domestic distilled spirits, it will be found that, after the imposition of the first tax of 20 cents per gallon in July, 1862, the rates were three times changed and largely advanced within the short space of ten months—namely, March, 1864, from 20 to 60 cents; July, 1864, from 60 cents to $1.50; and January, 1865, from $1.50 to $2 per gallon. There was, moreover, in each case—dating back to the imposition of the first tax—ample premonition to all interested that the tax would be imposed or largely advanced; and, after the enactment of the first tax, a feeling of almost absolute certainty, which experience afterwards confirmed, that Congress, under the influences to which it was subjected, would never make the advance applicable to stocks on hand. The first and general result of such legislation was to render the great business of distilling in all parts of the country almost altogether speculative and extremely irregular. A more special and immediate result of the first three and succeeding tax enactments was to cause an almost entire suspension of distilling, which was resumed again with great activity as soon as an advance in the rate of tax in each instance became probable. The stock of spirits which accumulated in the country under this course of procedure was without precedent; and as Congress, as already stated, refused to make the advance in taxation in any instance retroactive, it thereby virtually legislated for the benefit of the distillers and the speculators rather than for the Treasury and the country.

Under the first tax of 20 cents per gallon, imposed July 1, 1862, there was probably no very great fraud perpetrated. The idea of systematically cheating the Government was new; the persons concerned in the business of distilling did not fully know how to do it, and there was in addition an entire absence of that record and tradition of illicit practices in respect to matters of revenue that forms a part of the history and romance of almost every government of Europe, and entails an hereditary disposition to smuggle under the customs, to evade under the excise, and to socially ostracize every official charged with the execution of the laws and the detection of offenders. But there was nevertheless sufficient whiskey manufactured in anticipation of this low tax, or which evaded the tax after its enactment, to bring down the legitimate production of the country from ninety millions of gallons in 1860 to sixteen millions in 1862–3.

But early in the commencement of the new fiscal year, 1863–4, when it became evident that the great fiscal necessities of the Government would soon compel an increase of all taxes, and that distilled spirits would be one of the first subjects upon which the rate would be raised, the situation speedily altered; and with this anticipation all the distilleries of the country gradually got into full operation. The advance anticipated was made on the 7th of March, 1864, and was from 20 to 60 cents per gallon. The Internal Revenue Bureau assessed and collected the spirit-tax for that year upon 85,295,391 gallons. Of this great product—sixty-nine millions of gallons in excess of the product of the preceding year—at least seventy million gallons were manufactured prior to the 7th of March, and were released from Government control by the payment of the 20-cent tax only; and as after the 7th March, 1864, the market-price of the greater part of this increased product, which had not been allowed to pass into consumption, was advanced in accordance with the advance in the tax,—i.e., 40 cents per gallon,—it is clear that twenty-five millions of dollars at least were thus at once legislated into the pockets of the distillers and speculators.

Again, immediately after the imposition of the 60-cent rate in March, 1864, nearly all the distilleries once more suspended operation; the country was acknowledged to be overstocked with tax-paid whiskey, and the Government almost ceased to collect taxes upon its manufacture. In May, however, the project for a further increase in the rates began to be again agitated in Congress; and as soon as its realization became probable all the distilleries speedily resumed operations. How great at that time was the capacity of the loyal States for production, and how actively the distilleries temporarily worked under the stimulus of a prospective increase in the tax, may be inferred from the circumstance that in the month of June, 1864, the number of gallons distilled and on which the Government collected the 60-cent tax was 10,468,976, or at the rate of 125,000,000 gallons per annum; while the number of distilleries in the country, which according to the census of 1860 was 1138, or in the ratio of 27,540 persons to each distillery, had increased in 1864 to 2415, or in the ratio of 17,242 persons to each distillery; and how this increase in distilleries further continued will be hereafter noted.

On the 1st of July, 1864 (or of the succeeding month), the tax was again advanced from 60 cents to $1.50 per gallon; and during that month the entire product of the country of which the revenue officials could take cognizance was only 697,099 gallons. How great a " stock on hand," the result of manufacturing under the 20- and 60-cent rates of tax, was carried over the 1st of July and experienced the advance of 90 cents per gallon in market-price in consequence of the advance in the tax from 60 cents to $1.50, cannot be accurately known; but sixty millions of gallons would certainly be a low estimate; and on this amount the profit that accrued to private interests was at least $50,000,000. With the further advance in the tax on the succeeding 1st of January to $2, the operations above described were again repeated, with all the benefit derived from former experience, and with a very large extension of the sphere of participants in the resulting profits. What was the resulting profit from this last transaction was estimated, by those who had opportunities for forming an opinion, at from twenty to thirty million dollars.

In short, all the available evidence indicates that the profits realized by distillers, dealers, speculators, through Congressional legislation having reference to the taxation of distilled spirits from July 1, 1862, to January 1, 1865,—a period of two and a half years,—and exclusive of any gains accruing from evasions of taxes, and with every allowance for overestimates, must have approximated one hundred million dollars.

Such, then, is a brief but probably as exact a narration as it is possible to now give of what may be regarded as the first of a long series of subsequent and successful operations in the United States which have had for their object the spoliation of the general public for the benefit of the comparatively few through legislative enactments or the abuse of corporate privileges, and which was almost unnoticed at the time of its occurrence by reason of the far greater importance of other and contemporaneous events. The transactions under consideration, nevertheless, mark an era in the history of the United States almost as important as the war itself; for before that time frauds, in this country, against the Government, and trafficking in the interests of the community, were always comparatively small, and were never systematized on a large scale. The moral sense of the community previous to that time seems to have been also more impressible and less inclined to tolerate and overlook the prostitution of influence and position on the part of men prominent in public office or trusts for the sake of private gain. It was, moreover, the first occasion when the outside influences—subsequently termed the "lobby"—gathered round the halls of Congress in notable numbers, and with acknowledged influence and organization, for the purpose of influencing legislation in behalf of private and selfish interests. It was the opening of the flood-gates for an issue of corruption which has since then almost seemed to pervade the whole land, and which the press and the pulpit have not been able to roll back. Since then, also, nothing in this direction has been too audacious to venture, and there has been little in the way of attempt which the public has not tolerated, condoned, or speedily forgotten, more especially if the attempt has been accompanied by success.

One question, however, which naturally suggests itself at this point is, " What explanation can be given of the action of Congress in relation to this whole matter?" "How happened it that with the lesson of experience repeatedly before it and made a subject of discussion, Congress in successive instances, and always, refused to make the advanced rates on distilled spirits, enacted solely on account of the public necessity for greater revenues, applicable to stocks on hand, the greater part of which it was acknowledged had been manufactured solely for the purpose of profiting by the great advance in price certain to result from the advance in the tax?"

In reply it is to be said that it is not easy to satisfactorily answer these questions. It is certainly impossible to charge wholesale corruption or improper motives against the men in the two branches of Congress *who in the main* controlled and led the fiscal legislation of this period. Thus among those prominent in favoring exemption were Senators Fessenden, of Maine, and Trumbull, of Illinois—men against whom the voice of scandal never was and never could be raised; while on the other side were Mr. John Sherman, of the Senate, and Elihu Washburn, of the House. The arguments brought forward in opposition to making the whiskey taxes retroactive were mainly that it was contrary to sound policy for the Government, after having assessed and collected the taxes on an article of manufacture and released it for sale or use, to again reassess the same property before it had been subjected to use; and also that it would be a matter of no little difficulty and expense for the revenue officials to find and assess a product of spirits after it had once become an article of commerce and passed from the supervision and custody of the Government. On the other hand, it was urged in reply that it was the custom of the Government, Federal and State, to tax the same articles, while awaiting consumption and use, at successive periods—as stocks on hand, animals, and agencies of production and transportation; and that much of the whiskey which it was proposed to subject to the surcharge was held in warehouses in quantity (as was afterwards proved to be the fact), and so was not difficult of ascertainment and assessment.

In the case of the first two acts of legislation by which the tax was originally imposed and then advanced, there was probably not much speculation or participation of interest on the part of members of Congress and revenue officials. But in the case of the last two acts, speculation and participation in the results of legislation were very extensive. The answer to a question put by the writer, some twelve years subsequent to the period of the events related, to a somewhat prominent member of Congress during the war, " To what extent his associates participated in the speculation contingent upon their legislation respecting the whiskey tax ?" substantially was," that his personal and certain knowledge of such transactions was very limited, but that he inferred, from the interest displayed by members in the current market rates and prices of highwines, the participation to have been very extensive." A personal interest was confessed in a hundred barrels, purchased under the 60-cent tax and carried until disposed of under the $2 tax ; and regret was also expressed that, inasmuch as the legislation in question was inevitable, he had not been bolder and profited more largely by his opportunities. From conferences with persons who were formerly and at the time officially employed under the internal revenue, and spoke from personal knowledge, the writer also feels warranted in asserting that there was not a revenue district in the loyal States in which distilled spirits were manufactured or largely dealt in at wholesale, in which the officials of the revenue, collectors, assessors, inspectors, gaugers, clerks, and detectives, were not to a greater or less extent engaged in speculating in whiskey, and consequently personally interested in favor of Congressional legislation looking to an advancement of the rates; and that the transactions in question were not only no secret, but were regarded as perfectly legitimate. And as a single illustration of the profits accruing to private parties and in particular instances, a case made known to the Revenue Commissioners may be referred to, in which one firm manufactured or received under contract, for a period of several weeks prior to the assessment of the $1.50 tax, an average quantity of thirty thousand gallons of proof-spirits per day: the major part of which was held and sold after the advance in the tax in January, 1865, to $2 per gallon.

After the establishment of the $2 rate on the 1st of January, 1865, there was again a period of inactivity on the part of those interested in the manufacture of distilled spirits. The stocks on hand, manufactured in anticipation of the advances in rates, were very large, and, the markets being oversupplied, there was little legitimate inducement for activity on the part of distillers. The profits realized, or made prospectively certain, had been, moreover, enormous, and no further advance in the rate of tax could be anticipated. Under such circumstances there was an apparent disposition on the part of manufacturers and speculators to wait and see what developments in legislation and business would follow the now certain termination of the war.

It was just at this period that the writer was appointed chairman of the "Revenue Commission," created by Congress under an act of March 5, 1865, for the purpose of inquiring into the best methods " of raising by taxation such revenue as may be necessary in order to supply the wants of the Government," and also concerning " the sources from which such revenue should be drawn ;" and without any previous adequate preparation, and without any fund of experience available for guidance, other than what could be personally collected under the large powers

for investigation granted to the Commission, he entered upon his
duties. The task at the outset seemed as hopeless as to attempt
to tunnel a mountain with nothing but a crowbar; and one of
the chief sources of embarrassment was to determine, from the
immense number of points of detail, how and where to begin;
for the United States revenue system at this time actually
touched directly every art, trade, profession, and occupation of
the country, and drew from them, and largely by direct taxation, in a single year (1865), the enormous sum of $559,000,000.
After considerable deliberation it was determined to commence
the investigations with that one article or department of this
great tax system which furnished the greatest specific revenue,
which proved to be "distilled spirits." The theory which he
entertained at the outset respecting the situation was the common and popular one, so far as there was any such, namely, that
distilled spirits was a product upon which it was expedient to
impose the heaviest burden of taxation; that if the annual consumption of the country averaged ninety million gallons, as it
probably did before the war, a tax of $2 per gallon would suffice
to pay all the burden of interest on the immense public debt, and
provide for its ultimate extinguishment through a sinking fund;
and finally, that if the high tax resulted in restricting consumption, the gain to temperance and morality would far more than
counterbalance any reduction of revenue. The method of
investigation adopted was as follows: A typical distillery
was *first* visited, and a study made of its machinery and system of operations, including the assessment and collection
of taxes; *second*, the leading distillers of the country were
brought to a conference, and their views and wishes obtained,
and in conjunction a large amount of testimony from rectifiers,
wholesale and retail dealers, was also taken: *third*, the leading
officials of the Internal Revenue Office—assessors, collectors, inspectors, and detectives—were called together at Washington,
and their opinions and experiences noted. Finally, books were
consulted: and in this particular the situation in the United
States was like that of the snakes in Ireland—there were none;
while, apart from the British blue-books, the literature of all
other countries in respect to the taxation of spirits was exceedingly meagre. The result of a long and careful inquiry, how-

20

ever, abundantly satisfied the writer that all his preconceived ideas on the subject, and which were also very generally the ideas of Congress and the great body of the people, were entirely erroneous; that under the influence of a high tax and a resulting high cost the production and consumption of spirits, exclusive of the demand for drink, was greatly restricted; and that under the conditions of a sparse population scattered over a vast extent of territory, and a form of government that would not admit of the use of a despotic, inquisitorial, and numerous police, the attempt to collect a tax of a thousand per cent on the first cost of any article was utterly impracticable. In a report made to Congress in January, 1866, it was accordingly recommended that the $2 tax be abandoned and a tax of 50 cents per proof-gallon, conjointly with a license system for rectifiers and dealers, be adopted as the rate most likely to be productive of revenue and most efficient for the prevention of illicit distillation and other revenue evasions.

The report, altho attracting much attention by reason of the singular experiences of the preceding four years which it detailed, obtained no favor in respect to its recommendation of tax abatement; only two members of Congress of any prominence, namely, General Garfield and Hon. W. B. Allison, of Iowa, both then members of the House and of its Committee of Ways and Means, cordially accepting its conclusions. The result was no legislation, and a new chapter of experience; for when it became certain that the opportunity for realizing profits from manufacturing in anticipation of an increase in the tax had come to an end by the prospective maintenance of rate, the opportunity for profit offered by the imperfections of the law was at once eagerly embraced and improved. Thus, testimony subsequently brought to light repeated instances where individual distillers manufactured, conveyed to market, and fraudulently sold spirits, varying in quantities from 20,000 to 30,000 gallons and upward, without a suspicion on the part of local officials that the business was not in all respects conducted legally and honestly. It was sworn to before the writer that the determination of the strength of spirits, preparatory to assessment, was often made by mere physical inspection or taste, and that the use of instruments (for which no uniform

standard was provided) was regarded as something wholly unnecessary. It was also not unfrequently the case that barrels
were inspected and branded some days in advance of their
being filled, and their future regulation—filling and removal—
left entirely with the manufacturer. Distillers and their workmen were sometimes constituted inspectors of their own product; and in one instance an assessor was appointed who did
not possess sufficient intelligence to understand and correctly
use either a gauging-rod or an hydrometer. Thus it was at
the commencement of the period of high taxation; but subsequently, when the administration of the laws became somewhat
more intelligent and vigorous, and some degree of concealment
to the projectors of fraud became necessary, the expedients
successfully adopted for the evasion of the tax were in the
highest degree characteristic of the people. One of the most
fertile of these was made available through a provision of law
which allowed spirits to be made and stored in bond, or exported in bond, without prepayment of the taxes. Thus, for
example, spirits deposited in bond were, through the connivance
and corruption of ill-paid officials acting as guardians, secretly
withdrawn from bond, the barrels filled with water or very weak
spirits, and subsequently exported. On receipt of a "landing
certificate," obtained through a consul of an inferior grade at
some foreign port, the bonds given by the manufacturer for the
payment of the taxes were cancelled, and the profits derived
from the sale of the untaxed spirits in the domestic market, at
the tax-paid rate, were divided among all concerned. Warehouses from which spirits deposited in bond had been fraudulently withdrawn were also frequently burned, and the bonds
cancelled on evidence of loss, wholly fraudulent, but so strongly
supported by perjury as to be difficult of disproof. Large
losses were also sustained by the Government by the acceptance, as the basis of large transactions, of bonds which subsequent investigations, contingent on the exposure of more
open frauds, showed were purposely made and given by persons
of no responsibility, who in some instances by prearrangement
agreed to accept the risk of persecution and trial, with an
almost certainty of non-conviction by a jury, for a stipulated
compensation or a share in the anticipated fraudulent profits.

Congress enacted that in cases where spirits were sold for less than $2 per proof-gallon, the purchaser must show that the tax on the same had been paid. The immediate response to this legislation was a decline in the market price of spirits. For the best rectifying houses, alcohol distillers, and druggists, who had heretofore maintained themselves by buying their supplies (*i. e.* of illicit product) on the open market, asking no questions, now found that they must evade the law to meet competition, or give up their business; and very many chose the latter alternative. The methods of evasion adopted were numerous and simple. In some instances fictitious bills were given by the sellers at the legal valuation; others sold at the legitimate price and then made the purchaser a present of other whiskey sufficient to reduce the cost of the purchase to the market price. The officials, in many cases, aided in the violation of the law. Thus the statute forbade the sale of confiscated spirits at less than the rate of tax ($2) per gallon; and if not sold for so much, the liquor was to be destroyed; yet, at different sales by U. S. marshals, it was bid off at $2 and the purchaser charged with less than the actual number of gallons, in order to reduce the cost to the market price of illicit product. Then this law having proved a failure the Internal Revenue Department issued a stringent order that a Government receipt for the tax should accompany all sales in quantity; but immediately tax receipts for tax-paid spirits became abundant, and sold as freely in the market as the whiskey itself. Congress also attempted to check an important class of frauds through the removal of spirits from distilleries in barrels without payment of the tax, with the connivance of assessors and storekeepers, by the appointment of an inspector for each distillery, and requiring him to be paid by the distiller. But this made him in fact a creature of the distiller; and the inspector joining hands with the officials he was appointed to watch, the frauds soon became more gigantic than ever. Secret pipes, connected with the "worm tanks" or receiving cisterns, conveyed the spirits underground to rectifying establishments, often separated by considerable distance (and in the cities by intervening buildings) from the distillery. Brands upon barrels certifying to inspection and tax-payment were largely forged, to authorize removals; and the branding at that time being merely through the use of stencil plates, this forgery was very difficult of detection. The permission to remove spirits from the distillery to a bonded warehouse, in anticipation of the payment of the tax upon the same, was also most prolific of fraud. Thus a permit would be given to transport, say one thousand barrels, naming the destination. In place of one lot ten might be started at different times and by different routes. Should any lot be seized on the route, the permit would be offered and the spirits released. One lot would go on to warehouse, the remaining nine find their way into market with the taxes unpaid. The next steps would be to take the one lot that had found its way to the warehouse, out of the warehouse, under bonds for redistillation, or for a change of package; keep it out a few days, take out one half the spirit, and return it, when a pliant storekeeper would give the necessary certificates showing its return, and the bonds given for its removal would be cancelled. If the operators were determined, as they not unfrequently were, to steal from the Government to the last penny, the barrels would be returned filled only with water. Under such circumstances the warehouse would be speedily burned, with total loss of contents; and it was very remarkable how often, in severe thunder-storms, the warehouses for distilled spirits seemed to become the central point in a large district for the attraction of the electric fluid. In one instance where a rectifying establishment, alcohol distillery, and Government bonded warehouse—all in the same building—were seized and the transactions of the firm investigated, the bank-book of the storekeeper in charge, whose legitimate salary was $5 per day, was found to indicate transactions that could only have been expected of millionaire merchants; while among the papers of the firm was a letter from an agent abroad urging further speedy shipments of spirits (water?) in bond, and containing the gratifying announcement that the consul had assured him that he " would merely count the barrels exported, and not examine their contents." In New York City, landing consular certificates of spirits exported were made merchandise, and obtained without difficulty; and there can be but little doubt that the " whiskey-ring," in some instances, in order to have willing tools in foreign ports, actually had consuls appointed, and their appointments confirmed by the Senate.

As one further curious result and feature of this state of things during the last year of the continuance of the $2 tax, the Committee on Retrenchment of the House of Representatives reported in March, 1868, that the control of the business of rectifying spirits, distillation of alcohol, and also the wholesale dealing in spirits, had passed, to a very great extent, into the hands of the Jews; and that hardly any honest citizen was engaged in any of these departments of the business. "For three years," continues this same report, "efforts have been made to collect this tax (*i. e.* of $2); each year the frauds have increased, but not the revenue. The operators throughout have possessed more ability than Congress, more shrewdness than the Revenue Department. No sooner would a regulation of the department or an act of Congress be passed than means would be devised to evade it. The human intellect seems far more inventive, and skill far more effective, when to incentive to gain is added the chance of providing security against detection and punishment." "Men rush into schemes [for defrauding the Government under the spirit tax of $2] with the same zeal that enthusiasts do to new gold fields."

It is to be also noted that the number of licensed distilleries, which in 1864 was 2,415, or in the ratio of one to every 17,242 persons, had increased in 1868 to 4,721, or in the ratio of one to every 8,058 of the population. In short, the tax of $2 (amounting to 1,000 per cent. advance on the average cost of manufacture) and the enormous profits contingent upon the evasion of the law, coupled with the abundant opportunity which the law, through its imperfections and the vast territorial area of the country, offered for evasion, created a temptation which it seemed impossible for human nature as ordinarily constituted to resist; and the longer the tax remained at a high figure, the less became the revenue and the greater the corruption. Thus during the year 1866–7 the revenue directly collected in the United States from spirits distilled from other materials than fruits was $29,198,000, and in 1857 $28,-296,000, indicating an annual product respectively of 14,599,000 and 14,148,000 gallons. But during the succeeding year, 1868, with no apparent reason for any diminution in the national production and consumption of spirits, and with no increase,

but rather a diminution, in the volume of imported spirits, the
total direct revenue from the same source was but $13,419,092,
indicating a production of only 6,709,546 gallons; proof-spirits
at the same time being openly sold in the market, and even
quoted in price-currents, at from five to ten cents less per gallon
than the amount of the tax and the average cost of manufacture. We have also in these figures the materials for approximately estimating the measure and strength of the temptation
to evade the law, and the amount of profit that must have
accrued in the single year 1868 from the results of such evasion.
For as the consumption of distilled spirits in the country during
that year was probably not less than 50,000,000 gallons, and as
out of this the Government collected a tax upon less than
7,000,000, the sale of the difference at the current market-rates
of the year, less the average cost of production (even if estimated as high as 30 cents), must have returned to the credit
of corruption a sum approximating $80,000,000. To this must
be added a further unknown but undoubted loss of revenue,
growing out of the circumstance that the influence of successful fraud in the matter of spirits seemed to infect and
demoralize almost every other department of the internal
revenue.

But notwithstanding all these facts were for three years annually reported upon, and in detail, by officials of the Treasury,
and were also generally recognized and commented on by the
press, it was with the greatest difficulty that Congress could
be induced to take any action looking to remedies by the enactment of some perfect laws, by providing for more efficient
administration, or for diminishing the temptations to fraud by
diminishing the tax; and it was not until the revenue from distilled spirits bade fare to disappear altogether, and the popular
manifestations of discontent became very apparent, that any
thing really was accomplished ; a report from the Committee
of Ways and Means of the House of Representatives, in favor
of a new law and a reduction of the tax, having been actually
prevented in 1867, and action delayed thereby a whole year, by
an appeal of a leading member of the Committee—who has
since posed as a great statesman—for postponement of action,
on the ground that it would be derogatory to the honor of a

great nation to confess, "after having put down a great rebellion, that it could not collect a tax of $2 per gallon on
whiskey." There may have been instances in history where
one single speech of an individual has led a nation into war and
into consequent great losses and expenditures, but there probably never was a speech in reference to the civil polity of a
government which can be proved to have been as expensive as
the silly utterances above quoted. For reform being thus delayed, the *direct* revenues from *all* distilled spirits fell off in the
fiscal and succeeding year, 1868, to the extent of $14,874,000 as
compared with the receipts from the same sources for the previous year, 1867, or from $29,164,000 to $14,290,000; while on
the other hand, when by the act of July, 1868, the direct tax
was reduced to 50 cents per proof-gallon, the receipts for the
ensuing and incomplete fiscal year increased at once to the
extent of nearly $20,000,000, or from $14,290,000 in 1868 to
$33,738,000 in 1869; or, including all taxes on the manufacture
and sale of distilled spirits, licenses, etc., from $18,655,000 in
1858, to $45,071,000 in 1869. And as there is no question that
this advance might have been realized through legislation in
the previous year but for the influence of the speech of the
"statesman" in retarding action, the direct cost of his words
may be fairly estimated at over twenty-six millions of dollars,
to say nothing of indirect losses to the Treasury contingent
on the continuance for another year of a system which magni-
fied temptations and made frauds easy.

It is to be here stated that in preparing the law of July,
1868, by which the direct tax was reduced from $2 to 50 cents
per gallon, the intent of the writer, which was realized, was to
make the total aggregate tax 65 cents per gallon, but to impose
only 50 cents as a maximum tax on the spirit as an article
of manufacture, and to distribute the balance (15 cents) in the
way of licenses, fees, etc., at points intermediate between the
manufacture of the spirits and their final sale to consumers,
but so remote from and so disconnected with the process
of manufacture as to render collusion between producers and
distributors with a view to gain by evading the law almost
wholly impracticable. Another leading object was to fix the
direct tax at such a sum as would diminish the temptation to

fraud to the greatest possible extent consistent with the procurement of such an amount of revenue as was demanded by the necessities of the Government. The rate of 50 cents per proof-gallon, recommended by the writer, who was then "Special Commissioner of the Revenue," and subsequently adopted by Congress, was fixed upon, because investigations showed that on the average the product of illicit distillation costs through deficient returns, the necessary bribery of attendants and the expense of secret and unusual methods of storage and transportation, from two to three times as much as the product of legitimate or legal distillation. So that, assuming the average cost of spirits at that time in the United States to have been 20 cents per gallon, the product of the illicit distiller under the most favorable circumstances would cost from 40 to 60 cents, leaving but 10 cents per gallon as the maximum profit to be realized from fraud under the most favorable conditions—an amount not sufficient to offset the possibility of severe penalties of fine, imprisonment, and confiscation of property, which were made essential features of the new enactment. Another feature of the new laws, never before attempted, was a requirement that the original taxes on the spirit, as well as the license taxes on its subsequent manipulation and sale by rectifiers and wholesale dealers, should be paid by means of various stamps affixed to the packages containing the spirits,—which stamps, through their numbers, devices, and record, established the identity of the spirits wherever found, and their relations to the various tax requirements. This system, originally proposed and worked out by the writer, was at first violently opposed as wholly impracticable ; but was finally adopted, and, after some modifications suggested by experience, has proved in the highest degree practicable and successful. A similar stamp system for collecting the internal-revenue taxes on fermented liquors and smoking tobacco was also, on the recommendation of the writer, adopted by Congress, and has also proved successful.

In answer now to a question which those who have followed this narrative may naturally put, "What was the sequel to this radical change in this department of the revenue laws of the United States as it existed in 1868?" it may be said, without the possibility of challenge or contradiction, that in the whole

history of political economy, finance, and jurisprudence there
never was a result that so completely demonstrated the value of
careful scientific investigation in connection with legislation.
Illicit distillation practically ceased the very hour the new law
came into operation; and evasions of the law were confined to
occasional false returns, and a re-use, on a very limited scale, of
the stamps with which the tax was for the first time made payable by purchase and cancellation. Industry and the arts experienced a large measure of benefit from the reduction in the
cost of spirits, more especially in the form of alcohol; while the
Government collected during the second year of the continuance
of the new rate and system, with comparatively little friction,
three dollars for every one that was obtained during the last
year of the two-dollar tax.

OUR EXPERIENCE IN TAXING DISTILLED SPIRITS.

(This article is an original contribution to this series.)

IV.

IT is essential to the completeness of this history, and before proceeding further in the course of its direct narration, to specially notice, at this point, another extremely interesting phase of the attempt of the Government of the United States to assess and collect, during the years 1865–68, an extraordinary high tax on domestic distilled spirits.

As soon as it became evident that neither laws bristling with pains, penalties, and forfeitures, nor increased vigilance on the part of their administrators, would suffice to overcome the temptation created by, and ensure the collection of, the tax of $2 per proof-gallon, the American mind, with its fertility of resources, at once began to inquire if it was not possible to oppose and offset the exercise of great mental ingenuity for the furtherance of fraud with the product of equal ingenuity for the furtherance of honesty ; or, in other words, if it was not practicable to assess and collect the spirit taxes through mechanical devices that would neither lie, steal, nor be amenable to temptation to do other than what it was their legitimate function to do, and thus eliminate completely, or in a great degree, the element of moral responsibility from the office of government inspector. And this question had been hardly suggested before it began to be answered by the submission to the Government (Treasury Department) of such a variety and number of machines and devices for solving the involved problem, that the Commission appointed to examine into the matter, and of which the late Prof. Henry, of the Smithsonian Institution, was Chairman, characterized the exhibit and contributions " as truly astonishing," and as strikingly illustrative " of the prevalence in this country of the inventive faculty." [1]

---

[1] It is not the intent of the writer, however, to here convey the impression that the idea of attempting to collect the spirit tax through mechanical methods was altogether

Most of these inventions or devices were in the nature of "meters," designed to be attached to the "worm," or discharge pipe, of the still, and with such provisions of mechanism as to register automatically, and with security against unlawful interference, not only the quantity of liquid composed of alcohol and water that passes from the "worm," but also afford the data for determining the amount of proof-spirits (the basis for assessment) contained in the compound. The mechanical difficulties involved in the construction of such a piece of mechanism, or "meter," as will perform all the duties required of it, are exceedingly great, and, as experience so frequently proved, can only be approximately overcome under any circumstances. Thus, to illustrate, it may be stated that the quantity of spirits contained in a mixture of alcohol and water can only be determined by the less specific gravity of the compound as compared with pure water ; but which mixture, however, is not the same as the average specific gravity of the two liquids composing it, inasmuch as there is a shrinking of bulk when alcohol and water are mingled. " A quart of alcohol and a quart of water when mixed form a compound of less volume than the sum of the two ; besides which the specific gravity of the compound is largely affected by heat as well as by the quantity of spirits it contains. Hence for ascertaining the quantity of alcohol in a given amount of the mixture, recourse must be had to tables constructed by actual experiment, in which known quantities of alcohol are mixed with water and the specific gravity taken at different temperatures. From these tables the quantity of spirits in a given amount of the mixture is determined by inspection, when the specific gravity and temperature at which it is taken are known." The essential elements of a perfect spirit-meter are therefore as follows : " It must furnish automatically a registration of the data for determining the quan-

original with American inventors ; for the problem in question had for many years previous occupied the attention of the legislators and mechanicians of Europe, and had resulted in the practical employment, to some extent, of mechanical devices in both Austria and Prussia. But at the same time it is probably true that American inventors, at the time they interested themselves in the matter, had, as a general thing, no knowledge of any previous European experience in the same direction, and also (as it appeared from the examination of the best European results by the Commission) that in a very brief time they not only covered all the ground previously passed over by foreign inventors, but attained a much higher degree of successful achievement than had heretofore been accomplished.

tity, the specific gravity, and the temperature of the liquid which passes through it, or give the quantity and at the same time reserve samples, consisting of precise aliquot parts of the whole, for subsequent test with the hydrometer. In addition to all this, the construction of the meter must be such as not to render it liable to derangement by the ordinary operations or accidents of the distillery, or to be tampered with for the purpose of fraud."

Notwithstanding these inherent difficulties of the mechanical problem in question, a very large number of most ingenious pieces of mechanism, in the nature of meters, were, as already stated, offered to the Government, and for each of which a high claim for excellence or usefulness was preferred; the incentive to these inventions having been the prospect that in case of the acceptance of any one of them by the authorities, a large profit would result to the inventor from the manufacture of the great number of machines that would be required, and the royalty or compensation that would be given for their use. And Congress, in order to determine whether any of them were certain or likely to accomplish the result desired, authorized, in 1868, the appointment of a Commission of scientific men and mechanical experts, and the fitting up of a working distillery near Washington in order to thoroughly test the whole matter.

It is not the province of this article to either enumerate or attempt to describe in detail the construction of the various contrivances examined or tested by this Commission; but those interested will find all the information desired in a report submitted to the 40th Congress, at its 2d session. (See Executive Document, House of Representatives, No. 214, 1868.) It is sufficient to here say that the Commission reported that " none of the meters offered fulfils all the conditions deemed necessary for a perfect meter, particularly in regard to the quantity of proof-spirits dependent upon temperature"; and further, and speaking generally, " that no single apparatus or contrivance for protecting distillation against fraud is sufficient; although by the use of a meter and other appliances frauds may be rendered more difficult, and their detection more certain." It was, however, agreed that several of the meters submitted to them possessed a high degree of excellence and usefulness, and that one in particular so nearly fulfilled the requirements of such an instrument as to warrant a recommendation of its use on the part of the Government. This was the invention of the late Mr. Isaac P. Tice, a man who for ingenuity is entitled to rank among the most remarkable of American mechanics; and who had previously won distinction by the invention of a machine for cutting mouldings on irregular curved surfaces—as, for example, a stair-rail,—and during the war period, when cotton became scarce and most expensive, for the manufacture and extensive introduction of " string " or " twine " composed of paper. Mr. Tice was in fact the pioneer in the United States, in proposing to collect the tax on distilled spirits by mechanical methods; and a hundred sets of his meter, which was the first that was ready for practical use, were ordered by the Treasury Department, after practical testing, in 1867, or a year before the final report of the Government Commission and their obligatory use in all distilleries.

In addition to constructions in the nature of " meters," many other very curious devices, all having in view the prevention or restriction of frauds in the collection of the taxes upon spirits, were brought to the attention of the Commission. One fruitful source of fraud was the great difficulty of identifying any particular lot of spirits after it had passed out the distillery or warehouse, owing to the facility with which the official brands or marks of the inspectors could be removed or altered; spirits incapable of identification on seizure as being of illicit origin, being safe from forfeiture. To remedy this one inventor proposed the obligatory use of a peculiar barrel-head, which should be issued by the Government the same as stamps, and the peculiarity of which consisted in forming raised surfaces by turning concentric grooves in the head of the barrel, and on which surfaces the marks or brands required by law, and indicating inspection, were to be stamped. It was claimed that such branding could not be removed or altered without so cutting or defacing these raised surfaces, that the illegal re-use of a barrel with the prescribed head would be at once evident; and that every barrel, once marked or branded with the proper marks and numbers on such surfaces, would always carry with it its own history and identification. Other inventions related to the use of receipts and coupons for tracing and identifying the track of each barrel of spirits on the way from the distiller to the consumer; to safes for enclosing the meters when attached to the stills; to novel forms of hydrometers and other distillery adjuncts and appliances. Tice's meter continued to be used by the Government as an aid for the collection of the spirit tax for a period of about four years. There was always, however, and from the very first, an opposition to it on the part of the distillers; in the main, undoubtedly, for the reason that it rendered fraud more difficult than under the old methods of supervision, and partly because of its expense (first cost, erection, and supervision), which the Government made chargeable upon the distiller. With the reduction of the tax from $2 to 50 cents per proof-gallon in 1868, and the conclusive evidence subsequently afforded that the incentives to fraud had thereby been greatly decreased, and the necessity of a mechanical safeguard diminished, its employment was felt to be less necessary, and in 1871, by order of the Department, and in compliance with the wishes of the distillers, its obligatory use in distilling was discontinued; and from that time no meters of any kind have been in use in American distilleries.

The specific tax on distilled spirits of 50 cents per proof-gallon remained in force from July 1868 to August 1872, a period of a little more than four years. During this period the tax was assessed and collected on an average production of 67,175,822 proof-gallons per annum, yielding an average annual revenue of $33,563,161, and indicating an average annual consumption for all purposes of the country of about 1.65 proof-gallons per capita. For the period of four years immediately preceding the fiscal year 1868-9, under a tax of $2.00 per proof-gallon for three years, and $1.50 and $2.00 for one year (1865), the tax was assessed and collected on an average annual production of only 8,603,815 proof-gallons per annum, yielding an average annual revenue of $21,727,000, and indicating an average annual consumption of only about 0.25 proof-gallon per capita.

But, notwithstanding these satisfactory results, the law authorizing the reduction of the tax from $2.00 to 50 cents per proof-gallon had hardly become operative, when agitation commenced for its repeal or modification. Speculators had the idea that the old scheme of increasing the tax after a little lapse of time, without making the increase applicable to stocks on hand, was, with its gainful prospects, again within the range of possibilities. The distillers, as was natural, chafed at being made subject to new restrictions; while very many extreme advocates of temperance, untaught by, and caring nothing for, the record of recent experience, were inclined to regard the new and comparatively low tax as impolitic and in the light of the removal of a barrier against the spread of intemperance. Pending the continuance of the low tax, the Administration of the National Government also changed. Gen. Grant succeeded to the Presidency in 1869, and with that singular infelicity which characterized so many of his civil appointments, he selected in the first instance, for the head of the Internal-Revenue Bureau, a Western politician, with a large preponderance of the demagogue element in his composition; and after a service of about two years, replaced him with a former general of cavalry. It is almost needless to say that under the administration of these two appointees, the management of politics and patronage was the matter of prime consideration, and that neither of them evinced any interest in, or any knowledge of any economic principles or experiences. At the same time the new Administration, carrying out the principles of what was then (and even now) claimed to be "the best civil service in the world," removed for political considerations nearly all the other Internal-Revenue officials who had been appointed or continued in office by the previous President (Andrew Johnson), and replaced them for the most part with men having little or no acquaintance with the details of the revenue system; an experiment which cost the country nearly nine millions of dollars in a single year in the one department of distilled spirits; for to this extent, and mainly from this cause,[1] the revenues from this source declined during the year 1870–71; recovering three and a quarter millions in the succeeding year (1871–72), as the new officials became more conversant with their duties. The exceptional office of "Special Commissioner of the Revenue," which had

[1] Almost conclusive evidence of the truth of this assertion is to be found in the circumstance that, without any change in the fiscal or industrial condition of the country, or in the rate of tax, or law of administration during the year in question, the falling off of revenue above noted, occurred mainly in the single item of the "gallon tax" on the spirit product, which legitimately could only have occurred through decreased production ; while the revenues received from the sales of wholesale and retail dealers in spirits during the same year, collected under a different system of administrative inspection, in place of showing a corresponding decrease, actually increased ; a result that could only have been attained through an increased popular consumption.

expired by limitation of law, having been also discontinued by
Congress in accordance with the desire of the then Secretary of
the Treasury, and there being in consequence no officer whose
duty it was to *specially* report on the working of the revenue
system, all the circumstances for again effecting a change in
the rate of tax on distilled spirits were thus made favorable;
and this change, Congress in June, 1872, decided to make, by
advancing the direct tax from 50 to 70 cents per proof-gallon;
spirits on hand being again excepted. The argument which
carried weight, and was mainly instrumental in inducing action
by Congress, was exceedingly specious (apparently fair), and
involved so many points of economic interest, that any narrative
of the events under consideration would be incomplete that failed
to exhibit it with somewhat of detail.

Thus, when the proposition was first made to reduce the tax
from $2 to 50 cents per proof-gallon, the object was not to relieve
the manufacture of distilled spirits from any burden, for it was
generally agreed that it was desirable to collect as much revenue
as possible from this branch of production or business; but
wholly with a view of putting a stop to an acknowledged wide-
spread system of fraud, and of enabling the Government to
collect from spirits a reliable and legitimate revenue. And accordingly in advocating the reduction of the gallon tax to 50
cents, the writer, as has been before stated (see preceding article),
proposed, as an essential feature of this scheme of revenue reform
to compensate in part for such reduction, by imposing certain new
and supplementary taxes on the spirit product, at points so separate from the immediate results of manufacture—namely: measure-
ment, storage, and local transportation—as to prevent the collusion of separate interests, or the employment of any common
methods or agencies for the purpose of tax evasions; care being
at the same time taken to avoid fixing such supplementary taxes
at rates so high, as to create any new and undue temptations for
fraudulent practices. And with this intent, there was incorporated with the act reducing the gallon tax to 50 cents, the following other taxes which had not previously formed a part of the
(spirit) revenue system:

FIRST, a so-called "*capacity-tax*," or tax on each distillery,
proportioned to its capacity for spirit-production as determined

by a Government survey. Thus, on all distilleries having an aggregate capacity for mashing or fermenting 20 bushels of grain, or less, or 60 gallons of molasses, or less, in 24 hours, the capacity-tax per day was fixed at $2, and on distilleries of greater capacity, an addition of $2 per day was levied for every 20 bushels of grain, or 60 gallons of molasses, increased capacity. It was assumed, moreover, that every distillery worked continuously, unless a Government permit or certificate authorizing and defining its suspension could be exhibited. SECOND, a special annual tax was imposed on all distillers, proportioned to their aggregate annual production; distillers producing 100 barrels, or less, per annum paying $400, while for those distilling in excess of this quantity, $4 additional was charged for every barrel of product over 100 barrels. Each distiller, moreover, was compelled to reimburse to the Government all the expenses incurred by it for compensation to gaugers and store-keepers who were detailed to his establishment, and in this way an inducement in the shape of diminished expense was offered to every distiller to conduct his establishment in such a manner as to require the minimum of employment of governmental officials. The tax per gallon, therefore, although nominally but 50 cents, was in reality much greater, and in fact finally approximated to, if it did not fully equal, the sum of 75 cents.[1] How fully, furthermore, experience vindicated the correctness of the theory which prompted the idea of these supplementary taxes is shown by the fact, that the revenues of the so-called "capacity" and "barrel" taxes for the year 1871–2, the last full year of the 50-cent rate, were $2,010,986 and $6,489,786 respectively, or $8,500,772 in the aggregate; a sum representing nearly two thirds of the revenue directly collected in 1868 under the $2-gallon tax, from the entire spirit product of the country. Very curiously, however, the merits and success of these supplementary taxes were made the basis of the strongest and almost only argument presented to Congress, by those who had not sufficient intelligence to comprehend and appreciate the economic principle involved in them, or whose pocket interests were antagonistic, for a repeal of the 50-cent gallon tax and the imposition of a specifically higher rate; it being urged that it was in accordance with

---

[1] *A calculation made by the Chamber of Commerce at Cincinnati made the whole tax on a gallon of whiskey (in first hands) under the law of 1868, 63.47 cents.*

all sound principles of political economy to concentrate rather than diffuse and multiply taxes, and that if the "gallon," the "capacity," and the "barrel" taxes were all consolidated into one tax, and that imposed on the gallon, the same amount of revenue could be collected with much less friction and expenditure. And ostensibly under the influence of this argument, Congress, in June, 1872, by an act, which took effect in the following August, increased the "gallon" tax to 70 cents, and at the same time repealed the "capacity" and "barrel" taxes. The immediate result of this legislation is best indicated by the statement: that during the last year (1871–2) of the 50-cent-gallon tax, the quantity of spirits distilled from materials other than fruits upon which the Government assessed and collected the tax, was 65,145,880 gallons, while in 1874, the second year of the 70-cent tax, the quantity of like spirits upon which this rate was collected, was only 61,814,800 gallons, a falling-off of over 3,000,000 gallons, notwithstanding an increase in the meantime in the population of the country of about two millions. On the other hand, it should in fairness be also stated that the country, financially and industrially, was far less prosperous in 1874 than it was two years previous, or in 1872. But at this point commences the record of a period of such utter and shameless corruption on the part of high officials of the Federal Government, and in connection with the administration of the Internal-Revenue laws pertaining to distilled spirits, as finds no parallel in any previous experience of the country; and for the complete narration of which the opportunity has possibly even yet not arrived. The essential circumstances of the case are, however, as follows:

When the act of 1868, reducing the gallon tax on distilled spirits, was passed, illicit distillation, as before stated, practically ceased. In saying this, it is not pretended that it was absolutely and entirely suspended, for with any tax on such a product, there will undoubtedly be always some evasions of the law, as circumstances favor. But it existed, if at all, to a very small extent, and ceased to attract the attention of the public. The general removal and replacement of revenue officials during the earlier years of Gen. Grant's first administration undoubtedly, however, favored the revival of fraud, and in 1871 a large number of distilleries in Missouri were seized and proceedings against their proprietors instituted. The political excitement in this State was at that time very great. A strong party, nominally Republicans, headed by Carl Schurz (who at that time represented Missouri in the United States Senate), were opposed to Gen. Grant, and it was reasonably apprehended that their influence during the succeeding year would be most antagonistic to his renomination and election. To meet and overcome this opposition and secure the vote of Missouri for Gen. Grant's renomination was, therefore, regarded by the Federal office-holders of that State as their first duty, and for accomplishing such results a supply of funds (money) was most important. Under such circumstances the idea of taking advantage of the condition of the proprietors of the distilleries in difficulty with the Government, appears to have first suggested itself ; it being but reasonable to suppose that such proprietors, if their offences, with great contingent fines and other penalties, could be compromised or wholly abandoned in respect to prosecution by the suppression of evidence or other action on the part of the Federal officials, would in turn gladly contribute most liberally for such political expenditures as their friends might indicate. It is almost needless to say that this idea, once suggested, was promptly carried out. A general assessment was laid on all the distilleries in the Missouri district, with the understanding, on the one hand, that the proceeds were to be used as a campaign fund to promote the interests of the Administration, and on the other, that the contributors were to be favored and protected as far as possible by the revenue officials and the representatives of political power and patronage at Washington. How much money was raised in the year preceding the Presidential election of 1872, and professedly used in the preliminary State elections, is not known, but enough to buy the support of leading newspapers which were before in opposition, and accomplish generally the ends proposed. Writing on this subject at a later period, Col. Wm. M. Grosvenor, who at the inception of these transactions was editor of the *St. Louis Democrat,* and in a position to know whereof he spoke, said :

" More than one distiller has told me how he was induced to contribute, and how, if he objected to fraud, he was forced to choose between participation in the Ring or bankruptcy. If distillers or rectifiers declined to act with the Ring, care was taken to entrap them in some apparent or technical violation of the law. Then their establishments were seized, and they were told to see Mr. Ford (the Internal Revenue Collector). When they saw Ford they were told to go to some other parties not officially connected with the Government, who explained that if they (the distillers) did as was desired, there would be no trouble ; if not, they would be prosecuted and convicted of violation of law, and bankruptcy would be inevitable."

During the year of the Presidential election (1872) Mr. Grosvenor expresses the opinion that about a thousand dollars per week was paid to the editor of one Administration paper, but that this large sum constituted " but a very small part of that portion of the profits which distillers were required to pay," and that of the whole amount about 40 per cent. went into the pockets of the higher officials.

"One portion always went to the 'man in the country,' a phrase supposed to refer to somebody in Washington, for there was needed, and there was secured, somebody at Washington to give the Ring warning of the Treasury investigations and stop all complaints from reaching the Secretary or the President. Yet complaints were forwarded, sometimes to the Secretary and sometimes to the President himself, without result. If investigations were ordered, either the person selected and sent out (to investigate) was one whose eyes and ears could be closed with a bribe, or the Ring was warned by telegraph before he had left Washington, and had ample time to put every thing in readiness to receive him with equanimity. That complete immunity was thus secured at an early day is certain."

Whatever was mysterious in these statements of Mr. Grosvenor at the time they were written was, however, explained to a great extent at a later period, when the Private Secretary of the President of the United States, the Chief Clerk of the U. S. Treasury Department, who had previously been chief clerk of the Internal-Revenue Bureau, and the Supervisor of Internal Revenue for the Missouri District (who was appointed by Gen. Grant in spite of the earnest protest of Carl Schurz and other leading men in St. Louis), were all indicted and tried for frauds on the revenues, and the two latter convicted and sentenced to State Prison. It was also shown on his trial that $200 per week was regularly set aside by the Ring, as the compensation of the Chief Clerk.

The Presidential campaign of 1872 having ended with the

re-election of Gen. Grant, the motive originally assigned as a reason for collusion between the Government officials and the distillers could of course be no longer pleaded. It was not, however, to be expected, that a mine of wealth that had been so long and so profitably worked would be at once abandoned ; and as a matter of fact, the frauds, instead of decreasing, increased ; while the persons concerned became more audacious, and extended their operations to New Orleans and most of the other important Western and Southwestern cities. The members of the Ring, furthermore, says Col. Grosvenor :

" Openly boasted that it had a power at Washington which could not be resisted or broken. Moreover, the members undoubtedly believed it themselves. They did not go about like men who had any thing to hide. Diamonds, for which official salaries would not account, were worn openly and purchased several thousand dollars' worth at a time, without attempt at concealment. Officials with moderate salaries lived with their families at hotels, expending obviously more than their known incomes, and yet made open purchases of costly summer residences. If whiskey operators or discharged revenue officials threatened to make exposures at Washington, they were kindly invited to ' expose and be ——.' One at least tried it, and made a dead failure, came back to St. Louis, and was told he had better keep his mouth shut in the future, or he would get into the penitentiary for defrauding the Government. When McDonald (the supervisor afterwards convicted and sent to the State Prison) went to Washington, he was received by the President and rode with him on the avenue. When the President visited St. Louis, McDonald was usually in his company, and as late as October, 1874, when the President visited the Fair, in the presence of 50,000 people, McDonald was at his side."

At the same time the President (according to McDonald's subsequent confession) accepted as a gift from McDonald and his secretary, one Joyce, a pair of horses, a carriage, and gold-mounted harnesses, valued at more than $5,000.

Matters continued in much the same way, without attracting any marked attention on the part of the public, and without any serious interference on the part of the Government, until the commencement of the year 1875, when the Hon. Benjamin F. Bristow —a man of great ability and integrity,—who had been appointed Secretary of the Treasury in the previous June (1874), and who had been gradually growing suspicious that the Government was being largely defrauded in its collection of revenue from spirits manufactured in several of the large cities of the country, determined to institute a searching investigation.[1] And as a preliminary step, he ordered on the 26th of January, 1875, a change, to take effect on the 15th of February, in the location and assignment of the ten officers, known as "Supervisors," to whom, in pursuance of an act of Congress, the general supervision of the working of the Internal-Revenue laws, in as many different sections of the country, was intrusted ; the idea being, that through such changes frauds would be likely to be uncovered, by reason of a lack of understanding between the distillers and the new officials; or, in other words, if there really were any honest supervisors, they would readily detect the complicity or neglect of their predecessors, and the manner in which the frauds were being perpetrated. The mischief which such a measure entailed, being, however, at once apparent to the " Ring," its immediate suspension or annulment became to them indispensable ; and such was their influence at Washington, that on the 4th of February the President officially and indefinitely suspended the order of the Secretary, and the changes comtemplated were prevented. Then

---

[1] One of the most interesting and perhaps the primary incident that developed the suspicions of fraud entertained by the Secretary and the public into almost certainty, and one which the " Ring" could not have well anticipated, or if anticipated, could not have prevented, was the publication in 1874 by the Merchants' Exchange Association of St. Louis, in their annual report, of the movements—receipts and shipments—of distilled spirits in that city during the previous year. For when certain persons, curious in statistical inquiries, compared the receipts and shipments thus published, with the official (Government) reports of the spirits produced and paying tax in St. Louis, it at once became evident that the quantity locally consumed and shipped was greatly in excess of the quantity received and reported as manufactured ; which excess represented at that time a loss to the revenues, in the city of St. Louis alone, of about $1,200,000 per annum. This suggested a new mode of detecting the fraud—namely : an examination of the bills of lading, or other commercial reports of receipts and shipments ; and without communicating his purpose to any of the Treasury officials, Secretary Bristow commissioned Mr. Coloney, then the commercial editor of the *St. Louis Democrat*, to make the investigation. Mr. Coloney accordingly " proceeded first to collect, as if for his newspaper, a complete statement of every bill of lading or shipment during the year ; not of whiskey alone, but of all other important articles, so that his object was not suspected " And when this was accomplished, a comparison of the shipments by operators in whiskey at St. Louis with the reports transmitted to Washington by the revenue officials, furnished at once conclusive proof of fraudulent practices by a large number of persons and establishments, and made possible the complete overthrow of the most powerful conspiracy ever formed against the revenue service in this country.

followed an experience which has no parallel in recent times in any country in Christendom, and the mere recital of which carries one back in memory to the old-time governments of Central Asia, or of Turkey, or possibly to France, under the *ancien régime*, when intrigue, distrust of all surroundings, and ability to conceal and mislead in respect to real intentions, were regarded as the prime essentials of successful statesmanship. For it was to a policy akin to this, that the Secretary of the Treasury manifestly felt himself compelled to resort, when the suspension of his order for the change of supervisors clearly demonstrated that he must first outwit the officials of the Government with whom he was associated, if he was to be able to prosecute his investigations to the end of maintaining the law and of exposing and punishing corruption. In place, then, of giving any further instructions to the officers of the Government specially charged with the administration of the revenues to enforce the laws, he carefully concealed from them his intentions,—even resorting to the invention of a new cipher for telegraph and other correspondence; and in their place, employed new and unofficial agents to bring his plans to maturity. And so successful was he in this, that not only were the suspicions of the conspirators in a great measure allayed, but plans even were formed by them for inducing the President to summarily remove the Secretary himself from office.[1]

Meantime the subject of again increasing the gallon tax on distilled spirits had been brought before Congress, and, on the 3d of March, 1875, a bill was passed, raising the rate from 70 to 90 cents per gallon. There was comparatively little debate in either House of Congress on the merits of the proposition, members apparently feeling that the topic had already been sufficiently discussed, and only one prominent member of the dominant party in Congress—Hon. John Sherman—vigorously protested against its favorable consideration. It was, moreover, recognized, from the first, as a measure introduced and favored by the Ad-

[1] I stopped at the Arlington House (Washington, April, 1875), where I met Senator Dorsey, of Arkansas, and to whom I told my story of the manner in which Secretary Bristow was interfering with my affairs. The Senator advised me to join him in a determined effort to influence the President to dismiss Bristow, a suggestion which, if I had acted upon, would have undoubtedly prevented any exposure of the "Ring." —"Confessions of McDonald," p. 132.

ministration; the Chairman of the Commitee of Ways and Means in the House and his political associates stating in all seriousness, when the bill was first reported, and as a reason for their endorsement of it, that the Commissioner of Internal Revenue — the same official who, some three months later, was summarily dismissed from office for suspected complicity with fraudulent transactions—was of the belief, that a dollar tax " *could be collected with the same fidelity which accompanies its collection of seventy cents*";[1] and " *I agree with the Commissioner in his confident judgment that he can collect a tax of a dollar per gallon.*"[2] On the other hand it was brought out during the consideration of the bill in the House, that the Secretary of the Treasury had written to the Committee of Ways and Means, that he did not agree in opinion with the Commissioner, and regarded any increase of the tax as likely to prove injurious[3]; and it was also stated and not disputed, that " high wines manufactured in Cincinnati were at the time being shipped by the way of the Mississippi and the Gulf to New York, and there publicly sold, with all the contingent expenses of transportation, waste, interest, and commissions, at about one-half cent per gallon over the cost of their production in the very district in which the corn grows and the distillery runs." But all this availed little in view of the circumstance that the President, the Commissioner of Internal Revenue, and an active lobby favored the increase of the tax, and were undisguisedly desirous of the passage of the bill that required it. Had, however, the intentions and suspicions of the Secretary of the Treasury, and the conclusive evidence of extensive fraud and conspiracy which subsequently came into his possession, been then made public, the increased tax would unquestionably never have been authorized by Congress; for, reviewing all the circumstances, it can hardly be doubted that the idea of the desirability of an " increase " was in the first instance started by the Ring; and that its members subsequently and successfully advocated it, through a desire to make their work more profitable, and their ability to protect themselves, through command of greater resources and temptations, more effective.

[1] Henry L. Dawes.   [2] Ellis H. Roberts.
[3] See *Congressional Record*, Feb. 17, 1875.

While the bill was under consideration in the Committee of Ways and Means in the House, the matter of making the proposed increase of tax applicable to stocks of spirits on hand again came up for consideration, and it was agreed to recommend that such " stocks "—*i. e.*, in original packages, estimated as amounting to about 11,000,000 gallons—should be taxed under the new law to the extent of fifty per cent. of the increase. The proposition, however, as in all previous cases, found no favor with Congress, and the bill passing without any such retroactive clause, the sum of $2,200,000 was in consequence at once legislated into the pockets of the distillers.[1]

The increase of the tax was, however, the last measure of success which the " Ring " achieved; for, on the 10th of May following, the Secretary of the Treasury, having through his special methods of investigation secured evidence sufficient to render any further concealment of his plans unnecessary, commenced offensive operations by seizing a large number of prominent distilleries and rectifying establishments at the West, and five days later summarily dismissing from office the Commissioner of Internal Revenue. Then followed in rapid succession the indictment and arrest of McDonald, the Missouri Supervisor; Joyce, the Special Revenue Agent; Avery, the former Chief Clerk of the Treasury; Gen. O. A. Babcock, the President's Private Secretary; Wm. McKee, the proprietor of the *St. Louis Democrat;* Maguire, the Revenue Collector at St. Louis; and a great number of subordinate revenue officials and many distillers and rectifiers. McDonald, Joyce, McKee, and Avery were tried, convicted, and sentenced to the payment of heavy fines and lengthy terms of imprisonment. Maguire pleaded guilty ; while Babcock, who was able to enlist expert and able counsel for his defence, was ac-

---

[1] In connection with this matter, the following incident is not a little interesting, and from a legislative point of view somewhat instructive. When the Committee of Ways and Means, in secret session, agreed to recommend to the House that a provision taxing stocks on hand to the extent of half the proposed increase of rate be incorporated in the bill, special care was taken to keep the action of the committee secret, in order to avoid speculative action on the part of distillers and wholesale dealers. But within twenty-four hours exceptional orders for stamps, to the extent of half a million of dollars, came into the Department, for the purpose of taking whiskey out of bond and placing it beyond the reach of any prospective provisions for any additional taxation.

quitted. This result, in the minds of the public, was, however, regarded as having been due in a great measure to an extraordinary circular-letter written by the (then) Attorney-General of the United States, Hon. Edwards Pierrepont, to the United States District-Attorneys in charge of the case, and preceding the trial, to the purport that no immunity from subsequent prosecution was to be given to any guilty parties who might be inclined to purchase their safety by turning State's evidence. The obvious effect of this being to effectually prevent the Government from obtaining the evidence necessary to ensure conviction, Congress felt compelled to take cognizance of it, and by resolution of the House of Represenatives (Feb. 25th) the Attorney-General was asked for an explanation; which explanation (when given) being regarded as unsatisfactory, the whole matter was then referred to the Judiciary Committee with instructions to examine and report. And this Committee, after reviewing in severe terms the course of the Attorney-General, recommended the adoption by the House of a resolution to the effect, that, in their judgment, "the Attorney-General should immediately revoke the instructions covered and implied " in his letter, inasmuch as the position taken in it was in contravention of "the long-established rule relating to the testimony of accomplices in criminal actions," and which rule "is necessary to prevent combinations for criminal purposes, and greatly aids in the disclosure of conspiracies to commit crime." The trial of Babcock had, however, terminated before the Committee reported. Again, on the trial of Avery, Hon. John B. Henderson, formerly a United States Senator for Missouri, and a leading member of the St. Louis bar, was retained by the Government to assist the District-Attorney in the prosecution, and made the closing argument in its behalf to the jury. A portion of this speech being regarded by the President as personally offensive, he promptly manifested his displeasure by discharging Mr. Henderson from any further service as counsel for the Government.

The further and final incidents of note in this most extraordinary and disgraceful record may be briefly summarized by saying: that McDonald, Avery, McKee, and Maguire were all pardoned by the President (Gen. Grant) before the expiration of the terms of imprisonment to which they were sentenced, and their fines remitted; and that after the conclusion of the trials, the Secretary of the Treasury (Bristow) and the Solicitor of the Treasury (Wilson, who had been the Secretary's most earnest and active co-operator in exposing and breaking up the conspiracy) resigned and retired from their respective offices.[1]

Since the passage of the act of March 3, 1875, raising the tax on distilled spirits to 90 cents per proof-gallon, the rate to the present time of writing, 1885, has remained unchanged. Illicit distillation, as might naturally be expected under the temptations offered by such a rate of tax, constantly goes on, but on a very small scale in respect to quantity, and to a very limited extent in the Northern and Western States of the Union. For the period of seven years, from 1876 to 1883 inclusive, the experience of the Internal Revenue has been reported as follows: Number of stills seized, 5,498; officers and employés killed, 36; officers and employés wounded, 61. Of the 397 stills seized in the year 1883, five only were in the Northern and Western States, the others being mainly in the thinly settled and mountainous districts of the States of Kentucky, North Carolina, Georgia, Tennessee, and Virginia. In extensive regions in these States, the small farmers grow little besides corn, and in the entire absence of railways, and also to a great extent of roads, there is no way for them to bring their surplus corn to any market, except in the form of whiskey; and except for what may be paid them in cash for their whiskey, few farmers handle as much as twenty dollars in ready money in any one year. The result is that the inhabitant of these sections of the country feels that he has a right to transform his corn into whiskey, and that the Government is acting in a most tyrannical and unjust manner in seeking to prevent it. Hence the multiplicity of "moonshiners,"—as illicit distillers are termed,—the little rude stills among the mountains, and the murder of the revenue officials who attempt to make arrests and break up the business.

---

[1] Those desirous of more detailed information respecting the events of which a summary only has been here given, are referred to files of the leading newspapers and reviews of the United States for the year 1875, and the first half of the year 1876; also to a book entitled "Secrets of the Great Whiskey Ring," written by McDonald, and published in St. Louis (revised edition, 1880). This book, which is in the nature of a confession, purports to give documentary proofs, comprising, fac-similes of confidential letters and telegrams directing the management of the Ring, and in respect to most of its statements is probably unimpeachable.

The gross product that under these circumstances annually evades the payment of the tax is, however, comparatively inconsiderable.

Regarded from an economic or financial stand-point, the results of the 90-cent (gallon) tax, as compared with those obtained under the 50- and 70-cent rates, are exceedingly interesting. Thus, during the last full year (1872) under the 50-cent rate, the tax was collected on 65,145,000 proof-gallons of distilled[1] spirits, which, with an assumed population of 41,000,000, would include an average annual consumption of about 1.50 proof-gallons per capita.

During the last full year (1874) of the 70-cent rate, the tax was collected on 61,145,000 gallons, which, with an assumed population of 44,000,000, would indicate an average annual consumption of about 1.40 proof-gallons per capita.

During the year 1876, the first of the 90-cent rate, the tax was collected on 56,442,000 gallons, which, with the then population of the country, would indicate an average annual consumption of about 1.23 gallons per capita.

During the year 1880, under a continuation of the 90-cent rate, the tax was collected on 61,125,000 gallons, which, with a then known population of 50,155,000, would indicate an average annual consumption of about 1.21 gallons per capita.

The revenues from spirits for the years 1881–4 are valueless for estimating consumption; as the payment of taxes, during these years, was made compulsory on large quantities of spirits in bond, by limitation of the bonded period of tax exemption.

For 1885, the tax (90 cents) was collected on 67,689,000 gallons; but as large quantities of spirits were forced out of bond during this year also, there is reason for believing that the taxes were paid on a much larger quantity than actually entered into consumption. Assuming, however, the correctness of the official returns, the average consumption for 1885 would have been about 1.16 gallons per capita.

---

[1] In these comparisons account only is taken of spirits distilled from materials other than fruits, *i. e.*, grain. The revenue laws of the United States, with a view of favoring the business, have always discriminated, through lower taxation, in favor of spirits distilled from fruits, *i. e.*, brandies. The collections from such products are, however, comparatively inconsiderable, and in only one year (1873) have been in excess of two millions of dollars.

On the basis of these data an approximate estimate of the fiscal productiveness of the low (50 cents) and high (90 cents) tax system, becomes possible. Thus during the year 1872, the tax was collected on an average annual consumption of at least 1.5 gallons per capita. Had this rate been maintained, the quantity available for taxation in 1885 would have been 87,000,000 gallons. The number of gallons assessed in 1885 was 67,689,000.

Including the direct and collateral taxes the tax rate actually collected on distilled spirits, in 1872, amounted to 75.1 cents per gallon; which rate, if collected in 1885, on a per-capita consumption proportioned to that of 1872, would have afforded a revenue of over $65,300,000, as compared with an actual receipt from the same sources, under the 90 cent rate, of only $66,189,000; —a gain in revenue obviously insufficient to compensate for the advantages which would have certainly accrued under the lower tax through the reduction of incentives to illicit distillation, and of the first cost of spirits for industrial purposes.

In explanation of an apparent inconsistency between the fact that the Internal Revenue has not of late years been able to assess and collect the tax on as large a per-capita production and consumption of distilled spirits as in 1870, and the opinion above expressed, that there is at present but comparatively little illicit production in the country, it is to be said : that while nearly all who have carefully examined into this subject are agreed that Federal taxation of distilled spirits has not (except possibly at the outset) affected their demand for drink, and that their consumption for such purpose in the United States goes increasing regularly (if not in an equal ratio) with the increase of population, the evidence on the other hand is conclusive that their use for economic and scientific purposes has been greatly restricted by the present high rate of tax imposed on their production. Prior to the imposition of any taxes on spirits, or before the war, it is probable that 33 per cent. at least of the whole product of the country was consumed in the arts and industries; but at the present time (1885) it is estimated, by those well qualified to form an opinion, that not over 10 per cent. of the total product is thus used. Artisans, manufacturers, and pharmaceutists who formerly consumed untaxed alcohol in great quantities, and to a considerable extent also when the tax on proof-spirits was 50 cents, now regard its use under the present tax rate as unprofitable, and in consequence have either abandoned their old methods of procedure or preparations, or resorted to the employment of cheaper substitutes.

The aggregate amount of revenue received by the Federal Government from all the taxes which it has levied on the manufacture and sale of distilled spirits from 1863 to 1884 inclusive, a period of twenty-two years, has been a thousand and fifty-six millions of dollars, or, in exact figures, $1,056,137,946.79.

The magnitude of these results under the Federal system, and the apparent facility with which they have been attained, have naturally suggested from time to time to the several States of the Union, the special taxation of the manufacture and sale of distilled spirits within their own borders, as a means of increasing their local revenues. That the several States have the right to impose non-discriminating taxes on persons, property, and business within their own territorial jurisdiction, is not questioned ; but the almost insuperable obstacles in the way of the *special* taxation by any State of any of its local products—agricultural, mineral, or manufactured—are : that to just the extent to which such taxing increases the cost (price) of such State products, to a like extent is their export to and sale in other States, which do not similarly tax, restricted or prevented ; while, at the same time, as no State can impose taxes on importations from other States or from foreign countries, the imposition of special taxes on any of its products virtually constitutes bounties for the importation and competitive sale of the like products of other States which have not been subject to such special taxation. On the other hand, to attempt, with a view to obtaining large revenues, to impose and collect high taxes on the local sale and consumption of distilled spirits, was but to create undue temptations to fraud and to repeat the experience which the Federal Government had proved to be so disastrous. To overcome these difficulties the State of Virginia, some years since, enacted and put in operation an ingenious law, the object of which was to obtain a large revenue from taxes on the sale of spirits at retail, and to properly determine and ensure the collection by machinery. With this object, in addition to the payment in advance of a prescribed amount for a license to sell, each bar-room keeper or retail liquor-dealer was required to hire from the revenue commissioner of his district an "apparatus," which resembled a gas-meter in appearance, and was termed a "bar-room register." Its operation was not dissimilar to that of the familiar "bell-punch," or "indicator," employed for registering fares in the street-railway cars of our large cities. The law further provided, that each bar-room keeper, "immediately on the sale of each drink of wine, ardent spirits, malt liquors, or any mixture thereof, in the presence of the purchaser or person to whom it is delivered, should turn the crank of the proper register until the bell has struck once, and the indicator on its dial has moved one point or number for each drink sold by him." The registers were required to be inspected monthly, and the tax imposed was two and one half cents for each drink or half-pint of wine or spirits, and half a cent for the same quantity of malt liquor. Wild expectations were indulged in respect to the results of this system, which was popularly termed, from the inventor, the "*Moffat Bell-Punch Law*"; and some sanguine people, on the basis of an estimate of the average number of drinks purchased every day in the year throughout the State, were confident that revenue nearly or quite sufficient would be obtained from this source to meet all the requirements of the State for expenditures. The experiment was not, however, a success. The introduction of the "apparatus" was the only novelty in the law, and, with the exception of informers (who were allowed one third of the fine imposed for disobeying the law), and possibly also the manufacturer of the indicator, no one was particularly interested in its enforcement; while every regular toper felt bound to connive at the infringement of a statute, the immediate influence of which was to raise the cost of drinking. The system, after a brief but sufficient trial, was, therefore, adandoned; leaving as its only meritorious result, another illustration of the prevalent and apparently incurable delusion, that liquor laws can be made different in principle from all other laws; and that if one could be framed with sufficient ingenuity, the ordinary characteristics of human beings, their instincts, desires, motives, might be complacently ignored.[1]

[1] Additional light on the causes of the failure of the "Moffat Bell-Punch Law" may be gleaned from the following comment on it, at the time of its repeal, by one of the leading journals of Virginia, *The* (Richmond) *State* :

"To say the least, this law was not a success. The revenue from it was fast

CONCLUSION.

In concluding this most curious and not heretofore fully related record of recent economic experience, the writer would ask attention to what seems to him to be its most important and valuable lesson and moral, and that is: that whenever a government imposes a tax on any product of industry sufficiently great to sufficiently indemnify and reward an illicit or illegal production of the same, then such product will be illicitly or illegally manufactured ; and when that point is reached the losses and penalties consequent upon detection and conviction—no matter how great may be the one, or how severe the other—will be counted in by the offenders as a part of the necessary expenses of their business ; and the business, if forcibly suppressed in one locality, will inevitably be renewed and continued in some other. It is, therefore, a matter of the first importance for every government in framing laws for the assessment and collection of taxes, to seek to know when the maximum-revenue point in the case of each tax is reached, and to recognize that in going beyond that limit the government " over-reaches " itself.

But in an experience of now nearly a quarter of a century in making the manufacture and sale of distilled spirits, instrumentalities for collecting revenues for the support of the Government, the United States, as represented by the makers and administrators of its laws, has for the most part declined to seek for, or profit by, any such information ; but, on the contrary, as has been somewhat humorously expressed, " it has held out an undue temptation to defraud on the one hand, and a writ for seizure and indictment on the other, and thus equipped, has announced its readiness to proceed to business." And the consequences have become a part of the world's economic history.

growing less, not because the law hindered drinking, but because it gave every opportunity for fraud. Falling only on those who were honest enough to register their sales, it was never felt by those who chose to cheat the Government. As a law that could be obeyed or not at will, it could never be effective. Its inquisitorial nature made it repulsive, and the State is fortunate to be rid of it."

INFLUENCE OF THE PRODUCTION AND DISTRI-
BUTION OF WEALTH ON SOCIAL
DEVELOPMENT.[1]

LADIES AND GENTLEMEN:—In welcoming you to this first meeting in the States of the Northwest, of the American Association for the Promotion of Social Science, with the address which ancient custom and a recognition of the fitness of things seem to require should be made by the presiding officer on such occasions, I propose to ask your attention to a line of thought touching the agencies which, perhaps more than any other, are contributing to the moulding and development of society—namely, the production or accumulation, and the distribution, of that which we call wealth, or capital; meaning thereby abundance of all those things which contribute to our well-being, comfort, and happiness.

And, in so doing, the first point I would ask you to consider is, that, out of all of his present accumulations of wealth, man has never created any thing. What Nature gives he appropriates; and in this appropriation, or collection of natural spontaneous products, consists the original method of earning a living,—the method still mainly depended on by all uncivilized and barbarous people. The first advance upon this method is to make provision for the future by carrying over supplies from seasons of abundance to seasons of scarcity, or in learning the necessity and benefits of accumulation. But, in all this, man does nothing more than the animals, who, following what we term the promptings of instinct, gather and lay up stores in the summer for consumption in the winter; and he lifts himself above the animals only when, and proportionally so, he learns that he can tempt Nature to give more abundantly, by bringing various kinds of matter and various

[1] Annual address as President of the American Social-Science Association, Detroit, May, 1875.

forces together, or into such relations as will enable them to act upon each other under the most favorable circumstances. And it is in the attainment and application of this knowledge of how to tempt Nature to give,—or, as we term it, "*to produce*," using to express our meaning most correctly a word which signifies "*to lead forth,*" and not "*to create,*"—that the distinction is to be found between the civilized and uncivilized methods of earning a living; man in the one case being mainly a collector, and in the other a "*drawer-out,*" or producer. And herein, furthermore, is to be found the characteristic, or, as Chevalier the French economist expresses it, "the mystery and marvel, of our modern civilization—namely, that, through the attainment and exercise of increased knowledge and experience, we have so far come to know the properties of matter and the forces of Nature, as to enable us to compel the two to work in unison for our benefit with continually increasing effectiveness; and so afford to us from generation to generation a continually increasing product of abundance, with a continually diminishing necessity for the exercise of physical labor." And, as some evidence of the degree of success thus far attained to in this direction, we have the simple statement,—yet of all things the one most marvellous in our experience,—that at the present time, in Great Britain alone, the force annually evolved through the combustion of coal, and applied to the performance of mechanical work, is directly equivalent to the muscular power of at least one hundred millions of men; or, to state the case differently, the result attained to is the same as if the laboring population of Great Britain had been increased twelvefold, without necessitating any material increase in production for the support and sustenance of this additional number.

Another illustration to the same effect, but one more recent and less familiar, is afforded by the construction and operation of the Suez Canal. Thus, a few years ago, a swift voyage from England to Calcutta, *viâ* the Cape of Good Hope, was from a hundred and ten to a hundred and twenty days. Now steamers by way of the canal make the same voyage in about thirty days. Here, then, is a diminution of seventy-five per cent. on the enormous stocks of goods continually required to be held unused, involving continued risk of depreciation, loss of interest, and cost of insurance, to meet the requirements of mere transit. Add to which the fact, that the improvements in marine engines enable these vessels to work with about one tenth less coal, and therefore carry proportionally more cargo than they could seven or eight years before the canal was opened; and that the construction of the telegraph between England and India enables dealers and consumers also to regulate their supplies without carrying excessive stocks of commodities, and so keeps prices steady, and discourages speculation,—and we have in this single department of trade and commerce a saving and release of capital and labor for other purposes and employments that amounts to a revolution.

What is yet to be accomplished in the way of increasing the proportion of product to manual labor, time alone can show; but there is no evidence at present to indicate that we are approaching any limitation to further progress in this direction. A writer in *The London Economist* in 1873, evidently most conversant with his subject, claimed that the industry of the population of Great Britain at that time, taken man for man, was nearly twice as productive as it was in 1850; and I do not think that any one can review the industrial experience of the United States as a whole since 1860, but must feel satisfied that our average gain in the power of production during that time, and in spite of the war, has not been less than from fifteen to twenty per cent. And, if this statement should seem to any to be exaggerated, it is well to call to mind that it is mainly within this period that the very great improvements in machinery adapted to agriculture have been brought into general use: that whereas a few years ago men on the great fields of the West cut grain with sickles and with cradles, toiling from early morn to dewy eve in the hottest period of the year, the same work may be done now almost as a matter of recreation; the director of a mechanical reaper entering the field behind a pair of horses, with gloves on his hands, and an umbrella over his head, and in this style finishing the work in a fraction of the time which many men would formerly have required, and in a manner much more satisfactory.' I would also

---

¹ The following illustration is even more remarkable and interesting. Forty years ago or less, Indian corn was shelled by a man sitting astride the handle of a shovel and scraping the ears against the edge, or using the cob of one ear to shell the corn from another. A likely man could shell in this way about five bushels in ten hours, and received one tenth of the corn he shelled for his labor. Up to 1878, 378 patents had been

recall to you that, in the manufacture of boots and shoes, three men now, with the aid of machinery, can produce as much in a given time as six men unaided could have done in 1860; that we have forty thousand more miles of railroad now (1875)[1] than we then had to assist us in the work of exchange and distribution; that we can send our telegrams now for less than one half what it actually cost to do the work in 1866; and finally, taking the Pennsylvania Central Railroad as a type, that we can send our freight by railroad at an average of less than a cent per ton per mile, as compared with a charge of 2.41 on the same road for the same service in 1864.

And, as a curious instance of this continuous progress, it may be here also noted, that the abandonment of large quantities of costly machinery in most branches of staple manufactures, and its replacement by new, is periodically rendered a matter of absolute economical necessity, in order to produce more perfectly and cheaply, and at the same time avoid the destruction of a much greater amount of capital by industrial rivalry; thus strikingly illustrating an economic principle to which attention was, I think, first called by my friend Mr. Atkinson of Boston—that the absolute destruction of what has once been wealth often marks a greater step in the progress of civilization than any great increase in material accumulation; the breaking up and destruction of the old machinery, and its replacement by new, in the cases referred to, being the sole conditions under which a diminution of the cost of production could be effected, and the abundance of product be made greater.

We are often accustomed to speak of, and perhaps look forward to, a period which we call "millennial," which is to be characterized in particular by an absence of want of all those things which minister to our material comfort and happiness. But when

issued in the United States for corn-shellers; and the machinery for this purpose has been so perfected, that two men, with a machine driven by steam- or horse-power, can easily shell 1,500 bushels a day, the cobs being carried off into a pile by themselves or into a wagon, and the corn run into sacks or wagons, to be driven off in bulk. The corn crop of the United States for the year 1880 approximated 1,800,000,000 bushels. It would have required the entire population of the country at that time—every man, woman, and child of its fifty millions of people—to have spent the entire six working days of a week, and a part of Sunday, to have shelled the crop of that year by the old process.

[1] 80,000 more in 1885.

that period arrives, if it ever does, one of two things must take place : either man must so far change his nature as to be able to exist in comfort without a supply of all those objects which are comprised under the general terms, *food, clothing, shelter*, and *luxuries*; or else the forces of nature must be so much further subordinated and brought under our control as to do all our work for us, instead of, as now, doing but a part,—and thus become, in all respects, our all-sufficient ministers and servants.

But, when that time comes, then all material wealth, as we ordinarily use the term, must disappear; for that only is wealth which has exchangeable value, and that only has exchangeable value which is desired. But we can neither value nor desire that which, like the air, is at all times given in excess of any possible use or necessity.

But, fanciful as may be this speculation, it is nevertheless a most interesting and suggestive circumstance, that all of our true material progress constantly points in this same direction ; inasmuch as the great result of every new invention or discovery in economic processes is to eliminate or discharge value; making those things cheap which were before dear, and bringing within the reach and use of all what before were for the exclusive use and enjoyment of the few. Thus, in 1170, Thomas À Becket was counted extravagant because he had his parlor strewed every day with clean rushes ; and, four hundred years later, cloth was so scarce that Shakespeare makes Falstaff's shirts cost him four shillings per ell. But few are so poor nowadays as not to be able to afford some sort of a carpet for their parlor ; and, making allowance for the purchasing power of money at the different epochs, Falstaff's four shillings would now give him near *forty* times the same quantity.

Again : Sir Henry Bracton, who was Lord Chief Justice of England in the time of Henry III., wrote, in the way of legal illustration, that if a man living in Oxford engage to pay money the same day in London, a distance of fifty-four miles, he shall be discharged from his contract by reason of his undertaking to do a physical impossibility. But to-day, what Bracton regarded as impossible can be readily accomplished in from sixty to eighty minutes.

That this wonderful and continued increase in the gross prod-

uct of every department of human industry and enterprise has
been also attended with a general rise in the standard of comfort,
leisure, and enjoyment available everywhere to the masses, is
sufficiently proved by not only the most superficial of observation,
but also by a great variety of statistics, which, although not as
yet in any degree formulated or referred to an average, are
nevertheless exceedingly interesting.

Thus, for example, the British commercial reports indicate
that the ability of the populations of Russia and of Germany to
consume cotton has at least doubled since 1851; that in Swe-
den the increase has been fourfold; and, in Paraguay, fivefold.
And not merely has the consumption of cotton cloth increased in
near and remote regions, but the ratio of absorption among the
working classes of Europe, of articles which a generation ago were
luxuries to them, has also been most rapid and remarkable; the
ratio of increase having been most marked in the average *per
capita* consumption of meats, breadstuffs, tea, sugar, coffee, cocoa,
wines, and spirits.[1]

But, gratifying as these evidences of increasing abundance certainly are, the cry of the poor, at least to the superficial observer,
seems not less loud, and the difficulties of earning a living, or of
getting ahead in the world, seem not less patent than they have
always been; while the discontent with the inequalities of social
condition are certainly more strikingly manifested than at any
former period. To understand fully the origin of this social paradox, is to presuppose a full understanding of the whole domain of
social science, or of the laws and phenomena involved in all societary relations; a degree and comprehensiveness of knowledge
which it is safe to affirm has been attained by no man. But there
is, at the same time, a record of experience indicating the duties
incumbent on society in respect to some of these matters, which
cannot too often be pressed upon the public attention.

---

[1] Comparing 1883 with 1840, the increase in the consumption per head of various
articles of imported food by the population of Great Britain, has been as follows :

Sugar from 15 to 63 lbs.; tea, 1.22 to 4.59; butter, 1 to 7; bacon and hams, 1 to
11 ; wheat and wheat flour, 42½ to 250 ; cheese, 1 to 5½ ; rice, 1 to 12½. Of tobacco,
the increased consumption per head has been from 0.86 lb. to 1 43 lb.; and of spirits
from 0.97 to 1.09 gall. During the same period, the decline in prices has been in the
case of sugar from 9*d.* to 2*d.* cts. per lb. ; of tea, from 5*s.* to 2*s.* per pound ; and of
coffee, from 2*s.* to 1*s.* per pound.

In the first stage of society, property can hardly be said to exist at all, or it exists in common. In the second stage, individual 'rights appear; but property is to a great extent held and transferred by force, and the generally accepted principle governing its distribution is, *that might confers right.* As society has progressed, however, the reign of violence and lawlessness has gradually diminished, until now the acquisition and retention of property has come to depend on superiority of intellect, quickness of perception, skill in adaptation,—the cunning and the quick being arrayed against the ignorant and the slow,—while the principle which has come to be the generally accepted basis of all commercial, industrial, and financial transactions, is succinctly expressed by the coarse and selfish proverb: "*Every man for himself, and the Devil take the hindermost.*" And if we consider these terms as symbolical, and for the word "*Devil*" substitute absence of abundance—want, misery, and privation; and for the word "*hindermost*," the masses, who constitute the bulk of every densely populated community,—then it must be admitted, that the Devil thus far has been eminently successful. But the governing and controlling influences of society—meaning thereby the rich, the well-to-do, and most-intelligent classes—have for a considerable time found out one thing of importance, and are beginning to find out another thing of even greater significance.

The *thing which they have found out* is, that it is not for the interest of any portion of society, regarded simply from the point of view of individual selfishness, and not in accordance with the religion of Christ and humanity, to allow the Devil to take anywhere, or to any extent, the hindermost; and *the thing which they are beginning to find out* is, that the hindermost, who constitute, in this struggle for the acquirement and retention of property, the masses, are becoming fast conscious of their power and influence, and are determined of themselves, that they will not, if they can help it, be captured by this devil of civilization; and, if obliged to succumb to him, may, like the communists of Paris, endeavor to draw down with them the whole fabric of society into one common vortex of destruction.

Out of the *first* of these discoveries have come schools, hospitals, churches, sanitary and social reforms, the spirit and the power of charity, and all brotherly kindness ; out of the *second,* strikes, trades-unions, the crystallizing antagonism of labor against capital, the spirit and the teachings of socialism, the practice of communism.

It took society a good while to make the first discovery; but it has been forced upon it through bitter and costly experience. There was probably no less of kindness of heart five hundred years ago among individuals than now, no less of natural sympathy with the poor, no less of individual religious zeal to do as we would be done by. But society certainly did not act as now in respect to those things which society only can properly control and regulate; as, for example, sanitary reform, general education, protection of private rights, and the like. And for such neglect society paid the penalty; for, when the black-death and the plague came, they were no respecters of persons, and the rich in common with the poor went down to the slaughter. But when the well-to-do classes of society found out that these foes had their origin in want of drainage, and especially in lack of ventilation and cleanliness among the poor, and began to move in the matter, and provide remedies, then the black-death and the plague abated, and finally disappeared altogether.

During the reign of Henry VIII., seventy-two thousand thieves *are said* to have been hanged in England alone; which, if true, would indicate that "about one man in ten," during the reign, which extended over two generations, was, to use the words of the old historian, "devoured and eaten up by the gallows."[1] But society has now found out that hanging is one of the worst possible uses to which a man can be put; and that it is a great deal cheaper to prevent than to punish, to incur effort and expenditure to save the inefficient and the criminal from becoming such, rather than to save society from them after they have once become so; and that, of one of these two courses, society has got to take its choice. Furthermore, as showing how social-science investigations are taking propositions of this character out of the domain of philanthropic theory, and making them practical matter-of-fact demonstrations, I submit to you the following illustrations.

[1] Mr. Froude, while regarding this statement as wholly unwarranted, nevertheless admits, that the English criminal law of that period "was in its letter one of the most severe in Europe"; and that, "in the absence of graduated punishment, there was but one step to the gallows from the lash and the branding-iron."

Thus it has been estimated in England, that the ordinary expense of bringing up a child from infancy to fourteen, in the best-managed public institutions or asylums, cannot be put down at less than 4s. 6d., or somewhat over a dollar (gold), per week; and for the United States it is undoubtedly much greater. But taking the minimum sum as the basis of estimate, and allowing nothing for any outlay for education or amusement, the cost at fifteen would have amounted without interest to about eight hundred dollars; and at eighteen, allowing for all expenditures and for interest, each individual may be regarded as an investment by society of at least fifteen hundred dollars of capital economized for production.

Now, if from this period the individual fails to fully earn his own living, society loses not only the amount expended for his bringing-up, but other persons must be taxed on their labor and their capital to provide for his future support and maintenance; so that the general stock of abundance at the disposal of society is not increased, but diminished. If the individual turns pauper or mendicant, and does nothing whatever for his own support, the cost to society will be greater, though differently apportioned. If he turns thief or criminal, he will be supported even yet more expensively by society; for he will be maintained by plunder or in prison. But in whatever condition he may live, either idle or vicious, in prison or out of prison, the loss incurred by the community for each such individual for his life, which, after the attainment of fourteen years, is likely to continue until forty, cannot be less in the United States than five thousand dollars; a loss in Massachusetts alone, in which State at least one in fourteen of her entire population are paupers, criminals, or needlessly idle and dependent, which would be equivalent to an unproductive expenditure of over five hundred millions of capital—the results of some other person's labor—for each and every generation [1]

Another illustration to the same effect, drawn more directly from the domain of actual fact, and one of the most remarkable ever placed upon record, has been brought to the attention of the public by members of this association,—Dr. Harris and Mr. R. L. Dugdale of New York,—namely, the history of a female pauper

[1] For this illustration, I am indebted to the address of Mr. Edwin Chadwick, C.B., at the opening of the meeting of the British Association for the Promotion of Social Science, 1869-70.

child, who some eighty years ago, abandoned as an outcast in one of the interior towns of New York, and allowed by society to remain an outcast, has repaid to society its neglect by becoming the mother of a long line of criminals, paupers, prostitutes, drunkards, and lunatics; entailing upon the county of her residence alone an expense of over one hundred thousand dollars, and upon society at large an estimated cost of over one million of dollars; included under which last head, is an item of twenty-five thousand dollars for the simple prosecutions and trials of one hundred and twenty criminals and offenders, who received as the result an aggregate of one hundred and forty years' imprisonment.[1]

And thus it is, that reasoning from a purely economic point of view, and leaving all moral and religious conditions out of sight, we arrive at an absolute demonstration, that the very best thing society can do to promote its material interests, is to so far abandon its old principle of "*each man for himself*," that each man shall concern himself with the welfare of his neighbors and fellow-citizens to the extent at least of seeing that the Devil be nowhere permitted to take even the humblest and weakest of the hindermost. By many, perhaps by a majority of the community, the Association for the Promotion of Social Science is undoubtedly looked upon as an association of *doctrinaires;* clever men naturally, but at the same time men of seclusion and of study, unacquainted with the details of practical life, who like to meet

---

[1] Of the descendants of this pauper child and her sisters, 709 have been accurately tabulated ; while researches by Mr. Dugdale indicate that the total aggregate of their descendants reach the large number of 1,200 persons, living and dead.

"Of the 709, 91 are known to be illegitimate, and 368 legitimate, leaving 250 unknown as to birth. 128 are known to be prostitutes ; 18 kept houses of ill-fame ; and 67 were diseased, and therefore cared for by the public. Only 22 ever acquired property, and eight of these lost what they had gained ; 172 received out-door relief during an aggregate number of 734 years ; 64 were in the almshouse of the county, and spent there an aggregate number of 96 years ; 76 were publicly recorded as criminals.

" The crimes of the females were licentiousness, and those of the males violence and theft. But the record quoted is merely their public history of criminality, which is necessarily very imperfect. Great numbers of offences of this wretched family were never entered on any court records ; and hundreds were never brought to trial. Another appalling feature in this history of criminal inheritance, is the disease spread through the country by these vagrant children, and the consequent lunacy, idiocy, epilepsy, and final weakness of body and mind, which belongs to inherited pauperism, transmitted to so many human beings."—*Report of Children's Aid Society, New York,* 1875.

together periodically, hear themselves talk, and see their names appended to long articles in the magazines and newspapers. To any such I would commend, for instruction and conversion, a typical illustration of social-science work, as embodied in a paper, by Dr. W. E. Boardman of Boston, recently published by the State Board of Health of Massachusetts. In this paper it is shown that the rate of mortality in Massachusetts—twenty in a thousand—is higher than in most of the States of the Union; that it compares *quite unfavorably* with many of the larger cities of Europe, that it tends to increase rather than diminish, and more especially that there is an increasing amount of death and sickness from causes which are known to be avoidable ; also, that there is every reason to suppose, that by encouraging the study and following out the teachings of sanitary science, the death rate of the State can be speedily reduced from twenty to fifteen per thousand ; and that, in case this is done, the saving in the cost of sickness and disability to the working classes alone of the State will not be less than *three* millions of dollars per annum. Now, if the man who makes two blades of grass grow where but one grew before, is a public benefactor, how much more so is the individual who, by the patient gathering and study of statistics like these, convinces a community of a danger in respect to which it would otherwise be long ignorant ; and then, as the result of such conviction, initiates a reform which not only greatly diminishes the aggregate of human suffering, but also greatly increases the aggregate of material abundance? Nay, further, can any soil be cultivated, can any work be done, likely to yield so large fruition, so many blades bearing ears with full corn in the ear, as this work of the so-called *doctrinaires ?*

And there is yet one other thing which society is also beginning to find out ; and that is, that all these questions relating to the production and distribution of wealth, and the avoidance on the part of society of waste, and the economizing of expenditure, affect an infinitely higher class of interests than those measurable by dollars and cents ; and that the laws underlying and controlling economic progress are either identical with the laws underlying and controlling intellectual, moral, and religious progress, or at least are so far similar and closely connected as to be mutually interdependent. And we hold furthermore, that it is mainly from a lack of perception and appreciation of this truth, especially by those to whom the mission of making men better is particularly intrusted, that so much of the work undertaken in these latter days by philanthropic and religious associations has been like seed sown upon stony ground, productive of but little benefit.

"The study and investigation of these questions of taxation, currency, and the production and distribution of wealth," said one of our best-known philanthropists lately, "are all very well, and undoubtedly most important; but somehow they do not interest me. They seem to me to be wholly material, while the great thing, in my opinion, to be worked for on behalf of society, is the attainment of a larger life."

Now, as to the ultimate issue and end of all our effort, I fully agree, a larger life is the one thing essential. It is the consummation of all social progress, the crowning glory of all Christian civilization, the aspiration of a future state of existence. But on this earth, and while we continue in the flesh, in order that there may be a larger life, there must be an exemption from such servitude of toil as precludes leisure; and, in order that there may be more leisure with less want, there must be a greater abundance; and, in order that there *can* be greater abundance, there must be larger production, more economical using, and a more equitable distribution. So that instead of there being any real or fancied antagonism, or diversity of interest, between the work of investigating and determining the laws which govern the production and distribution of wealth, and the business of calling men to a larger and a higher life, the former, as society is at present constituted, must be the forerunner and coadjutor of the latter; or the labor of the latter, as has been too often the case, will be labor in vain.

When Van der Kempt, a Dutch missionary, first entered upon his work in South Africa, he devoted himself in the outset to the labor of reconstructing and improving the dwellings of the natives; and for this purpose followed for a time the business of the brickmaker, the mason, and the carpenter. When taken to task for doing these things, rather than devoting his whole time to the preaching of the gospel, he is said to have made answer substantially as follows: that while he had no doubt that the Spirit of God would enter a brush hut with a mud floor, and dwell therein, he felt equally certain that it would come more readily into a house with a tiled roof, dry floor, and glazed windows; and, when there, would be more likely to abide permanently. And he was right; for the reason that it is not easy—nay, all but impossible—to lead a life of intellectuality, purity, and righteousness, amid filth, poverty, and all the adjuncts of physical debasement. And, if this proposition be correct, then it is a condition precedent to the future progress and well-being of society, *first*, that there shall be continually increasing abundance; and, *second*, that this abundance shall also, to the greatest extent consistent with the retention and exercise of individual freedom, be equally distributed among the masses. And the great question of the age, one which the course of events shows that we must before long, either voluntarily or involuntarily, meet and answer, is, How can these ends be best accomplished?

By the majority of those who have undertaken to discuss these questions in the interests of labor, the idea is put forth that the ends desired can be most fully and rapidly attained through the enactment of law; but, in respect to the extent to which the law is to be made operative, the ideas which are entertained and expressed have no little of diversity.

In Europe, the masses emerging from the sluggishness and torpor in which for centuries, like brutes, they have been content to suffer and to wait, and grasping at once the idea—long familiar to the people of this country—that all men are created equal, have speedily passed to a conviction that, because thus created equal, they have, in common with all, an equal right to all acquired property. And hence we find such leaders in the labor-movement as Proudhon and others in France and Germany, assuming and maintaining the position " *that property is theft*," and demanding that through legislation the State shall take possession of all property, and provide for all its citizens an equal and adequate support.

Now, it would seem as if no argument could be needed in this country to expose the wickedness and folly of such a proposition; and yet such doctrines, in a thinly disguised form, are continually preached in this country by men claiming to be respectable and intelligent to a much greater extent than the community are generally aware; and not only preached, but received with an apparently increasing favor and interest. Thus, for example, in a tract issued by one of the recognized leaders of the eight-hour movement in Massachusetts, I find the statement that the ultimate end and meaning of this special labor reform is to be the compulsory limitation of labor by legislative enactment to six hours per day; *and that*, out of such a law and co-operation, it will follow, *that "the commonest or the most obscure laborer will live, if he chooses, in dwellings as beautiful and as convenient as any which are now monopolized by the wealthy."* [1] To render his plan, however, in any degree practicable, the author singularly omitted to provide by statute that all men should be born with an exact physical and mental capacity for production, and that, if any one by increased industry or frugality should perchance produce more than another, the surplus should be forcibly taken from him without compensation. Under such circumstances it cannot be doubted that all at no distant day would come to live in houses of equal similarity; but the style of architecture which would prevail would probably closely resemble that which now characterizes such truly free localities as the Desert of Sahara, the interior of Caffre-land, or the domains of the Esquimaux.

Other illustrations to the same effect may be found in the circumstance that a paper is now issued regularly in New England, which is devoted mainly to the object of combating the receipt of interest or hire for the loan or use of capital, or, what is the same thing (whether the editors be or be not conscious of it), of combating abundance or accumulation; that the same idea finds favor in numerous pamphlets recently issued in various parts of the country, some of which exhibit no small ability; and finally in the disposition so frequently evinced by our legislative bodies, to deal with corporate property in accordance with the principle of *might*, rather than in accordance with the principle of right.

It is therefore well for us, even here in this boasted land of freedom and intelligence, occasionally to go back to first principles, and see where these ideas about the distribution of wealth by direct or indirect compulsion, or about diminishing the incentives for personal accumulation, are likely to lead us.

It is evident, in the first place, that such notions are wholly antagonistic to the idea of personal freedom, unless we mean to

[1] The Meaning of the Eight-Hour Movement. Ira Steward, Boston, 1868.

restrict the meaning of freedom simply to the possession and control of one's own person irrespective of property, which would invoive little more than the right to free locomotion ; and, second, that they tend to impair the growth of, if not wholly to destroy, civilization itself. For if liberty is not afforded to all, rich and poor, high and low, to keep, and to use in whatever way they may see fit, that which they lawfully acquire, subject only to the necessary social restraint of working no positive ill to one's neighbor,— then the desire to acquire and accumulate property will be taken away ; and capital, meaning thereby not merely money, which constitutes but a very small part of the capital of any community, but all those things which are the accumulated results of labor, foresight, and economy,—the machinery by which abundance is increased, toil lightened, and comfort gained,—will, instead of increasing, rapidly diminish.

And, in order to comprehend the full meaning of this statement, allow me to call your attention to an illustration of the extreme slowness with which that which we call capital accumulates, even under the most favorable circumstances.

By the census of 1870, the aggregate wealth of the United States, making all due allowances for duplication in valuation, was probably not in excess of *twenty-five thousand millions.* But vast as the sum is, and difficult as it certainly is for the mind to form any adequate conception of it in the aggregate, it is, nevertheless, most interesting to inquire what it is that, measured by human effort, it represents. And the answer is, that it represents, *first,* a value, supposing the whole sum to be apportioned equally, of about six hundred and twenty dollars to each individual,—not a large amount, if one was to depend on its interest at six per cent. as a means of support ; and, *second,* it represents the surplus result of all the labor, skill, and thought exerted, and all the capital earned and saved, or brought into the country, for the last two hundred and fifty years, or ever since the country became practically the abode of civilized men.

Now, with capital, or the instrumentalities for creating abundance, increasing thus slowly, it certainly stands to reason that we need be exceedingly careful, lest, by doing any thing to impair its security, we impair also its rate of increase ; and we accordingly find, as we should naturally expect from the comparatively high education of our people, that the idea of any direct interference with the rights of property meets with but little favor upon this side of the Atlantic. But at the same time we cannot deny that many of the most intelligent of the men and women interested in the various labor-reform movements in this country, taking as the basis of their reasoning the large nominal aggregate of the national wealth, and the large advance which has recently been made in the power of production, and considering them in the abstract, irrespective of time or distribution, have nevertheless adopted the idea—vague and shadowy though it may be,—that the amount of the present annual product of labor and capital is sufficient for all ; and that all it is necessary to do to insure comfort and abundance to the masses, is for the State somehow to intervene,—either by fixing the hours of labor, or the rates of compensation for service, or the use of capital,—and compel its more equitable distribution.

Now, that a more equitable distribution of the results of production is desirable, and that such a distribution does not at present take place to the extent that it might without impairing the exercise of individual freedom, must be admitted ; but, before undertaking to make laws on the subject, is it not of importance to first find out how much we have really got to divide ?

Let us see.

Stated in money, the maximum value of the annual product of the United States is not in excess of $7,000,000,000 (probably less); of which the value of the annual product of all our agriculture,—our cotton and our corn, our beef and our pork, our hay, our wheat, and all our other fruits,—is returned by the last census with undoubted approximative accuracy, at less than one half that sum ; or in round numbers at $2,400,000,000.

But while this sum of estimated yearly income, like the figures which report the aggregate of our national wealth, is so vast as to be almost beyond the power of mental conception, there is yet one thing about it which is certain, and can be readily comprehended ; and that is, that of this whole product, whether we measure it in money or in any other way, fully nine tenths, and probably a larger proportion, must be immediately consumed, in order that we may simply live, and make good the loss and waste of capital previously accumulated ; leaving not more than *one tenth* to be applied in the form of accumulation for effecting a future increased production and development.[1]

Or to state the case differently, and at the same time illustrate how small, even under the most favorable circumstances, can be the annual surplus of production over consumption, it is only necessary to compare the largest estimate of the value of our annual product, with our largest estimate of the aggregate national wealth, to see that, practically, after two hundred and fifty years of toiling and saving, we have only managed as a nation to get about three years and a half ahead, in the way of subsistence ; and that now if, as a whole people, we should stop working and pro-ducing, and repairing waste and deterioration, and devote our-selves exclusively to amusement and idleness, living on the ac-cumulation of our former labors or the labor of our fathers, four years would be more than sufficient to starve three fourths of us out of existence, and reduce the other one fourth to the condi-tion of semi-barbarism ; a result, on the whole, which it is well to think of in connection with the promulgation of certain new theo-ries, that the best way of increasing abundance, and promoting comfort and happiness, is by decreasing the aggregate and oppor-tunities of production.

In fact, there are few things more transitory and perishable than that which we call wealth ; and, as specifically embodied in the ordinary forms we see about us, its duration is not, on the average, in excess of the life of a generation.

The railroad system of the country is estimated to have cost more than four thousand millions of dollars[2] ; but if left to itself,

[1] According to the more reliable data furnished by the U. S. Census of 1880, the aggregate wealth of the country has been estimated at about forty thousand millions of dollars ($43,642,000,000 ; which, if equally divided among the whole population, would have amounted to $880 per head ; or, omitting the value of land, the value of the actual wealth of the United States, created by the hand of man during the whole period of its history, could not have been more, in 1880, than from $400 to $500 for each person.

The value of the annual product of all the labor and capital of the United States for 1880, according to estimates based on the census data of that year, was $8,500,000,-000. As the population of the country, in 1880, was fifty millions (50,155,783), the average annual share of each person of this product would have therefore been about $170 ; which would make the average individual expenditure permissible to meet the expenses of living, provided each person was obliged to live on the results of his own labor, about 47 cents per day.

[2] The share capital and funded and floating debts of the railroads of the United States, for the year 1883, have been estimated at $6,765,000,000.

without renewals or repairs, its value as property in ten years would entirely vanish ; and so also with our ships, our machinery, our tools and implements, and even our land when cultivated without renovation. For it is to be remembered, that those same forces of nature which we have mastered, and made subservient for the work of production, are also our greatest natural enemies, and if let to themselves will tear down and destroy much more rapidly than under guidance they will aggregate and build up. A single night was sufficient in Chicago to utterly destroy what was equivalent to one quarter of the whole surplus product which during the preceding year the nation had accumulated ; and of all the material wealth of the great and rich nations of antiquity,— of Egyptian, Assyrian, Tyrian, and Roman civilizations,—nothing whatever has come down to us, except, singularly enough, those things which, like their tombs and public monuments, never were possessed of a money valuation.

But the inferences which we are warranted in drawing from these facts and figures are by no means exhausted. Supposing the value of our annual product to be equally divided among our present population : then the average income of each individual would be about $170 per annum ; out of which food, clothing, fuel, shelter, education, travelling expenses, and means of enjoyment are to be provided, all taxes paid, all waste, loss, and depreciation made good, and any surplus available as new capital added to former accumulations.

Now, if at first thought this deduction of the average individual income of our people seems small, it should be remembered that it is based on an estimate of annual national product greater both in the aggregate, and in proportion to numbers, than is enjoyed by any other nation, our compeers in wealth and civilization ; and, further, that this $170 is not the sum which all actually receive as income, but the average sum which each would receive, were the whole annual product divided equally. But as a practical matter we know that the annual product is not divided equally ; and, furthermore, that, as long as men are born with different natural capacities, it never will be so divided. Some will receive, and do receive, as their share of the annual product, the annual average we have stated, multiplied by hundreds or even thousands; which of course necessitates that very many others shall receive proportionately less. And how much less is indicated by recent investigations which show, that for the whole country the average earnings of laborers and unskilled workmen is not in excess of four hundred dollars per annum,—the maximum amount being received in New England, and the minimum in the Southern, or former slaveholding States; which sum, assuming that the families of all these men consist of four, two adults and two children, would give one hundred dollars as the average amount which each individual of the class referred to produces, and also the amount to which each such individual must be restricted in consumption; for it is clear, that no man can consume more than he or his capital produces, unless he can in some way obtain the product of some other man's labor without giving him an equivalent for it.

We are thus led to the conclusion that, notwithstanding the wonderful extent to which we have been enabled to use and control the forces of nature for the purpose of increasing the power of production, the time has not yet come, when society in the United States can command such a degree of absolute abundance as to justify and warrant any class or individual, rich or poor, and least of all those who depend upon the product of each day's labor to meet each day's needs, in doing any thing which can in any way tend to diminish abundance; and furthermore, that the agency of law, even if evoked to the fullest extent in compelling distribution, must be exceedingly limited in its operations.

Let the working-man of the United States, therefore, in every vocation, demand and strive, if he will, for the largest possible share of the joint products of labor and capital; for it is the natural right of every one to seek to obtain the largest price for that which he has to sell. But if in so doing he restricts production, and so diminishes abundance, he does it at his peril; for, by a law far above any legislative control or influence, whatever increases scarcity not only increases the necessity, but diminishes the rewards of labor.

Street processions, marching after flags and patriotic mottoes, even if held every day in the week, will never change the conditions which govern production and compensation. Idleness produces nothing but weeds and rust; and such products are not marketable anywhere, though society often pays for them most dearly.

But if law, acting in the manner proposed by the representatives of the working-men, is not likely to avail any thing, and if abundance is not as great as it might be, and distribution not as equitable as it ought to be, wherein is the remedy ? Shall we let things drift along as in times past, trusting that Providence will finally do for us what we are unwilling or unable to do for ourselves?

My answer to this is, that the first step towards effecting a solution of the problem under consideration is to endeavor to clearly comprehend the conditions involved in it ; and that, when we have entered upon an investigation for that purpose, we shall soon see that the causes which tend to diminish abundance, and restrict the rewards of labor, in the Old World, are not the same as exist in the New ; and that therefore the agencies adopted for relief in the one case are not likely to prove remedial in the other.

In the Old World, the prime cause of the lack of abundance, and its resulting pauperism, is an over-crowded and increasing population, and the enormous waste and expenditures contingent on great standing armies and a continued war policy.

All the natural resources, originally the free gift of Nature, have long ago been fully appropriated, and in part exhausted. Every foot of arable land has its owner or tenant ; every mine, quarry, forest, or tree-bearing fruit, its possessor ; and even the right to fish in the waters, or capture the wild beasts of the field, or the fowls of the air, has become in a great degree an exclusive privilege.

When there is but *one to buy*, and *two to sell*, the *buyer* fixes the price. When there are *two to buy*, and only one to sell, the seller has the advantage.

Now, Europe, in respect to labor, has been for centuries the *seller*, rather than the *buyer*, of labor ; and the buyer, therefore, has always been, and is now, all-powerful in fixing its price, and controlling it to his advantage. Again, in a country whose natural capital or resources—*i. e.*, fertile and cheap land, abundant timber, food, minerals, etc.—are unexhausted or unappropriated, as in the United States, the rewards of labor, or wages, will be necessarily high ; and on the other hand, where the reverse condition of things prevails, as in Europe, the rewards of labor, as expressed in wages, must be comparatively less. In other words, as has been pointed out by Prof. Cairnes : " So far as high wages and profits are indications of cost of production at all, high wages and profits are indications of a low cost of production, since they are indications—being, in fact, the direct results—of high industrial productiveness." Nothing, therefore, more strikingly illustrates the difference in the conditions of the labor-problem in Europe and the United States, than the difference in the average rate of the wages of labor in the two countries ; and also the fallacy of the popular notion, that legislative interference is necessary in the United States to protect domestic industry against the pauper-labor of Europe ; or, in other words, to protect the people of the United States against the evils of abundance.

Under such a state of things, therefore, the efficient remedy, and indeed the only remedy, against pauperism in an overcrowded country, must· be emigration ; and it is one of the most curious of social phenomena, that, while the results of the most recent investigations show that thousands in the great cities óf Europe are annually crowded out of existence by the mere fact of their numbers, there are yet almost continental areas of the earth's surface, healthy, easy of access, and comparatively uninhabited, where the amount of labor necessary to secure all the essentials of a simple livelihood is but little in excess of the instinctive requirements of the system for physical exercise ; as, for example, in the delicious islands of Polynesia, where a temperature obviating any requirement for artificial heat prevails uninterruptedly, and where the plantain, the cocoa-palm, and the bread-fruit spring up and flourish spontaneously ; and also in the West Indies, where the late Charles Kingsley, in his book " A Christmas in the West Indies " (1871), says, that one of the first things which a visitor learns in landing at " Port of Spain," in the Island of Trinidad, is, that there are eight thousand persons, or about one third of the population of the city, who have no visible means of support, or who live without regular employment, and yet are evidently strong, healthy, and well fed. The same author also describes the life of an English emigrant in this island, whom he visited, as follows :

" The sea gives him fish enough for his family. His cocoa-palms yield him a little revenue. He has poultry, kids' and goats' milk more than he needs. His patch of provision-ground gives him corn and roots, sweet potatoes, and fruits all the year round. He needs nothing, fears nothing, owes nothing."

But, *per contra*, Mr. Kingsley adds:

"News and politics are to him like the distant murmur of the surf at the back of the island,—a noise which is nought to him. His Bible, his almanac, and three or four old books on a shelf, are his whole library. He has all that man needs, more than man deserves, and is far too wise to wish to better himself"; which last expression is equivalent to saying, that, the animal wants being abundantly satisfied, he wishes to remain an animal. And this conclusion, furthermore, may be regarded as the result of necessity rather than of choice; for, if man resident in the tropics is desirous of any thing much beyond what Nature furnishes almost as a free gift, the realization of the desire can only be attained through labor under conditions of climate so exhausting that the white race shrinks from its execution, and for the most part is incapable of its endurance; as is seen, for example, in the raising of cotton, coffee, sugar, and other similar tropical productions. And it would indeed seem as if Nature, in view of the fact that great physical exertion and an elevated temperature are incompatible, had made provision for man's residence in the tropics by furnishing him, with the minimum of exertion, those vegetable products which are especially adapted to maintain and support a physical existence. And whether we admit the example of design or not, it is certainly curious to note how man, when transferred from temperate zones to tropics, instinctively adapts himself to these conditions, and exchanges a life of activity for one of indolence. Of this, the description of the European emigrant in the West Indies, which I have quoted from Mr. Kingsley, is one illustration. Another is to be found in the fact, often noted and commented on, of the rapidity with which young men of New England, sent out as clerks or factors to Singapore, Manilla, or Calcutta, exchange their original physical and intellectual activity for the listless indolence of the native population. And, descending to the animal kingdom, it is said that the northern honey-bee, transported to the tropics, ceases after the first season to make provision for the winter, and, laying aside its habits of industry with the necessity for exertion, becomes not only a drone, but a veritable pest to the community.

In the United States, on the other hand, the case is entirely different. We have, in the first place, no excess of population in proportion to the area of country inhabited; but, on the contrary, we have, as a source of abundance and a certain barrier against want, that which no nation of Europe possesses; namely, an almost unlimited supply of cheap, fertile land. We have such a variety of soil, of climate, and of crop, that a deficiency of food, which in very many civilized countries is ever a source of anxiety, is with us a matter of impossibility; for the very conditions which tend to reduce the aggregate of the crops in one section tend to increase their fruition in some other. We have, as it were, the monopoly of the staple textile fibre of the world's clothing. We have more of coal, the symbol and the source of mechanical power, than exists in all other countries. We have every facility, natural and artificial, for the transportation and exchange of products. We have a form of government in which the will of the people constitutes the law. We have, in short, all the conditions which give to labor its greatest productiveness, and to capital its greatest reward. And if to-day these conditions are not fulfilled; if there is not to-day unison between labor and capital; if there is not a sufficient degree of material abundance, and a sufficient equity in its distribution, to lift up life among the masses, and make it somewhat more than a struggle for existence, —then we shall be forced to one of two conclusions: either the obstacles which militate and prevent these results are all artificial; or that it is in accordance with the designs of Providence that there shall always be a needy and dependent class, that there is a natural antagonism between labor and capital, and that the capacity of the earth for production is not adequate to meet the natural increase of the population that Providence has placed upon it.

Now, I, for one, fully accept the first of these conclusions, and wholly reject the latter. And although there is much about us which would seem to indicate that the characteristic evils which affect society in the *Old* World are being transferred to the *New;* though the present tendency seems to be toward a concentration of wealth in a few hands, to make the rich richer and the poor poorer,—I nevertheless feel certain that the causes which have led to these results, and which for the present stand in the way of a greater abundance and a larger life, are wholly within our control, and essentially different from the causes which in Europe are recognized as working disadvantageously to the interests of the masses. To specifically enumerate them, and to point out the degree in which each is operative, may not as yet, through lack of reliable data, be practicable; but, generalizing broadly, three causes may be mentioned as especially militating against the augmentation of abundance in the United States:

First, Failure to secure the proper and possible maximum of production in industrial enterprises which have long since passed beyond the domain of experiment.

Second, Inexcusable and inordinate waste in using.

Third, Inequalities in distribution, due to obstruction created by legislation.

I have thus reviewed, as briefly as the subject will admit, some of the principal obstacles which at present, in this country, seem to me to stand in the way of a greater material abundance, a more equitable distribution, and a larger life. Did time and opportunity suffice, an almost infinite amount of curious and interesting illustrations, drawn from our recent national experiences, might be given; but, apart from any further detail, the general results of our economic progress since 1860 may be summed in brief as follows: We have increased the power of production with a given amount of personal effort throughout the country, probably at least *twenty-five*, and possibly forty per cent. We have not decreased the cost of living within the same period, to the masses, to any thing like the same extent.[1] But startling as is this statement, the truth of which any man can verify if he will, the attainment of a better result is entirely within the power of society in this country to effect, if it will only avail itself of remedies whose simplicity and effectiveness long experience has proved beyond all controversy.

But herein consists the difficulty. Like Naaman the Syrian, we are anxious to be cleansed; but, like Naaman, we expect to be called upon to do some great thing, and experience a measure of disappointment when-told that the simplest measures are likely to prove the most effectual.

[1] An analysis of the business of manufacturing pig-iron indicates an increased product in 1879 as compared with 1860—capital remaining the same—of forty-six per cent.; diminution in the number of hands employed $6\frac{5}{100}$ per cent.; increase of wages per hand, $37\frac{6}{100}$ per cent.

In point of natural resources, Providence has given us all that we desire. And that these resources may be made productive of abundance, great and overflowing, to all sorts and conditions of men, there must be, *first*, industry and economy on the part of the individual; and, *second*, on the part of society, a guaranty that every man shall have an opportunity to exert his industry, and exchange its products, with the utmost freedom and the greatest intelligence ; and, when society has done this, we will have solved the problem involved in the relations of capital and labor, so far as the solution is within the control of human agency ; for in giving to each man opportunity, conjoined with feedom and intelligence, we invest him, as it were, " with crown and mitre, and make him sovereign over himself."

www.ingramcontent.com/pod-product-compliance
Lightning Source LLC
Chambersburg PA
CBHW030731280326
41926CB00086B/1101